Essential Article

Articles, opinions, arguments, personal acc
opposing viewpoints

In print in this book & online as part of Complete Issues

Complete Issues
articles · statistics · contacts

Complete Issues
articles · statistics · contacts

www.completeissues.co.uk

Your log in details:

Username: _____

Password: _____

Essential Articles 2017

For effective independent learning

Essential Articles 2017 is part of Complete Issues, a unique combination of resources in print and online.

Complete Issues

Complete Issues gives you the articles, statistics and contacts to understand the world we live in.

The unique format means that this information is available on the shelf and on the screen.

How does Complete Issues work?

Using www.completeissues.co.uk you can view individual pages on screen, download, print, use on whiteboards and edit to suit your needs. It makes Essential Articles even more flexible and useful.

Complete Issues has been redesigned this year to make it even more user-friendly and flexible.

All the articles are available to view online and download as PDFs and there are references and links to other parts of Complete Issues - the archive of articles, the statistics and the website and contact details of relevant organisations.

The articles in the Essential Articles series, the statistics in Fact File and online contacts work seamlessly together on the Complete Issues website to produce a choice of relevant writing, figures and links.

When you search for a topic you instantly generate a list of relevant articles, figures and organisations with a thumbnail of the page and a short description.

The **advantages of Complete Issues** over just googling are:

- **varied & reliable sources**
- **moderated - so appropriate for student use**
- **properly referenced**
- **beautifully presented**
- **adaptable for classroom use**
- **cleared for copyright**
- **links that are checked for safety and relevance**

You can search and browse individual elements of Complete Issues or all the parts together, past and present editions.

You can research a topic secure in the knowledge that you will find reputable sources and considered opinions.

Our **Focus Guides** offer a selection from Complete Issues as a starting point or quick and easy access to information on the most searched topics.

In addition to the online service, you have this attractive printed version always available. Its bright, magazine-style format entices readers to browse and enjoy while learning about current issues and dilemmas, making even difficult issues approachable.

Because you have both the book and online access you can use Essential Articles in different ways with different groups and in different locations. It can be used simultaneously in the library, in the classroom and at home.

Your purchase of the book entitles you to use Complete Issues on one computer at a time. You can find your access codes on your covering letter or by contacting us. It is useful to record them on page 1 of this volume.

You can also buy an unlimited site licence to make the service and the material available to **all** students and staff at **all** times, even from home.

If you do not yet have the other resources in Complete Issues - the statistics and the contacts - you can sample the service and upgrade here:

www.completeissues.co.uk

Complete Issues

articles • statistics • contacts

Contents

> 66 **You need to be white, you need to be male, and you need to be middle class** 99
> Page 30

Photo: YouTube

Contents

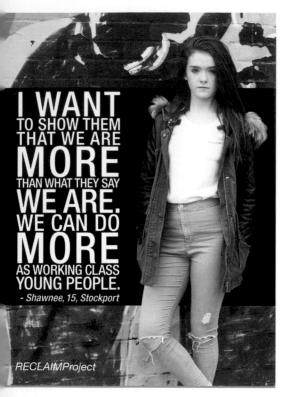

I WANT TO SHOW THEM THAT WE ARE **MORE** THAN WHAT THEY SAY **WE ARE. WE CAN DO MORE** AS WORKING CLASS YOUNG PEOPLE.
- Shawnee, 15, Stockport

RECLAIMProject

❝ My boyfriend never notices. Unlike me he's never had to develop a 'racism radar' ❞

Page 46

© WashedAshore.org

❝ Like the rest of British dads, all Muslim fathers think their daughter is smarter than everyone... and that their son is a heartbreaker! ❞

Page 50

> " Part of me went through a kind of mourning for the child I thought I had "
>
> Page 107

Contents

> **The digital revolution breaks down borders**
>
> Page 142

> **I had lived a secret life of ritualised handwashing, hair pulling, counting syllables**
>
> Page 122

Contents

❝ I now felt ready to take on whatever boys' football threw at me ❞

page 157

❝ I've been in a civil partnership for almost ten years and I gave birth to our beautiful daughter 12 weeks ago ❞

page 152

Contents

> " In recent years women-only metro cars, cafes, gyms, pools and beaches have emerged "
>
> Page 184

Abortion

Photos posed by models

Shout your

In September 2015 a new movement, with a distinctive, even shocking, hashtag, was started by two US writers who had both had a moment of sudden insight into their own lives. Amelia Bonow and Lindy West had both had abortions. Statistics told them that many of their friends must also have had abortions, since the official figure is that one in three women have had one. Yet they realised that they had never talked about it.

Their silence wasn't a conscious decision but the result of a powerful social expectation, mentioning your abortion was not normal or accepted. As Lindy West later told the Guardian: "We don't talk about it because we don't talk about it because we don't talk about it." It was in response to this self-imposed wall of silence that the hashtag #ShoutYourAbortion was created. Amelia Bonow has said, "A shout is not a celebration or a value judgment; it's the opposite of a whisper, of silence".

The spark for this movement came when some US politicians tried to take away financial support from Planned Parenthood, an organisation that provides contraception, cancer screening, and treatments for sexually transmitted diseases, as well as abortions. Its patients were mainly those who could not afford treatment within the expensive American healthcare system. Amelia Bonow realised that she had never told people how grateful she was for her abortion at her local Planned Parenthood clinic and what a difference it had made to the rest of her life. So she posted her experience on Facebook, concluding, "Having an abortion made me happy in a totally unqualified way. Why wouldn't I be happy that I was not forced to become a mother?" After Lindy West shared this post the hashtag and the movement was formed. In very little time they could claim in a tweet: "#ShoutYourAbortion has

SOME ISSUES:

Why do you think there is so much secrecy around abortion?

How does this issue affect women and men differently?

Why is it important to talk more openly about your experiences?

Will this movement help women to feel they do not have to keep their experiences secret?

> Just as the decision to have an abortion is rarely taken lightly, the decision to speak out can also be a major one

changed the conversation. Abortion is a part of reproductive healthcare and not 2 b whispered about." The idea of breaking the stigma about 'confessing' to having had an abortion had immediate appeal. The hashtag has been used over 250,000 times by women and men who want to tell their personal stories of abortion as part of a normal discussion.

It became clear that the preconceptions of society

abortion

and the way abortion is usually dramatised on TV and in film did not match the experience of a whole range of women. Portrayals in the media would have us believe that those seeking abortions are young and feckless, or at least naïve and unfortunate. For dramatic purposes, the woman should regard her decision as a shameful secret and later be wracked with guilt and regret. The truth is that 60% of women who seek an abortion already have at least one child - they often want an abortion precisely because they already have children.

Just as the decision to have an abortion is rarely taken lightly, the decision to speak out can also be a major one. The movement helped to uncover cases in the past where women were made to feel ashamed and guilty. Karen Harris Thurston wrote in a blog for the Sea Change Project about how she lived with the secret of her first abortion from the time she was 13 to the time she was 40. She recalls, "You must tell no one," my father commanded, "not even your husband when you are grown and married." A second

abortion at 19, when she was in an unhealthy relationship, left her convinced she was contemptible. "Without the Internet and no one to talk to, I lived in solitary confinement around my abortions. I feared everyone I loved would abandon me if they discovered the truth." At 40 she confided in a friend and by the time she was 56 she could tell her story to a roomful of strangers and encourage others to share too.

On a Buzzfeed thread, one woman revealed: "I told my mum a few days later that I'd had one and then found out that not only had she had an abortion too, but so had my grandmother. I hadn't expected it and wished she had told me years ago, even though I understand why she didn't."

On that same thread, others revealed how they were surprised by their own feelings: "After my abortion I told my boyfriend about how I felt relieved and how I was a little surprised by just how relieved I felt, because normally the post-abortion reaction that you see in TV and movies is regret, sadness, etc. So I asked him, 'Is it weird that I feel super happy right now?' His answer was, 'Not at all, that's just your sign that it was the right decision.'"

Others had been led to believe that 'payback' would come in time, particularly when they experienced birth and motherhood. Instead: "My son was born in 2014. As I held him and looked at his perfect little fingers and toes I waited for the repressed shame to wash over me….

> 'Is it weird that I feel super happy right now?' His answer was, 'Not at all, that's just your sign that it was the right decision.'

Instead, I was overwhelmed with gratitude for the abortion I had 11 years earlier…And I realised that… it was only through choosing to not be a parent then, that I got to be a great mom now!" Doctor Pratima Gupta wrote: "When I was pregnant, patients often asked me if it was hard/weird to do their abortion. My response was simple, 'Not at all. It is not the right time for you, but it is for me. Later on, if you decide to become a parent, I will be by your side then too."

Obviously with such a controversial subject, there has been loud opposition to the movement. The hashtag #ShoutYourAdoption was set up to put forward anti-abortion views. Twitter posts insulted and threatened the women who had shared their experiences: "You will pay for the murder of babies. You will pay."

However, it seems likely that this silence, once shattered, cannot be reinstated. The next task for the campaigners is to try to get women to the stage where they don't need to explain, and therefore justify, their choices. "One of the final hurdles is getting it into people's heads that the reason for an abortion doesn't matter," says Lindy West. "Women own their own bodies, and you just can't force someone to bring a baby into the world."

Sources: Various

United Kingdom, but not united laws

Women in Northern Ireland do not have the same rights as the rest of the UK

In England, Wales and Scotland abortion is legal if you are less than 24 weeks pregnant and two doctors agree that it is necessary. The reasons for the abortion can include risks to your mental or physical health, risks to the baby or to your existing children. Unlike the rest of the UK, abortion is only allowed in very restricted circumstances in Northern Ireland.

The 1967 Abortion Act, which introduced legal abortion, was not applied to Northern Ireland, which then had a separate Parliament (it now has a Legislative Assembly in charge of law-making). The law makers at that time simply ignored what was happening on the mainland and kept to the 1945 law which allowed abortion only where the mother's life was threatened or there was a substantial risk of severe disability in the baby. This means that circumstances which would make an abortion legal in most of the United Kingdom - such as abnormalities in the foetus, rape and even incest - are not permissible there.

The consequence of this is that while there were 16 terminations in Northern Ireland hospitals in 2014/15, at least 837 women from the province had abortions in England. The actual number is certain to be higher as some would have travelled to Wales or Scotland, while others would have concealed their home address.

For women in the rest of the UK, terminations are available as part of the National Health Service. However, women from Northern Ireland who seek a termination in England have to pay for their medical care as well as for travel and accommodation costs - meaning that treatment is not available to the poorest. As a result of this, some women in the region have resorted to buying pills online to induce a miscarriage. It is a method which is cheap, accessible and, normally, secret.

In 2014, a 19 year old woman from Belfast, who was between ten and twelve weeks pregnant, used pills to terminate her pregnancy since she could not afford to travel to mainland UK. Her housemates found the aborted foetus in the rubbish bin. For a week they did nothing, feeling, according to one of them that "It wasn't our decision to make. We just thought we can't do anything, it's not our place to say anything." However, apparently without realising how serious the sentence could be, and despite the woman's pleas, eventually they told the police.

The young woman was taken to court. In Northern Ireland the potential penalty for procuring a miscarriage is life imprisonment, but in April 2016, she was given a three month suspended jail sentence after she admitted two offences - procuring her own abortion by using a poison, and of supplying a poison with intent to procure a miscarriage. The judgement may seem to show some sympathy for the woman but, as her barrister told the court, had she lived anywhere else in the UK she would not have found herself before the courts.

Just as laws there differ from those in the rest of the United Kingdom so do some attitudes, particularly when it comes to religion, sexual matters and

SOME ISSUES:

Do you think that different countries within the UK should have different laws?

Is it fair that women from Northern Ireland could not have terminations on the NHS?

Do you think abortion is a human right?

What should happen now in Northern Ireland?

In Northern Ireland she would be forced to continue with the pregnancy and deliver a child who could never have survived.

politics. A much higher proportion of Northern Irish people (82%) describe themselves as Christian compared to the rest of the UK (less than 60%). It is the only part of the UK where same-sex marriage is not legal.

An opinion poll in 2014 suggested that more than 60% of people would be in favour of legal abortion in the case of foetal abnormality and for pregnancies which are the result of rape or incest. Despite this, and the ruling by a High Court judge that these strict laws were a breach of human rights, when the Northern Ireland Assembly has had the opportunity to vote on relaxing the legislation the proposals have been defeated. The two main parties representing the religious and political divide, the Democratic Unionist Party and the Social Democratic and Labour Party, are united in opposing any concessions towards choice. The Greens (who have 2 seats) are the only party in the province to support bringing the abortion law in line with the rest of the United Kingdom.

The young woman's sentence produced opposite reactions. The anti-abortion group Precious Life described the sentence as "very lenient" and called for it be reviewed since "It's sending out a dangerous message and could set a dangerous precedent for future cases of illegal abortions here in Northern Ireland."

In contrast, Amnesty International said it was "appalled" by the conviction. "A woman who needs an abortion is not a criminal - the law should not treat her as such," Patrick Corrigan, Amnesty International's Northern Ireland director, said. "This tragic case reveals that making abortion illegal does not stop women in Northern Ireland needing or seeking terminations."

The case of Sarah Ewart illustrates how harsh the law can be. 20 weeks into a much-wanted pregnancy she was told that her baby had a fatal abnormality and had developed without a brain or a skull. In Northern Ireland she would be forced to continue with the pregnancy until the baby died and then go through an induced labour to deliver a child who could never have survived. Doctors were not even allowed, by law, to advise her on any alternatives. When she went to a private clinic for advice, she was confronted by anti-abortion protestors. She eventually made the journey to London for a termination. Sarah Ewart had been an opponent of abortion but her personal experience of the law turned her into a pro-choice campaigner.

The consequences of the recent judgement will be far reaching and will have an effect on individuals, reinforcing a culture of fear for those who have purchased these pills. One of the housemates who reported the young woman made it clear that a judgement about her behaviour and attitude was part of their reasoning: "She showed no remorse, she really didn't," the housemate told a radio interviewer. "She was completely fine about it." How many women will be afraid to seek medical help if they fear a risk of a similar judgement - and its consequences? And the burden of fear, and possibly unwanted pregnancy, is more likely to fall on those who cannot afford a discreet trip to the mainland. Meanwhile, individuals continue to find their own solutions and fall foul of the law. The next case to come before the courts will be that of a 35-year-old woman who is being prosecuted for obtaining the pills for her young daughter.

Sources: Various

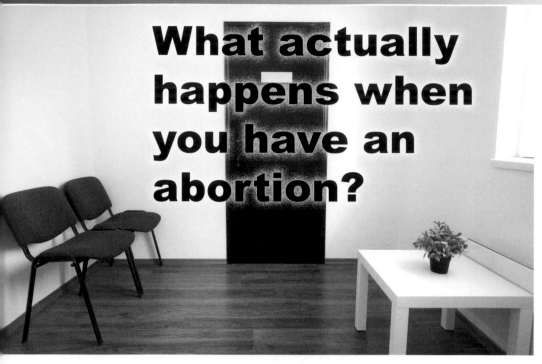

What actually happens when you have an abortion?

In most of the UK, abortion is legal and available. Generally, the earlier an abortion takes place the easier and safer it is. 90% of abortions take place before the 13th week of pregnancy and almost all are performed before 20 weeks. The legal limit is 24 weeks.

Consultation

This can be with your doctor or a specialist clinic. It will look at your health, how far advanced the pregnancy is, what your situation is and what contraception choices you might make afterwards.

90% of abortions take place before the 13th week of pregnancy

SOME ISSUES:

Do you think there is enough information available about abortion?

What sort of information and advice do people need when they are considering this step?

What sort of aftercare should be provided for people who have had an abortion?

Is it important that abortion remains legal?

Medical abortion - pills

An early medical abortion - up to nine weeks since the last period - involves taking two pills 36 to 48 hours apart. This results in bleeding and pain like a heavy period. Some patients stay in hospital for this part of the procedure but others return home while the medicine takes effect.

For a late medical abortion - 9 to 20 weeks - more pills may need to be used and the process will take longer. The effect is similar to having a miscarriage. Most women can return home on the same day.

Surgical abortion - suction

This can be done from 7 to 15 weeks after the date of the last period under local or general anaesthetic. The process sucks out the foetus and surrounding tissue. This usually takes about 5 to 10 minutes. After 15 weeks of pregnancy the process to remove the foetus and tissue is done with small forceps as well as suction.

Women who have had a local anaesthetic go home after about 30 minutes, those who have had a general anaesthetic go home after a few hours. Patients often experience heavy bleeding in the 2 or 3 days following and lighter bleeding can last for as much as 3 weeks.

Late abortion

At 20 to 24 weeks an overnight stay in hospital will be required.

A medically induced abortion is like a late miscarriage as a medicine brings about contractions to expel the contents of the womb - this usually lasts 6 to 12 hours. Women stay awake during this and are given pain relief.

Alternatively a surgical two-stage abortion is carried out under general anaesthetic. Stage one stops the heartbeat of the foetus and softens the neck of the womb. Stage two, a day later, is the removal of the foetus and tissue.

Sources: various

Animals

Why are we shocked that a lion is dissected in public?

Alex Forrest

This morning I was a guest on Danish TV News, TV2, where I was asked to discuss why Britons are so shocked that a Danish zoo is dissecting a dead lion. My live studio interview ran alongside pictures of a previous dissection - leaving nothing to the imagination. You can watch it, but please be warned that there is graphic content. (No broadcaster in the UK could ever use images like this before the 9pm watershed.)

The nine-month-old lion, along with two others, was culled back in February because Odense Zoo had too many of the animals. Today just one - a male - was taken out of the freezer and, as I write, is being cut up in front of huge crowds, including children.

Only last year, Copenhagen Zoo walked into a media frenzy when it decided to kill a healthy giraffe named Marius, dissect him in front of crowds and then feed him to the lions. So have these Danish zoos learnt nothing? Well yes because this time round, Odense Zoo decided not to publicise the cub's death at the time, and not to give him a name.

Zoologists and most Danes in general are adamant that dissections are important

SOME ISSUES:

Do you think there is ever a good reason for a zoo to kill a healthy animal?

What alternatives are there?

Do you think it is helpful for children to see a dissection?

Is the author right to imply we are concerned about zoo animals, but not the animals we eat?

Let's not kid ourselves - hundreds of 'big' animals in zoos across Europe are culled every year

But zoologists and most Danes in general are adamant that dissections are important - they say they are for educational purposes and not entertainment. They've done it before and they'll do it again.

Which goes to show how culturally different Danes are to Brits (as well as Americans and other nationalities). There is no way on earth that a British zoo would or could do this in public. Let's not kid ourselves - hundreds of 'big' animals in zoos across Europe are culled every year for many reasons, including having the wrong gene pool. And whatever we may think, it happens in the UK too - but in secret. Remember the storm that followed after it was revealed by the Daily Mail that Longleat Safari Park had put down six lions, including four cubs, because there were simply too many? I am, though, still shocked that killing 'healthy' zoo animals needs to happens at all - in the US they use contraception.

I certainly wouldn't allow my five-year-old son to watch a dissection, even if he wanted to. That prompted the TV presenter to ask me if I was playing into the 'Disneyfication' of animals? Perhaps I am. But even though I know that children of all ages regularly visit abattoirs and watch animal dissections here in Denmark, it just doesn't sit well with me. Does that make me, a meat-eater, a hypocrite? Probably.

This article first appeared on Alex's personal blog
alexfw.com
15 October 2015

No place for a child

Childhood is sacred, a time for magic and innocence. I take my children to the zoo because they love the animals, knowing all the different types from their story books and the Disney films. Why on earth would any parent want to destroy that illusion by taking their child to a dissection? That is no place for a child. I do not agree that if you are happy going to a zoo you should be happy to see this (and I don't care to tell my children either about the realities of abattoirs, it's difficult enough getting them to eat a balanced meal without a warts and all description of how their chicken nugget came to be). There is plenty of time for reality when they grow up, for now, I think enjoy the magic!

Kids are more clued up than you think

I took my 8 year old daughter to see the dissection, and I would again. We've always raised our children to know the truth about things; how zoos work, where their food comes from, and biological facts. We want our children to be well informed and educated, not ignorant and potential hypocrites. She has a keen, lively, inquisitive interest in animals, science and the natural world, so of course we took her to see the dissection. She was really interested in it all and came away with all sorts of interesting questions about how the zoos work and what parts of the body do what. Some of the children were a little squeamish, but they got over it. Kids are a lot more clued up than you think, and far less soft than us grown-ups would like to kid ourselves.

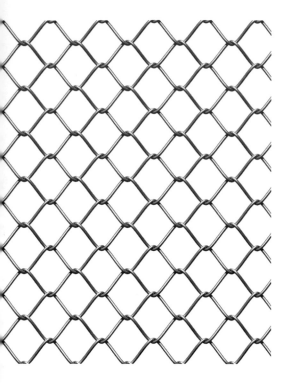

FROM CAGE TO GRAVE: THE SHORT, UNPLEASANT LIFE OF A GAME BIRD

**Dr Toni Shephard
Head of Policy and
Research at the League
Against Cruel Sports**

SOME ISSUES:

What surprises you about how
these birds are raised?

Should these birds be protected by
law like farmed animals are?

Can you understand why some
people enjoy hunting and
shooting?

What can be done to raise
awareness about these issues?

The writer represents a certain
organisation. Does this affect how
you respond to her views?

The pheasant shooting season starts today, and while many people instinctively oppose the killing of animals for sport, most have no idea just how miserable the short life of 'game' birds really is.

Around 35 million pheasants and red-legged partridges, both non-native species in the UK, are released on shooting estates each year. These are not wild birds who roam freely until killed quickly by a competent shooter. No. They are factory farmed in much the same way as intensively reared chickens, yet are not covered by humane slaughter laws and probably won't end up on someone's plate.

According to the Department for Environment, Food and Rural Affairs (Defra), almost all partridges released on UK shooting estates come from breeding birds confined in wire mesh cages with less space per bird than an A4 piece of paper, often for their entire life. An increasing majority of breeding pheasants are now also confined in wire mesh cages for at least three months a year.

The League has filmed inside these farms many times, both in the UK and abroad. The conditions are little different to battery cages for laying hens which were outlawed in the EU in 2012. Most hens are now kept in colony

These are not wild birds who roam freely until killed quickly by a competent shooter.

cages housing 60 to 80 birds, with the space per hen approximately 20 percent larger than an A4 piece of paper. Nest boxes, litter and perch space must be also provided. Most people think this still falls short of 'barely adequate', yet game birds fare even worse.

There are no minimum legal space requirements for caged pheasants and partridges, and enrichment is barely mentioned in Defra's voluntary Code of Practice for the Welfare of Gamebirds. Moreover, these are still semi-wild birds, unlike domesticated chickens, who find confinement highly stressful as evidenced by repeated jump escape behaviour.

Many of the 35 million birds released in the UK start their lives on intensive farms in continental Europe - at least 50% according to Defra. These young birds can spend 20 hours or more crammed inside a crate stacked in the back of a lorry travelling from farm to shoot.

Shooting estates buy young birds from breeding farms and rear them in crowded sheds and pens, releasing them just a few weeks before shooting begins. What happens on the day of a shoot is little different to 'canned' hunting - where animals such as lions are tamed and confined in an enclosed area to make killing them easier.

Birds which have been farmed, fed and 'protected' from predators are driven towards paying shooters by employees called beaters who stomp noisily through vegetation and scare birds out towards the guns. Dozens of birds fly overhead simultaneously while the shooters fire. Many, up to 40% according to a former employee of the British Association for Shooting and Conservation, are wounded not killed. Some are left to die slowly where they fall.

More than 500 birds can be shot on one estate in one day. This is not one for the pot. Most birds are dumped in makeshift pits along with the spent shotgun cartridges.

The League Against Cruel Sports is calling on the government to:

1) ban breeding cages for game birds as they are totally unsuitable for semi-wild species

2) hold an independent inquiry into the commercial shooting industry to examine the welfare and ecological impacts of farming millions of non-native birds simply to be shot for sport.

View the League's new exposé of the short, unpleasant lives of pheasants www.league.org.uk/cruelgame

Huffington Post Blog, 1 January 2015

They are factory farmed in much the same way as intensively reared chickens, yet are not covered by humane slaughter laws and probably won't end up on someone's plate

protection and destruction

Human attitudes to animals are complicated, contradictory and not always subject to rational explanation. The complexity of our reactions, especially to our nearest relatives the apes, was brought to the fore by a recent incident at Cincinatti Zoo in North America. One Saturday in June 2016, a 3-year-old child managed to get into the gorilla enclosure and into the domain of Harambe, a 17 year old male Western Lowland Gorilla.

In the wild

Gorillas are often thought of as gentle giants. They are mainly vegetarian and in the wild live in stable groups with a dominant male gorilla whose role is to protect the group. He does this with a display intended to frighten the threat away, dragging large branches about and slamming them down, tearing up vegetation, beating his chest and running from side to side. It's a noisy show of power and strength - the mature silverbacks are very large and very strong, probably as strong as ten men. But the display is a bluff, designed to prevent aggression, not an invitation to a fight.

What happened

When the child fell into the moated enclosure the two female gorillas were brought inside, but Harambe climbed down into the moat. The huge gorilla at first stood in front of the boy, between him and the screaming, panicking crowds of onlookers on the viewing platform above. Harambe's posture was tense, his movements abrupt. It seems likely that he was preparing to make a display in the face of something unknown which could be a threat. He then dragged the toddler through the water of the moat, and placed the boy in front of him, extending his finger to examine the boy's clothing and seeming to

SOME ISSUES:

Do you think we have the right to keep animals in captivity?

Should humans stay away from animals in their natural habitat?

Could the zoo have prevented the accident from happening?

Was the way the zoo reacted justified?

What should we do to protect animals?

Gorillas are often thought of as gentle giants.

Harambe before he was killed. Image from YouTube   *Harambe with the child in the enclosure. Image from YouTube*

position the child's arms before once again dragging him through the water to a corner of the enclosure further away from all clamour.

What happened next caused controversy and an outpouring of hatred on social media - the zoo called in their emergency team who shot Harambe in order to rescue the child.

Social media reaction

First to bear the brunt of social media blame was the zoo - why weren't their barriers more secure? Why shoot the gorilla and not tranquillise it? Wasn't the gorilla just trying to protect the child? Why didn't they value the life of the animal they were supposed to be protecting? The focus of attention was turned too upon the parents. How did the child manage to get in to the enclosure? What were they doing?

Social media users were quick to condemn "poor parenting", there was even a petition, signed by hundreds of thousands of people, which accused the parents of negligence and said that "This beautiful gorilla lost his life because the boy's parents did not keep a closer watch on the child". This shaming centred particularly on the mother with many tweets under the hashtag *#justice4harambe* like this one [spelling errors have not been corrected]:

> RESPONSIBILE (along with #CincinnatiZoo) for HARAMBE'S DEATH. #MichelleGregg Take their kid away!

and a picture of Harambe with the words:

> "Not sure why they killed me - I was doing a better job of watching that lady's kid than she was".

Since the family was black, there was a fair helping of racism along with the misogyny.

How could the child get in?

Like most zoos, this one wanted to give its visitors the best possible view that was consistent with safety - so people can see in and animals can't get out. In this case the barriers consisted of a 91cm fence, up to 1.8 metres of ground densely planted with vegetation and a moat, more than 3.5 metres wide and 4.5 metres deep, with steep concrete sides. About 40 million visitors had passed safely through this enclosure before this. The barriers appeared to be adequate until this incident occurred. The boy's mother, Michelle Gregg, posted on Facebook:

'As a society we are quick to judge how a parent could take their eyes off of their child and if anyone knows me I keep a tight watch on my kids. Accidents happen but I am thankful that the right people were in the right place today.'

Why didn't they tranquillise Harambe?

Tranquilliser darts don't work instantly, there was a risk that a semi-conscious gorilla might have harmed the child before the anaesthetic took full effect or that the gorilla could have fallen on the boy, possibly in the water, drowning them both.

The report of the emergency crew says:
"Arriving within a few minutes at the Gorilla World complex, the crews from Engine 32 and Medic 9, under the supervision of Capt. Ken Lemaster, witnessed Harambe, a 425-pound, 17-year-old male gorilla, violently dragging the young boy through the water in the moat and at times throwing him to the side.

Several times the boy's head went under water and struck the concrete bottom and sides. The child remained conscious throughout the approximately 10 minutes from his fall into the moat until the Cincinnati Zoo's Dangerous Animal Response Team neutralized the gorilla with a single shot from a long rifle.

At the time the shot was fired, the gorilla was holding the young boy between his legs."

What was the gorilla's intention towards the child?

In parts of the video of the incident Harambe can be seen reaching out tentatively and exploring the child's clothing. This has caused people to claim that he was protecting the child. Certainly it seems he was anxious to get himself and the boy away from the noise of the crowd, but his 'care' probably amounts to curiosity and wariness. Without any malicious intent, this powerful animal, alarmed by the arrival of another creature in its enclosure and by the commotion, could easily have harmed or killed the little boy.

There have been instances in the past where children have fallen into gorilla enclosures and apparently been cared for by the animals. In 1986, 5-year-old Levan Merritt fell into a dry moat which surrounded the gorilla enclosure at Jersey Zoo. As the child lay unconscious a huge male gorilla, named Jambo, came over to him and began to stroke him and appeared to stand guard over him. When the child woke and started to scream, Jambo retreated to the interior, where the zoo staff had already enticed the other gorillas. In this incident one major difference was the degree of agitation around the incident, the child was unconscious and not moving and the crowd were much quieter, the gorilla was not agitated and was not actually in physical contact with the child when Levan began to move and cry out.

What are zoos for?

What was clear was that many people valued the life of the gorilla very highly and some thought it was worth more than a human child's life. The question was also raised as to whether the animal should have been in captivity at all, touching on the more general subject of what rights animals have.

Modern zoos claim to be protecting animals by maintaining a gene pool (in case of complete extinction). Harambe was a Western Lowland Gorilla (scientific name Gorilla gorilla gorilla). It's an endangered species and zoos have a strategy, which Harambe was part of, of keeping a healthy breeding stock by avoiding inter-breeding (sperm

It was clear that many people valued the life of the gorilla highly and some thought it was worth more than the child's life

was taken from Harambe after his death). But, at best, this is an insurance policy. Although it ensures that there will be genetic material to draw from in the case of near extinction, what it really guarantees is that zoos will always have a stock of animals available, animals who will be born and die in captivity.

Most zoos also feel that they have a conservation mission, but their main function is entertainment. In designing a habitat, the needs of the animals are considered but the needs of the paying public generally take precedence. By allowing the public the thrill of seeing real wild animals close up zoos feel that they are educating them about the need to preserve them in the wild. However, there is the contradiction that the larger species, that people like to see, do not thrive in zoos. Elephants for example, have a much shorter life span in captivity. Research also shows that while people feel better informed after a zoo visit there is no evidence that it changes their behaviour.

And now?

After this incident parents may hold on a little tighter to their children for a while. Zoos will re-examine their security and people will lay flowers on a shrine to the dead gorilla. But will we also re-examine the purpose of zoos and the relationship between humans and animals - particularly endangered animals?

Western lowland gorillas have two predators, humans and, occasionally, leopards. Humans hunt them for meat, sell their body parts for use in medicine and magic remedies and capture their babies to sell as pets. Humans destroy forests for logging and mining. And the gorilla population has been devastated by the Ebola virus which has killed off perhaps one third of them.

If half of the people who wept for the death of Harambe considered the threat to the nameless gorillas in the wild, and acted upon it, then something constructive could emerge from the outpouring of blame and the zoo, ironically, would have justified its conservation claims.

Sources: Various

Art & culture

Creating is not just a 'nice' activity; it transforms, connects and empowers

Paula Briggs

SOME ISSUES:

Do you enjoy making things?

Is enough school time given to creative activities?

How can making and creating benefit people and society?

What can be done to highlight the importance of creativity?

As a child, when I wasn't eating, sleeping or at school, I was making.

My memories of childhood relate to stuff – smell, material and texture: digging up the garden to make heavy, grogged clay; melting wax crayons to make 3D shapes; building matchstick houses; casting plaster in Disney latex moulds; and cutting out. Always cutting, shaping and sticking.

Since then, I've studied, made and taught sculpture. I know what it feels like to submerge my hands and mind in making, occupied with the struggle to transform and connect material. Since 1995 I've been working with friend and colleague Sheila Ceccarelli through AccessArt to explore how we can enable making in others. We've seen over and over again how making transforms people, just like makers transform materials.

It feels so fundamentally good and right to use our hands to manipulate materials – to use tools to extend our ability; to put stuff out into the world. The urge to alter our environment is part of our genetic makeup. The skill of making lies latent within all of us.

We now know that creativity is good for the economy too. The UK creative industries generate £84.1bn a year and account for 2.8 million jobs. It's the fastest-growing sector of the economy.

It's looking good for makers.

We work a lot in schools and see 10-year-olds who can't use scissors. We see art squeezed into obedient slots that require no mess, quick results and easy success. We see children who have never had to solve the problem of a sculpture that doesn't balance; never had an argument with a lump of stuff; and never learnt the need to rebuild.

We see children who have never felt success from using a tool to help them manipulate material, never felt the pride of producing something for others and never felt the optimism of daring to ask: "would it work if … ?"

Somehow, somewhere along the line, making became seen as a "nice" activity, but one we could do without.

So are we really preparing our children for their creative futures?

Making connects the hand, eye and brain in a very special way. It's empowering for both maker and viewer

There are so many reasons not to make and we need to talk about them. Let's get the reasons our children aren't making out in the open.

It takes time and energy: making with a class of 30, or even a household of one or two, can be exhausting.

There's enough to be getting on with: pressure from other subjects means making and the arts can get squeezed out.

Homework encroaches on spare time at home, which could be spent making.

It creates mess: wouldn't it be nice if we could make like a singer sings, without the mess to clear up afterwards?

Making can be risky: a child might burn their finger on a glue gun or cut themselves with a saw.

There's enough stuff in the world: do we really need to make more?

Making uses resources: aren't we meant to be trying to use less?

We don't need to make to survive: we generally buy what we need, so we don't need to learn the skills first-hand any more.

We don't need to make to entertain ourselves: in the past we might have kept our hands and eyes busy with making in our spare time, but now we occupy ourselves through binary code.

But when we give children the time and space to make – and present them with a pile of materials – they fall to it with such a will. The appetite to make is there, even when no one speaks of it.

Making connects the hand, eye and brain in a very special way. It's empowering for both maker and viewer. The act of making is optimistic; it's an act of faith. People of all ages feel better for doing it.

We really need to be preparing children for their creative futures

Making can also be very social – conversations can meander while hands are kept busy. But it can also be very personal and give confidence to children who listen to their own internal monologue that takes place as they make in solitude.

If we want a world full of creative, entrepreneurial thinkers, we need to enable and sustain making from a very young age. Not all of us will become sculptors or engineers or designers, but we will become more connected, rounded and creative people.

So while making may sometimes seem inconvenient, we need to find the time, space and resources to make it happen.

The Guardian, 17 March 2016
© Guardian News & Media 2016

Don't Wait, Create Now!

Phillip Krynski

I don't know where to start with this. But I'm not alone. I've heard many people who don't consider themselves "artists" say, "I wish I could draw/write/think like that". What they don't realise, is that it doesn't come so easily to most. In fact it can be painful knowing you're capable of creativity, yet you have a blank slate of ideas. The key is to just jump in and start creating without too much conscious thought. How many times have you sat with a blank piece of paper thinking strenuously about what to draw or write and eventually turn away to go get a bite to eat or watch tv?

Passive engagement is such an easy route, because you're still doing something yet nothing productive. It's a nice way to relax once in a while, but not to live. Instead of trying to think and force ideas, just begin to draw. The sketch takes form if you just continue putting pencil to paper. The same goes for writing. A blank screen is incredibly daunting. Just start typing.

There are a few elements of creativity that should be considered:

SOME ISSUES:

Why do you think creativity is important?

What creative things do you like to do?

Do you think there is enough creativity in your education?

How and why should we encourage more creativity in everyday life?

Does the advice 'just begin' work? Can it be applied to other aspects of life?

1. MISTAKES

If you make a mistake, you can change it. If you mess up badly enough, you can start again.

2. JUDGEMENT

If some people don't like what you've created, why does it matter? Do you like it? If yes, it's not a worry. It's a guarantee that if you like it, others will too.

3. LEARNING

At the end of the day, if it really does suck - and a lot of things do - then what's the worst that happens? You don't even need to show anyone. Just rip it up and take it as a learning experience. You will succeed.

4. SUCCESS

Success is difficult to measure in the creative world sometimes. Unless you are a well known highly paid artist/writer etc, you need to be prepared for people not to care about your work. The key is for you to care. Positive responses will follow naturally from here.

It's time to take your creative dreams and turn them in to reality. Life is too short. You've picked up the pen, now it's time to throw down some ink.

14th October 2015,
Read more from this author here: huffingtonpost.co.uk/phillip-krynski
and follow his progress on Twitter: @phillipklionel

Beulah Devaney

The Illegal, Underground Ballerinas of Iran

Dancing is illegal in the Middle Eastern state, but that hasn't stopped renegade ballet teachers and students from staging classes in secret.

SOME ISSUES:

Could you imagine not being allowed to take part in dance or music?

What makes people continue to want to dance even if they might be severely punished?

Why do you think those in power think the arts are such a threat?

Should access to the arts be a human right?

The first time I met Ada* was at a rooftop party in Amsterdam. We had gravitated towards the snacks table and, reluctant to give up a prime position that offered both uninterrupted access to the fries and a view of drunk tourists falling into the Prinsengracht canal, we began swapping stories. Ada, a web developer from Iran, told me about dodging Tehran's morality police as a teenager, once dashing into a shop in the hope that they'd run past - only to realise that they had followed her in.

"They used to check our nail varnish to make sure it wasn't too bright or enticing," she laughed. "All the police had different ideas about what was going to turn men on too much and it was difficult to know how they'd react. But I knew they'd hate purple so I ran into the shop. The shop owner saw me and opened the back door and I ran out into the back alley while he told the police he hadn't seen me."

"It sounds like something out of the French resistance."

"It was resistance! We would wear gloves to hide our hands and use tricks to get away with wearing as much makeup as possible. That's what [the government] does to us. They make us feel like painting our nails was a really rebellious thing to do. They make you care about such little things, so you don't have the energy to fight for the big things."

Six months after our conversation, Ada emailed me from Tehran. She had just attended her first ballet class in years and was buzzing. She told me about covertly scanning the local newspapers for the "right kind of advert," stalking online message boards, calling mysterious numbers, drafting in friends as character references and, finally, gaining entry to the secretive classes.

Dance is illegal in Iran. Before the 1979 Iranian Revolution, the country poured funding into the arts, especially dance programmes that combined elements of traditional dance with Western disciplines like ballet. After the Shah's government was overthrown, dance was declared sinful. The Iranian National Ballet Company was disbanded in 1979, shortly after all its foreign dancers fled the country.

Their Iranian counterparts were left with three choices: Give up on their life's work and find another way to pay their rent; leave Iran and revive the company somewhere else (Les Ballets Persans is currently operating out of Stockholm), or stay in Iran and - through a combination of subterfuge, bribery, and outright defiance - keep dancing.

Ada was 20 when she attended her first ballet class; she is now 28. "I'm not a risk taker and I never went to any of the illegal parties at college," she says, "but dance classes seemed worth the risk." It's not just dance that is banned in Iran; any music that makes your body move spontaneously is considered sinful. "It's OK as long as it doesn't give you pleasure," Ada explains. "As soon as dance or movement gives you pleasure, it's a sin."

> "It was resistance! We would wear gloves to hide our hands and use tricks to get away with wearing as much makeup as possible. That's what [the government] does to us.

Coming from an English town that was obsessed with three year olds in pink tutus wobbling to Swan Lake, it's difficult to picture ballet as a risky or illicit activity. While I was whining to my mum that I wanted red, not pink, ballet shoes, Ada had to keep her dance classes a secret from her parents. Her parents would have banned Ada from attending - police regularly broke up the classes, especially if the teachers hadn't paid a big enough bribe, and Ada's arrest could have led to a prison sentence and expulsion from university.

These days, classes are held in abandoned hospital basements, office blocks, or silently conducted in the teachers' homes. More often than not, a teacher counts out the beat for the dancers, rather than risk playing music and alerting the neighbours.

Ada's old dance teacher, Azar*, reflects on the constant threat of police intervention. "At any time there is a chance that police will arrive and arrest all of us," she says. "I keep telling my students that I cannot guarantee their safety. However, I try to be very careful. I only accept students who have been referred by other students. I do not try to fill in all my hours by advertising, like some other teachers who give out business cards on the street."

While the 1979 Revolution ended many dancers' careers, it did create unusual opportunities for people like Nassrin*, a young dancer who has - almost by chance - become one of the only suppliers of dance shoes in Tehran. Before the Revolution, professional and amateur dancers could buy their shoes from multiple places, and take their pick from cheap and cheerful basics to high-quality ballet shoes. Thirty-five years on, Tehran's shoemakers have largely moved on, died off, or given up. Nassrin advertises her work via Instagram and is fairly philosophical about the risks: "I make dance shoes. They cannot forbid making shoes."

I put the shoes' photos on my Instagram and it has a specific audience, most people don't know about it. When some of my friends saw it they said they did not know that they were shoes for dancing. They did not recognise them."

> Coming from an English town that was obsessed with three year olds in pink tutus wobbling to Swan Lake, it's difficult to picture ballet as a risky or illicit activity.

Nassrin's attitude is a fairly recent development in Tehran's dance scene. When Ada first started attending classes, people were a lot more worried about being arrested. Now she tells me that they have settled into a familiar rhythm with the police. "They [the government] still say dance is sinful so you must not dance, unless you pay bribes, and then you can dance, but only in secret... Because it's sinful..."

Dancers still have to keep their lessons secret from their families, teachers continue counting out the beat in silent rooms, and shoemakers remain few and far between. But opportunities to dance in public are increasing, although it remains illegal for women to dance in front of men - the only attendees allowed are other women.

Yassi explains that things have changed with the election of President Hassan Rouhani in 2013. "There are a lot more chances to perform but they ask a lot of money for it. We have to pay a big amount of money for each performance, so it will cost us about 200 million rials ($6,630) per performance, which is a lot of money."

An informal compromise has been reached after decades of jostling between fundamentalist Islam and the Iranian public's reluctance to characterise dance as sinful: Pay up and you can dance. When she recently returned from Tehran, Ada reminded me that genuine progress remains painfully slow.

"This new pay-to-dance scheme seems like a good development for Iranian dancers [but] the regime is still benefitting from not having a clear border between what is legal and what is illegal," she says. "It makes it harder to challenge them and majority of the people live even more limited lives by trying to stay away from danger. Ambiguity and fear are the easiest ways to control people."

There is something inherently ludicrous about the idea that a room of seven year olds doggedly practising La Bayadère is sinful. But until this is acknowledged by the Iranian government, Ada and her dance partners must continue to view every small public performance as a triumph in the bigger battle to keep ballet alive in Iran.

Dancers still have to keep their lessons secret from their families, teachers continue counting out the beat in silent rooms, and shoemakers remain few and far between

* Names have been changed

11 July 2016, broadly.vice.com
You can find out more about
Beulah Devaney by visiting her website:
beulahdevaney.com

Whose role is it anyway?

Idris Elba and Michaela Coel, winner of Female Performance in a Comedy Programme for Chewing Gum at the Royal Festival Hall, Southbank, London. Image © Doug Peters/EMPICS Entertainment

Does it matter who gets the best parts? How do gender, race and class affect creative success?

In recent years there has been a great deal of discussion of opportunity in the arts - or the lack of it - with the charge that only those with a relatively wealthy background can succeed.

In 2016 the question of privilege in TV and film hit the headlines when a number of stars boycotted the Oscars Ceremony because no black actor or director had been nominated for an award. The hashtag #OscarsSoWhite was trending on Twitter. Critics pointed out that it was the second year in which outstanding films and actors had been passed over. The suspicion was that the voting was biased because 94% of the voters were white.

Of course, it is also possible to put the counter argument that there were no black candidates who were worthy of an award - that there were good performances but that their white colleagues were simply better this time. But both those arguments collide in one word - opportunity.

The Economist analysed the Oscar results and found that the problem was much wider than awards: 'an analysis of Oscar selections since 2000 suggests that the imbalances are industry-wide, not primarily to do with Academy voters. And they affect all ethnic minorities. Oscar nominations have not dramatically under-represented black actors. Instead, they have greatly over-represented white ones. Blacks are 12.6% of the American population, and 10% of Oscar nominations since 2000 have gone to black actors. But just 3% of nominations have gone to their Hispanic peers (16% of the population), 1% to those with Asian backgrounds, and 2% to those of other heritage."

Black actors are under-represented in top roles and top box office films but when they get those parts they do well, statistically, at the Oscars, winning 10% of best actor nominations and 15% of the actual awards. Where there is a lack of diversity is in the areas where films are written, financed, cast and directed. The problem begins well before an actor starts to work on a performance.

SOME ISSUES:

If TV is the "window on the world" what sort of world do you think it represents?

Why is diversity important among actors and creatives?

What should schools and colleges do to promote and support people who have fewer opportunities because of their gender, race or class (or all three)?

What can be done to improve opportunity in general for people?

An analysis of appearances on TV and film from the University of Southern California concluded:

'The film industry still functions as a straight, white, boys' club. Girls and women are less than one-third of all speaking characters....Characters from under-represented racial/ethnic groups are also excluded or erased. Behind the camera, the conglomerates are sending a strong message to females, especially women of colour. That message is: Your talents are uninvited.'

In 2015, Viola Davies nailed the deep roots of the problem in film and TV. She became the first black actress to win an Emmy for drama and in her emotional acceptance speech she said, 'The only thing that separates women of colour from anyone else is opportunity. You cannot win an Emmy for roles that are simply not there.'

Denied a chance

In interviews in the *New York Times* in February 2016, some of the most successful actors and directors spoke about early setbacks based on ethnicity and class. Wendell Pierce, who starred in *The Wire*, recalled: 'In 1985, I'm sitting in the casting office of a major studio. The head of casting said, "I couldn't put you in a Shakespeare movie, because they didn't have black people then." He literally said that. I told that casting director: "You ever heard of Othello? Shakespeare couldn't just make up black people. He saw them." '

America Ferrera, star of *Ugly Betty* and now a producer, spoke about facing a sort of quota for non-white actors: 'I was 18 and putting myself on tape for a movie I really wanted. I got that phone call: They cast a Latino male in another role in the film; they're not looking to cast [a Latina].'

Class and money

In the UK an extra dimension - class - was added to the debate. It was noted that many of the leading actors in film and TV, people like Benedict Cumberbatch, Eddie Redmayne and Tom Hiddleston, were the products of elite public schools where education costs thousands a year.

According to a survey from the London School of Economics, 73% of actors came from middle class backgrounds - while the

Black actors are under-represented in top roles and top box office films

middle class proportion of the population amounts to only 29%. One actor, whose parents were both doctors, said that his very existence as an actor depended on financial top-ups from mum during lean spells. A black actor from London says: 'If I had inheritance or something I would have been able to take more risks. I would have been able to see more theatre and meet people.'

But disadvantage starts well before the struggle for jobs. The cost of training in the performing arts is high. Student loans are not available for professional courses. Anyone who fails to gain a scholarship faces fees of approximately £18,000 per year over a 3 year course. Without some support, training is not an option.

Those who try to find cheaper ways to get professional training in provincial schools hit

Eddie Redmayne arrives at the Oscars in Los Angeles. Image © Dan Steinberg/ Invision/ Press Association Images

"You need to be white, you need to be male, and you need to be middle class."

another obstacle, the bias towards London. London-based agents select clients from the main drama schools at an early stage. There is less opportunity to train 'on the job', to hone skills and to develop a good CV as there are fewer regional theatres.

Established actors from working class backgrounds have often said that they would not have succeeded if they started now because of the need for parental support and a London base. Maxine Peake, Julie Walters, David Morrissey and Christopher Eccleston are among those who have expressed concern that working class actors are being erased from the scene because of lack of finance, not lack of talent. Christopher Eccleston has a recipe for acting success in the current climate: 'You need to be white, you need to be male, and you need to be middle class.'

The reality of TV

Why does it matter that the people we see on TV and in films are not drawn from the whole of our society? Idris Elba offered some answers when he spoke to Members of Parliament in January 2016 about the need for diversity in TV. 'The TV world helps SHAPE the real world,' he told them. 'It's also a window on our world. But when we look out the window, none of us live in Downton Abbey. … Talent is our lifeblood – we can't afford to WASTE it, or give it away. But when you don't reflect the real world, too much talent is trashed.'

Like others, Elba found that his options were limited by the way people saw him: 'I was getting lots of work, but I realised I could only play so many "best friends" or "gang leaders". I knew I wasn't going to land a lead role. I knew there wasn't

"Talent is everywhere, opportunity isn't. And talent can't reach opportunity."

enough imagination in the industry for me to be seen as a lead.' His move to America brought him fame and the possibility of better, more varied parts but he summed up his concerns about the narrowness of TV portrayals: 'The Britain I come from is the most successful, diverse, multicultural country on earth. But here's my point: you wouldn't know it if you turned on the TV.'

Other art forms

Lack of diversity isn't confined to TV and film. Stuart Maconie, the DJ and music critic, has written on the subject of too many upper class people in music. He argues that 'The best art, and the best pop music certainly, has always been made by smart, impassioned outsiders…The silencing of other, rougher voices brings with it a creeping blandness.'

Others have pointed out that closing libraries, disparaging any education which isn't directed towards making money and saddling students with debt are all ways in which entry into creative professions is blocked to those without the 'right' background whatever potential they may have. And if youngsters don't see themselves on our screens how can they even aspire to find their own path into that creative world.

In the current climate access is blocked, talent is wasted, progress is held up and our culture is misrepresented. But is it merely sour grapes to complain about a lack of diversity? Is singer James Blunt (ex Harrow public school) right to attribute such complaints to jealousy? Is actor Tom Hiddleston (Eton) correct to think the predominance of 'posh' actors and musicians is just a fashion? Will talent always rise to the top?

The argument is not with the talents or merit of those awarded the big prizes and the big roles. Rather it is that the overwhelming presence of relatively privileged people - because of their skin colour, background, gender and absence of disability - highlights the lack of opportunity for those who are not so privileged. To quote Idris Elba again: 'Talent is everywhere, opportunity isn't. And talent can't reach opportunity.'

Sources: Various

Body image

Enhancing Male Body Image

The National Eating Disorders Association, a non-profit organisation in the United States which supports individuals and families affected by eating disorders, provides some tips on how to survive and thrive under this physical pressure

SOME ISSUES:

Why do you think that so many people struggle to feel confident about their bodies?

How do you think that our culture - celebrity culture, our news and media - affects our ideas about how we should look?

What do you think of the suggestions in this article?

How do you think we should help promote a positive sense of self?

Recognise that bodies come in all different sizes and shapes. There is no one "right" body size. Your body is not and should not be exactly like anyone else's. Try to see your body as a facet of your uniqueness and individuality.

Focus on the qualities in yourself that you like that are not related to appearance. Spend time developing these capacities rather than letting your appearance define your identity and your worth.

Look critically at advertisements that push the "body building" message. Our culture emphasizes the V-shaped muscular body shape as the ideal for men. Magazines targeted at men tend to focus on articles and advertisements promoting weight lifting, body-building or muscle toning. Do you know men who have muscular, athletic bodies but who are not happy? Are there dangers in spending too much time focusing on your body? Consider giving up your goal of achieving the "perfect" male body and work at accepting your body just the way it is.

Remember that your body size, shape, or weight does not determine your worth as a person, or your identity as a man. In other words, you are not just your body. Expand your idea of "masculinity" to include qualities such as sensitivity, cooperation, caring, patience, having feelings, being artistic. Some men may be muscular and athletic, but these qualities in and of themselves do not make a person a "man".

Find friends who are not overly concerned with weight or appearance.

Be assertive with others who comment on your body. Let people know that comments on your physical appearance, either positive or negative, are not appreciated. Confront others who tease men about their bodies or who attack their masculinity by calling them names such as "sissy" or "wimp."

Demonstrate respect for men who possess body types or who display personality traits that do not meet the cultural standard for masculinity; eg men who are slender, short, or overweight, gay men, men who dress colourfully or who enjoy traditional "non-masculine" activities such as dancing, sewing or cooking.

Be aware of the negative messages you tell yourself about your appearance or body. Respond to negative self-talk with an affirmation. For example, if you start giving yourself a message like, "I look gross," substitute a positive affirmation, "I accept myself the way I am," or "I'm a worthwhile person, fat and all."

Focus on the ways in which your body serves you and enables you to participate fully in life. In other words, appreciate how your body functions rather than obsessing about its appearance. For example, appreciate that your arms enable you to hold someone you love, your thighs enable you to run, etc.

Aim for lifestyle mastery, rather than mastery over your body, weight, or appearance. Lifestyle mastery has to do with developing your unique gifts and potential, expressing yourself, developing meaningful relationships, learning how to solve problems, establishing goals, and contributing to life. View exercise and balanced eating as aspects of your overall approach to a life that emphasises self-care.

National Eating Disorders Association, www.nationaleatingdisorders.org

Photos posed by models

What (and what not) to say to someone who has lost weight

Saying nothing is absolutely OK, says Viv Groskop. But begging for tips isn't

Sometimes you realise that the problem you have is a good problem to have. And my problem is not that I have lost weight. That's good. (I was previously too heavy. Let's leave it at that.) My problem is that I find it difficult to deal with other people's reactions to the fact that I've lost weight. Especially when they say "You've lost weight" and then don't say anything else. It's a bit like saying, "It's raining today." Yes. It is. And? Your point is? We can all see it's raining. Why are you telling us what we already know? Are you concealing some deeper meaning we are supposed to surmise?

Since April this year I have lost close to three stone. So I understand that I look different. But do I look radically different? This is where other people can only be the real judge. Some people don't notice at all and say nothing. Perhaps I like these people best. I like to think that they didn't notice I was that heavy to begin with. So now that I'm not, they don't really notice that either. Fair enough.

The people I like second best are the ones who say: "Have you lost weight? You look great." It's the second part that is crucial: "You look great." I say this not because I need people to tell me that I look great. But because if they don't say that then by implication they are saying the opposite. This is also a conversational exchange that allows us both to move on. "We acknowledge there has been a change here and it's not a big deal."

The ones who consider it a big deal immediately want to apply your experience to themselves, regardless of whether they need to lose weight or not. In fact, the less weight they need to lose, the more likely they will be to quiz you on the intimate details of how you lost the weight.

SOME ISSUES:

Why do you think we are so interested in how other people look?

What is a compliment and what is offensive when it comes to commenting on how another person looks?

Why do people think it is ok to comment on how other people look?

Do women receive this sort of comment more than men?

> I have lost close to three stone. So I understand that I look different. But do I look radically different?

Essential Articles 2017 • www.completeissues.co.uk

The ones who consider it a big deal immediately want to apply your experience to themselves.

(Here's how: eat less, exercise more. I'm hoping for a book deal. The book will contain those four words and a lot of pictures.) They are very disappointed when you don't have some magic bullet that they didn't know about. "Is it gluten-free? Is it Atkins? Have you gone vegan? Dairy-free? Sworn off carbs? Do you only drink coconut water now?" A bit of all these things, my friends, but not religiously. I repeat: stop looking for the magic bullet! There isn't one!

Which brings me to the worst people. The people who say: "You've lost weight." Then they leave a gap in the conversation where I am supposed to say... what? I usually say quizzically, "Yes, that is correct." Because all they are doing is stating a fact. Are they worried that I am ill and so they're embarrassed to say anything? If so, this is also wrong as I don't want to know

Someone saying "You've lost weight" and then not saying anything else is a bit like saying, "It's raining today." Yes. It is. And? Your point is?

that I look like I might be ill so they should pretend that I look fine.

Or are they doubting their own eyesight and expecting me to say: "No, I haven't lost weight. I am exactly the same as the last time you saw me. You have gone mad"? Or is it that they are

scared of saying the one thing you are not supposed to say: "You've lost weight. Thank God. You were massive." I think it is. I kind of wish they would just say it. Then I could punch them and we could all get on with our lives.

The Pool, 24 November 2015
www.the-pool.com

Advanced style

Our society can be extremely age-ist when it comes to what we think people should and should not wear as they get older, yet one man's blog sets out to highlight that style is not only free for everyone to explore, but in fact gets better with age!

SOME ISSUES:

Why do you think our society is so judgemental about who should wear what?

Is there such a thing as "dressing appropriately"?

If people become more carefree with age, is that the best time to explore style?

Are young people more likely to stick to a coventional look and more frightened to be different?

Is style just clothing or personal expression?

Ari Seth Cohen trawls the streets of New York looking for the most stylish and creative older folks he can find. He believes strongly that you should respect your elders and let these ladies and gents teach us a thing or two about living life to the fullest. Roaming the streets of New York, Ari finds glamorous, outrageous and outright extrovert followers of fashion, or indeed creators of style themselves, and takes images of them for his blog and social media accounts.

His blog-based ode to the confidence, beauty and fashion that can only be achieved through the experience of a life lived glamorously is a collection of street fashion unlike any seen before. It is focused on the over-60 set in the world's most stylish locales. Inspired by his grandmother's unique personal style and his own interest in the put-together fashion of vibrant seniors, this collection of timeless images and words of wisdom provides fashion inspiration for all ages and proves that age is nothing but a state of mind.

His blog and social media built up a huge following. People all over the world are so interested in the outfits of senior style icons that he has now brought some of his favourites together in a book.

Advanced Style offers proof from the wise and silver-haired set that personal style advances with age.

You should respect your elders and let these ladies and gents teach us a thing or two about living life to the fullest.

Source & images:
www.instagram.com/advancedstyle
www.advanced.style

BORROWED OR STOLEN?

Is imitation of other cultures appreciation or oppression?

SOME ISSUES:

What cultural appropriation examples can you think of?

Is copying from other cultures wrong?

Why is it that some cultures that are discriminated against are also copied?

What can we do to make sure we are more respectful of other cultures?

What arguments could you put in favour of such imitation?

The UK, especially the big cities, can be a melting pot of different cultures. And social media, globalised business, TV and film mean that we are familiar with the dress, customs and mannerisms of places far removed from our own. Food, too, is part of this shared world-wide mixture of fashions, tastes and experiences. But when something is used by everyone, does it then belong to no-one? Do the original owners lose possession of a symbol that matters to them when it becomes part of someone else's 'dressing up'? Is taking from another culture a sign of appreciation and integration? Or is it the case that such casual use of an aspect of another culture just hides contempt for its deeper meanings? And what does all of this mean if the original, authentic cultures are at the receiving end of abuse and discrimination while others select aspects of their customs for fun or fashion? These are the questions behind the concept of cultural appropriation.

What is cultural appropriation?
Culture appropriation is a one-way street which involves members of a dominant culture 'helping themselves' to aspects of another group, often a minority. This is done without reference to the other way of life, without any deep understanding or appreciation, and often without giving the minority group credit. The item taken over could be clothing, decoration, dance, music, folklore, a symbol, a remedy - the list is extensive. It can be especially harmful when this careless borrowing relates to something as sensitive as a religious symbol, but also when the minority group feels that something of value, something exclusively theirs, has been removed.

Borrowed or stolen?
From the beginnings of modern pop music, white musicians copied styles, rhythms and even pronunciation from black counterparts. In the 1950s it was white musicians who made successful careers as rock-n-roll artists even though they had been introduced to the form by black innovators. These originators got no credit and very little money.

In recent years, several music stars have been accused of exploiting other cultures. Perhaps the most notorious example is that of Miley Cyrus twerking at the MTV awards in 2013. Cyrus, a white, former child-star, used the dance, which originated in the African American community, as a way to assert a 'grown up', sexualised image for herself, while surrounded by black women backing dancers. She was criticised harshly for imitating black style while pushing actual black women into a background role - her performance was a visual metaphor for cultural appropriation.

She is not the only pop star to be criticised. Taylor Swift was accused of appropriating the whole of Africa in her video for "Wildest Dreams". The video uses the idea of a vintage film, set in colonial Africa in the 1950s. Its lack of a single distinguishable black face was justified by its director as historically accurate. This, and the fact that Swift had given the proceeds of the video to an African wildlife charity, did not deter critics who said she had packaged the continent as her backdrop while ignoring its people and romanticising a time that was actually brutally cruel - distorting both Africa's appearance and its history.

Fashion is an area where a level of unacknowledged copying is rife. Designers discover or 're-invent' patterns and styles from other lands as innovations. When a fashion magazine suggests that dreadlocks or Afros are a new trend because a reality TV personality has adopted them - ignoring the fact that they have been around for centuries - it is not just the claiming of the style that is the problem. The underlying message is that its origin can be disregarded as unimportant. It also cruelly overlooks the everyday reality for many black people themselves - ignorance and discrimination based around their natural hair - making it galling that white people are free to copy it just as they please.

It isn't only black culture that is absorbed and diluted in the interests of pop music and trend setting. When Katy Perry performed as a Geisha at an awards ceremony she described it as a homage to Asian culture. But others felt that it was both disrespectful and perpetuating a stereotype of a subservient Asian woman that reinforced a Western perspective of the East.

This pattern of lifting cultural artefacts and making them fit our own purposes is widespread. While music and film personalities may have been seen wearing a bindi, a dot or pattern between the eyebrows, the spread of this style has more to do with festivals and retro-hippiness. For the girls at Glastonbury or Latitude wearing a bindi is less an embrace of Indian culture than a statement about their (temporary) alternative lifestyles. The anonymous creator of #reclaimthebindi has something to say about a religious and cultural symbol being used this way: "You shouldn't take cultural artefacts with immense amounts of significance and reduce them down to a fashion statement. While you are appreciated as 'trendy' and 'hipster', I am forced to deal with the harassment and racism because of the colour of my skin".

hidden meanings

It may be argued that all these borrowings are just an expression of how liberal and multicultural our society has become. You could say there is no harm in Native American headdresses being used as festival wear. But when a member of a dominant (that is white, western) civilisation makes use of something associated with a less advantaged, and far more less privileged group there is a large element of oppression. It is a sort of play-acting that suggests that the 'other' culture is exactly that - other: not mainstream but edgy, not everyday but exotic, not meaningful but trivial, and there to be rifled as and when and at a whim. This is an option that only those in positions of privilege can take - copying the trappings of another culture without having to face the hardships and prejudices that frequently go alongside.

It was once acceptable mainstream entertainment for white men to put on blackface make-up to perform. Al Jolson was a huge silent-movie star and the *Black and White Minstrel Show* was once popular TV entertainment. We now understand that this mimicry was demeaning and damaging. How long before we wake up to all the other messages we send out by treating someone else's culture as fancy dress?

Cultural appropriation is so deep rooted in our society that much of it is completely unknown and goes by unnoticed – by white westerners. Stealing from other cultures and disregarding the consequences is exactly what colonialists did. Yet in a multi-cultural and progressive society, we still need to open our eyes to the fact that this is not ok. As *Hunger Games* actor Amandla Stenberg asks in her YouTube vlog "What would America be like if we loved black people as much as we love black culture?"

We, too, need to ask what the world could be like if we learnt more about, and connected with, other cultures, instead of merely taking from them.

Sources: Various

From the beginnings of modern pop music, white musicians copied styles, rhythms and even pronunciation from black counterparts.

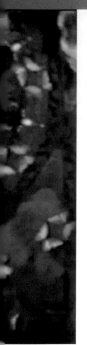

BLACK LIVES MATTER. SO DOES ISLAMOPHOBIA. BEYONCÉ IN A SARI? NOT SO MUCH

Some cultural appropriation is insensitive. But not every battle is worth having if it segregates culture and distracts from battling real prejudice - Nosheen Iqbal

SOME ISSUES:

Is wearing something from another culture damaging to that culture or flattering?

Does it matter what culture the things you are wearing come from?

How can you explore other cultures and ways of expression without contributing towards the problem?

Does knowing about cultural appropriation make you reconsider any choices?

"Is it OK to use the black emojis if you're not black?" As conversation starters about identity politics go, few seem more juvenile and current than this one. (FYI, to avoid the tedium of this real-life chat I had recently, it's easier to stick with your own skin tone.) And yet, here we are, at the frontier of "being woke". On one hand, this means being socially aware about issues such as #blacklivesmatter, racial profiling, privilege, Islamophobia etc — all the big guns. On the other? Not every battle is worth having. To clarify, this isn't a discussion about the very real and very insensitive cases of cultural appropriation in recent years — the most obvious being native American headdresses — a sacred tradition regurgitated as cheap and crass festival costume fodder (so two summers ago, keep up). No,

"being woke" - being aware - especially about what's going on in the community about racism and social injustice.

privilege - the advantage that a person or a group has because of their position in society. Often the person with privilege is unaware that being, for example, rich, white or male gives them an advantage that others don't have.

cultural appropriation - members of one group adopt or use parts of the culture of another group. This is often the dominant group borrowing from minorities, for fairly trivial purposes, without appreciating that what they are using for decoration may have a deeper significance. As one tweeter put it "because my culture, my heritage and my religion is not your trashy fashion statement"

Beyoncé in Coldplay's Hymn for the Weekend
Photo: YouTube

HAVING BEEN EMBARRASSED ABOUT YOUR HERITAGE AND MADE FUN OF WHEN YOU WERE YOUNGER...

... IT'S JARRING THEN TO SEE THAT ETHNIC FESTIVAL LOOK.

what we're seeing more and more of now are the minority voices within minorities who are policing communities and culture to the point of ridicule.

Take, for example, the #reclaimthebindi movement. I understand the frustration: having been embarrassed about your heritage and made fun of when you were younger for your mum's funny clothes and accent, it's jarring then to see Becky at Latitude co-opting sari tops and henna for that ethnic festival look a decade later. It's not necessarily racist, but it is definitely high on the scale of Dumb, Annoying Shit People Do. To be ranked in that same file: colour runs (the Hindu spring festival Holi

reconfigured as an Instagram opportunity in Hyde Park); the fact that Black Twitter is rarely credited for setting the agenda for contemporary pop culture; Coldplay's cringe discovery of India on their last album. However, to claim that Beyoncé committed a heinous, culturally insensitive crime by wearing south Asian-style gold and henna in the video for Coldplay's *Hymn for the Weekend*, or that only African American women can truly appreciate [Beyoncé's album] *Lemonade*, segregates culture in an aggressively retro way. It's a parody of earnestness that does us no

favours. How did we even get here?

Tribally marking off permission rights on who can and who cannot enjoy certain music and certain fashion – both industries where creativity and innovation depend so much on borrowing from so-called "other" cultures – is inane. It also distracts from bigger-picture arguments: say, the disproportionately high numbers of non-white deaths in police custody, or the rights of Bangladeshi factory workers, still stitching your H&M vests for less than a living wage.

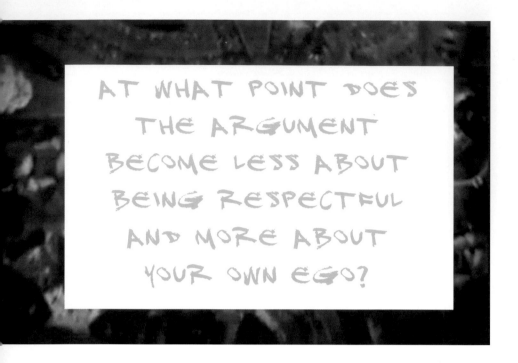

AT WHAT POINT DOES THE ARGUMENT BECOME LESS ABOUT BEING RESPECTFUL AND MORE ABOUT YOUR OWN EGO?

See the energy expended on Blake Lively last week. A relatively innocuous actor slash lifestyle brand – the B-side to Gwyneth Paltrow, if you will – Lively was called out as a racist for posting a picture of her arse on Instagram with the caption: "LA face with an Oakland booty." Which is, for clarity's sake, a lyric from *Baby Got Back* by the connoisseur of big butts, Sir Mix-A-Lot. Lively may well be dim to sensitivities around race and privilege (she did, after all, host her 2012 wedding to Ryan Reynolds at a plantation in South Carolina), but that's by the by. The alleged furore she sparked in this instance was because, to quote women's website Jezebel, she "touts a diametrical opposition: that Los Angeles can equate to elegance and/or beauty (read: whiteness) and that Oakland is its foil (read: blackness)".

Sure, yes, I get it. But is this the hill we want to die on? The Daily Mail would like its readers to think so. Like many sections of the press, it will routinely, hysterically, report on tiny corners of the internet shrieking racism at every minor outrage – arguably, because it's easier then to undermine social justice warriors as sensitive keyboard ninnies even when they're battling legitimate prejudice.

Should we really be wearing out moral outrage and energy in pretending that Sir Mix-A-Lot belongs not to those coming of age in the 90s, but exclusively to the African American experience? And, if so, where do we stop When Cultural Appropriation Goes Bad? Once you put down dodgy markers, where only people of colour have the right to write about race, only black people can rap, only my mum can make authentic palak gosht (that last one is true, actually), where do you draw the line? And at what point do we admit that the argument becomes less to do with being respectful of "other" cultures and more about your own ego as a minority voice? While it's one thing to stick it to white privilege and remind the mainstream that not everything is made for and about white people, it's quite another to cordon off culture into ever tinier boxes, where the right to enjoy and be influenced by what you consume is narrow and prescriptive.

Suddenly, that utopian optimism about embracing, sharing and celebrating one another's differences seems so quaint. The struggle isn't about one-upmanship. Nor is it about the racial politics of your emoji.

The Guardian, 22 May 2016
© Guardian News & Media 2016

Blake Lively - In May 2016 this American actress caused controversy when she tweeted photographs of herself from the front and from the back at a film premiere. She accompanied the pictures with a line from a song: 'LA face with an Oakland booty'. Since Oakland is considered as a black area of California, some tweeters were offended, "Unbelievably problematic, using women of color's bodies as a joke."

Britain & its citizens

The grim reality of being an interracial couple in Britain

Singer FKA twigs has been subjected to online abuse for having a white boyfriend, Twilight actor Robert Pattinson.

Radhika Sanghani reports on the casual racism experienced by many interracial couples

SOME ISSUES:

Why do interracial couples get 'looks' from some people?

What should be done to stop people receiving abuse for their choice of partner?

Do you think these attitudes will change as time goes on?

When FKA twigs started going out with Robert Pattinson, the gossip sites went crazy.

R-Patz from the Twilight franchise - a man swooned-over by womankind and probably quite a few Hollywood stars too - was seeing a singer from London, who gelled baby curls on to her face.

Some online commentators showed their surprise by saying how 'alternative' FKA twigs was.

Reading between the lines, it was clear part of their issue was with white Pattinson dating dark-skinned twigs, with her mixed Jamaican, Spanish and English descent.

They suggested twigs was part of his 'edgy' phase, and he'd soon come to his senses and go for someone more 'on his level' - such as his Twilight co-star and ex-girlfriend Kristen Stewart.

Until the news came out that he'd reportedly proposed to his singer girlfriend.

Interracial couples 1. Narrow-minded idiots 0.

Such sites may have made uncomfortable reading. But it's nothing compared to what twigs was directly subjected to.

She recently told the Sunday Times Magazine that when her relationship with Pattinson became public, she started receiving abuse. Lots of it.

Legions of Twilight fans would send her racist messages, calling her "monkey" — and they're still going. Unsurprisingly, it's made her break down and cry.

It's depressing that, in 2015, people can still have a problem with interracial couples.

But they do.

It's something I've experienced personally as a British Indian. I had my first taste of this racism — because that's what it is, no matter how subtly or politely it's disclosed — when I was 18.

I went on a double date with my female Jewish friend. My partner for the evening was a white, Jewish guy. Hers was Indian.

The reaction we had from family and friends? 'You two should swap dates'.

It was delivered in a jokey way and we laughed it off, but there was always that sense that being with someone of the same race was the 'right' thing to do. By that token, interracial dating wasn't.

Seven years on and I still have problems with my current boyfriend, a white New Zealander. Obviously we're not subjected to online abuse from gossip sites (being that we're not in any Hollywood film franchises, or performing at Glastonbury).

We do get 'looks' when we're walking down the street together – especially when we leave London.

Robert Pattinson and FKA twigs attending The Metropolitan Museum of Art Gala, 2016

Photo: © Doug Peters/EMPICS Entertainment

But we do get 'looks' when we're walking down the street together - especially when we leave London.

Sometimes they're glances of pure disgust. Much of the time it seems to be confusion and uncertainty ('are they even allowed to date in her culture?')

My boyfriend never notices. Unlike me he's never had to develop a 'racism radar', where you instinctively know that people are staring because of your skin colour.

But I do.

Lots of my black and ethnic minority (BAME) friends, who date white people, tell me the same thing. Their partners never realise.

I know of one couple — a black man and white woman — who've had much worse experiences. Her middle-class British family often make racist remarks about his skin colour ("didn't see you there in the dark — you should have smiled").

On holiday in Europe, waiters have rudely ignored him and only spoken to his girlfriend.

But such racism doesn't just come from white people trying to process the fact that someone might want to date outside their race. It can come from inside the BAME community too.

An Indian girlfriend of mine, whose ex was white, tells me that when they used to walk around in London, holding hands, other Indians would stare.

"They'd look at us and do this subtle head shake thing. It always felt like they were trying to say I was betraying my culture and religion by choosing to be with someone outside of it."

She knew that's what they were thinking because that's how her extended family felt about him - and they'd give her the same disapproving looks.

Other friends tell me they don't even bother telling their relatives about new partners if they're not the same race. One jokingly refers to her boyfriend as her 'vanilla secret' as her extended family in India have no idea he exists.

For many interracial couples, this is perfectly normal. They take it all in their stride. We expect the jokes about how our skin colours (mine brown; his freckled) look different on the

> My boyfriend never notices. Unlike me he's never had to develop a 'racism radar', where you instinctively know that people are staring because of your skin colour.

beach. We know people will be curious about how our families feel about it (absolutely fine). Most of the time we laugh it off.

But when that veers into nasty looks, comments or even outright abuse, it becomes something no couple should have to deal with. Famous or not.

It's plain racist and it's time Britain outgrew it once and for all.

Daily Telegraph, 11 August 2015
© Telegraph Media Group Limited 2015

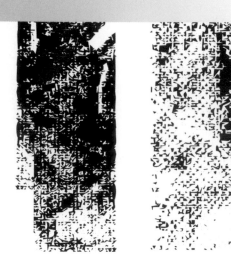

A conversation with a Muslim London taxi driver after the Paris attacks that should shame us all

Chris Hemmings

"What am I supposed to tell my son? He's only ten. Every time I turn the news on, people are talking about Islam, about Muslims, about the religion I'm bringing him up to love."

SOME ISSUES:

What might help Ahmed feel less alienated?

Where do people's opinions about Islam come from?

Why is it wrong to blame a whole community for acts committed by others?

How could you explain to Ahmed's ten year old son what he is hearing in the media?

In the early hours of Sunday morning, at 2am, I met Ahmed. Ahmed drives a cab, lives in London and has a young son. As we drove, the news briefly came on the radio - he quickly turned it off. "No more news for me," he said.

When I queried why, he let loose. Our conversation carried on long after we'd reached my house. And what he said was so extraordinary, I began to record him.

Ahmed speaks English. Perfect English, with only a hint of a Pakistani accent. He's a second generation immigrant, a British Muslim man, and his experience of living in the UK now is utterly depressing to hear.

"What am I supposed to tell my son? He's only ten. Every time I turn the news on, people are talking about Islam, about Muslims, about the religion I'm bringing him up to love."

Following yet another attack by "Muslims", Ahmed feels his religion is again being assaulted. His friends and family feel so ashamed, they feel compelled to apologise for what happened. They hold up 'Not all Muslims' signs. Like we have to be reminded that not every follower of Islam is out to murder us in the name of Allah. It proves how pervasive this mentality has become.

"My community is becoming alienated from everyone else. We don't feel we belong here anymore."

His religion has become a synonym for evil.

He went on to explain that, each time one of the attacks happens, it gets increasingly difficult to feel secure on the streets of London. "I don't feel like I belong here anymore," he said.

I then asked if he'd ever considered leaving, tired of the abuse and the anti-Islam rhetoric. "All the time," he said, "but where would I go?" He explained how he has family here, a home, a job. He couldn't go to Pakistan - "I'm too Westernised". The same goes for other Islamic countries, too. "Plus, I'm British, and don't want to go anywhere." Why should he?

Ahmed has a magnificent beard. The sort I'm unable to grow and am jealous of. Now, because beards have somehow become a symbol of terrorism, he's genuinely considered shaving it off - "just to blend in". He no longer wants to be recognisable as a follower of Islam in the UK. "My community is becoming alienated from everyone else. We don't feel we belong here anymore."

With each of these assaults on our freedoms, there's a predictable swell of right-wing rhetoric. Anti-foreigner, anti-immigrant, anti-Muslim sentiment becomes the default setting. But for the sake of Ahmed, his son, and the future of a civilised world, we have to fight the urge to join in with that mentality.

We have to stop blaming the world's 1.5 billion Muslims for the acts of a singular death cult. We have to ensure more young people aren't lured to Syria under the false promise of belonging, after being convinced that they can never live side-by-side with their fellow citizens because of their religion. We have to re-welcome Ahmed, beard and all, back in to society where he belongs.

More importantly, we have to stop calling the perpetrators of these attacks Muslims. They are extremists, terrorists, murderers - anything but 'Muslim'.

As if that needed emphasising, it's recently emerged that the leaders of Islamic faith groups told Muslim women they "should avoid going out in public places and stay vigilant" after what happened in Paris. Said Khan told LBC (a London based talk radio station) his daughter asked him if it was safe for her to leave the house, and a mosque in Glasgow has been set alight. We cannot allow this to continue.

I promised him I wouldn't publish our recording, so he wouldn't become a recognisable target of hate. But Ahmed, if you're reading this, please know you're not alone, not hated, not feared.

As I finally stepped out of the car, I turned to him with one last question.

"When you get home in the morning, what will you tell your son?"

"I just don't know anymore," was his exhausted answer.

What can we, as fellow British citizens, tell Ahmed's son? We should tell him to be proud of his heritage, proud of his religion and proud of his father for having the courage to speak out. Hopefully, we can give him a country to be proud of too.

The Independent, 18 November 2015
www.independent.co.uk

15 things I learned about Islam and British values as a gay boy living opposite a mosque

Photo © George Daley
Geodaley

Thomas Mauchline

The media stories about Islam meant that I was genuinely a little nervous about moving in across the road to a mosque. What I have learned in the four years since I moved is that the ridiculousness of British culture is universal. We all love tea, are really polite and tut rather than saying something, no matter what our religion

SOME ISSUES:

How do the media tend to represent British Muslims?

There are many different cultures living in the UK, how can we promote community cohesion?

Why is it important to try to understand different cultures and communities?

How much of what the writer is saying relates to you and your community?

1. No mosque has enough parking and Muslim men love to complain about it. I don't care how young or trendy they are; within seconds they will be pointing at bits of pavement and muttering about the number of cars you could fit in there - like my Granddad from Manchester does at Sainsbury's.

2. You can do that look British people do to each other, when someone nearby is making a scene, in a full face veil.

3. Muslims pray a lot.

4. You will be happy they pray a lot if you have been stabbed on your doorstep and are too scared to go outside, so you time your trips to the shops to coincide with these prayers as the streets are full of friendly people.

5. Muslims, like all British people have that one problematic uncle that kinda ruins family occasions.

Like the rest of British dads, all Muslim fathers think their daughter is smarter than everyone...

Photo posed by models

... and that their son is a heartbreaker!

6. When confronted with something out of their comfort zone, like me and my boyfriend in full drag dancing down the road, Muslims - like all British people - get flustered and overcompensate by being overly polite -a bit like Hugh Grant.

7. When finding out you have been dating your boyfriend for five years, your Muslim neighbours will be disgusted that you haven't proposed. You hear "Get a civil partnership - for your mother's sake" a lot.

8. Apparently there is usually half a cup of tea next to the prayer mat when praying at home - especially for morning prayers.

9. Like the rest of British dads, all Muslim fathers think their daughter is smarter than everyone, even though she is only 6 years old...

10. ...and that their son is a heartbreaker even though it's clear to everyone else that he spends all his time on his Xbox.

11. Young Muslim women are really, really, really ambitious.

12. British people's dry sarcasm works really well when confronting the times the more traditional parts of Islam come face-to-face with modern gay culture. For example, when I donated three sequined crop-tops to the Islamic Relief Syria clothing drive, one of the older guys there smirked while shaking my hand and said, "Our brothers and sisters in Syria thank you for the evening wear."

13. There is always an aunt who gets too involved in the wedding planning and annoys the bride.

14. During ramadan and eid there will be so many people on the streets going to mosque that the drugs dealers will have to move to other places - making your area really safe for a while.

15. Mothers will say anything to stop their kids nagging them. I once saw a Muslim mother tell her kid who wanted some fried chicken after Friday night prayer, that the shop wasn't halal - even though there was a 5ft square neon halal sign in the window. Reminds me of when my mum told me that the chip shop was closed for a private event as she wanted some peace.

This blog post first appeared on medium.com.
To read more from Thomas Mauchline visit:
medium.com/@tommauchline

I WANT TO SHOW THEM THAT WE ARE MORE THAN WHAT THEY SAY WE ARE. WE CAN DO MORE AS WORKING CLASS YOUNG PEOPLE.
- Shawnee, 15, Stockport

19 PRIME MINISTERS FROM ETON, BUT NOT **ONE** FROM STOCKPORT.

WE'RE GOING TO CHANGE THIS.
www.disruptiveleaders.org.uk
#DisruptiveLeaders
RECLAIM

How old is old enough?

Should 16 year olds be allowed to vote?

SOME ISSUES:

What is the right age to be allowed to vote?

In your experience, are young people interested in politics?

What are young people concerned about and passionate about?

How should politicians make sure they connect with young people?

If there is a minimum age for voting, should there also be a maximum age? Is age the only way to measure whether someone should have the right to vote?

Currently in the UK a person must be 18 or over to vote for their MP but there is a move to lower the voting age to 16. Is a 16 year old responsible enough to be given that right? Yes or No?

16 year olds are generally classified as being children. They can't legally buy alcoholic drinks or drive a car. For the most part they are still living at home, still dependent on their parents for financial and other support. They are still in education and their parents are still legally responsible for their care and wellbeing. All of this suggests that they are not ready to participate in the decisions that will shape the future of the country.

A 16 year old can legally consent to sex, choose a doctor, decide on medical treatment, work, pay tax, order a passport and become a millionaire by buying a lottery ticket. With parental support 16 year olds can get married, rent somewhere to live and join the armed forces. To some extent the state regards them as adults, after all, they have a National Insurance number and can claim benefits. But they have no say in decisions about their legal status or about their future - which is also the future of the country.

Do 16 year olds even want the vote? In recent elections the 18-24 year olds have been the least likely to turn out. It is the older age groups who are the most likely to vote and consequently political parties can afford to ignore the young while courting the old. Would 16 and 17 year olds be any more likely to vote than those slightly older? Are they even interested in politics? It's not good for our democracy that large percentages of the population aren't bothered about voting. If 16 year olds are given the vote and don't use it then politicians will have every reason to ignore them and concentrate on the proportion of the population who do vote. Ironically, giving them the vote could make them less influential.

Social media and direct action provide them with the interest and the influence that is missing from their experience of traditional politics.

Declining interest in politics is not confined to the younger age groups. The total turnout in the 2015 election was 66.1% of eligible voters. This is better than the lowest ever turnout of 59.1% in 2001 but compares very badly with the 83.9% turnout in 1950. Many people are disenchanted with party politics. Young people, though, are engaging with issues such as environmental campaigns and local issues in ways that seem more natural and accessible and simply possible to them. Social media and direct action provide them with the interest and the influence that is missing from their experience of traditional politics.

Even if they are interested, 16 year olds have other priorities. They are right in the middle of important exams. Understanding and participating in politics would be just another burden and a stress at a time when they have all the stresses of adolescence to contend with.

The illustrations we have used are from RECLAIM, a Manchester-based youth leadership charity with a bold aim - to end leadership inequality within a generation.

RECLAIM is not party political and is led by the young people it supports and the issues they face. Its aim is to help young people use their potential for leadership 'irrespective of postcode, school or family background'.

The organisation believes that current leaders in all fields - politics, economics, media, culture and sport - are too alike and the voices of young, working-class people need to be heard.

www.reclaimproject.org.uk
@RECLAIMProject
Working class young people being seen, being heard and leading change.

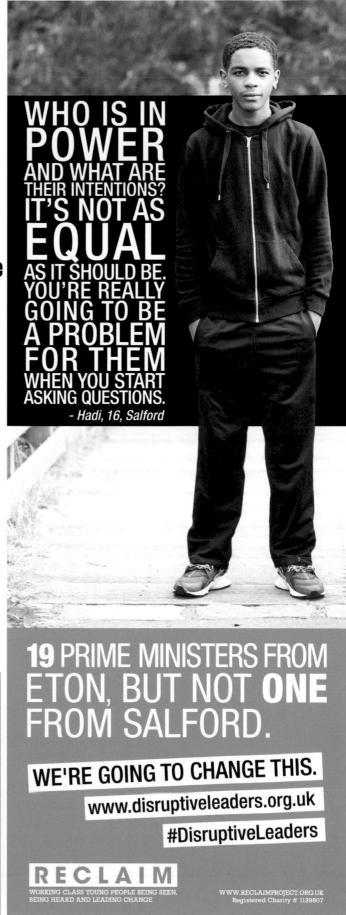

WHO IS IN POWER AND WHAT ARE THEIR INTENTIONS? IT'S NOT AS EQUAL AS IT SHOULD BE. YOU'RE REALLY GOING TO BE A PROBLEM FOR THEM WHEN YOU START ASKING QUESTIONS.
- Hadi, 16, Salford

19 PRIME MINISTERS FROM ETON, BUT NOT **ONE** FROM SALFORD.

WE'RE GOING TO CHANGE THIS.

www.disruptiveleaders.org.uk

#DisruptiveLeaders

RECLAIM
WORKING CLASS YOUNG PEOPLE BEING SEEN, BEING HEARD AND LEADING CHANGE

WWW.RECLAIMPROJECT.ORG.UK
Registered Charity # 1139807

Voting wouldn't be compulsory.
No one would be forced to participate. Having the vote would be an opportunity not an obligation. Just like the rest of the population, some people would choose to be active and many would not - but they would have the right to have a say in decisions about their future.

There's another worry. Giving 16 year olds - young, inexperienced, naive and easily influenced people - a say in the future of the whole country is a big risk. They don't have enough knowledge about life or its complexities to be able to make sensible long-term decisions. Young people are easily fired up, easily enraged about things and attracted by simple solutions. They get their news and information from social media - with no idea about how reliable it is. They respond in short simplistic soundbites. Do we want someone whose analysis of problems takes just 140 characters to make decisions that affect everyone?

If we care about the future of the country, we should make sure that 16 year olds are educated about the way our democracy works, what its values are and how to protect them. We should educate people not just for exams but to be clear thinkers. If 16 year olds felt that their vote was important, that it would make a difference, then they would have an incentive to find out about it. If the people who vote most are older then they are making decisions for someone else's future. Older doesn't always mean wiser or better informed.

Many of the arguments used to deny the vote to 16 year olds are exactly the same as those used when the voting age was lowered from 21 to 18 in 1969 and even to deny the vote to women at the beginning of the 20th century - too irresponsible, too easily influenced and emotional, not as knowledgeable as others (that is men) who would make better decisions on their behalf. We recognise them as wrong - and they are still wrong 100 years later when applied to another group.

Sources: Various, including: www.votesat16.org, www.electoral-reform.org.uk, kennyimafidon.com, www.parliament.uk/briefing-papers/sn01747.pdf

The current situation - and the future

Who can vote now?
To vote in a UK general election a person must be registered to vote and also 18 or over, a British citizen (or a qualifying Commonwealth citizen or a citizen of the Republic of Ireland) and be legally allowed to vote.

Who can't vote?
Members of the House of Lords and prisoners who are in jail are banned from voting (although the European Court of Human Rights has ruled that prisoners should be allowed to vote, the UK government has refused this).

What about the future?
16 and 17 year olds were allowed to vote in the Referendum on Scottish Independence in 2014 and the law has been changed to allow voting at 16 for elections to the Scottish Parliament and for local government elections in Scotland.

The National Assembly for Wales will be given the power to lower the voting age to 16 for Assembly elections.

16 and 17 year olds in the Isle of Man, Jersey, Guernsey, Brazil and Austria already have the vote. They can also vote in some elections in Germany, Malta and Norway.

The Labour Party, the SNP, the Liberal Democrats and the Green Party all support voting at 16, but the Conservative party is opposed to it.

The House of Lords wanted to extend voting in the EU referendum to 16 and 17 year olds, but in December 2015 this was blocked in the House of Commons.

A petition to give them the right to vote has been started: petition.parliament.uk/petitions/119706

If we care about the future of the country, we should make sure that 16 year olds are educated about the way our democracy works

"We've grown up with some frightening events"

UK teenagers' hopes and fears

It's tough being a teen – especially, a WHO study found this week, in Britain. From social media to job prospects, five teens explain the challenges they face

Emine Saner

Jodie Ginger, 19, apprentice business administrator, Leicester

When I was at school I was worried about the way I looked. Social media didn't help, even though you knew people had changed their photos to make themselves look better. I don't spend much time on social media, particularly now I have a job. I don't like the way sites like Facebook and Twitter have become a way to bully people.

When I was younger, there was a point when I was smoking and drinking and doing stuff that I shouldn't. I had gone through some negative experiences at school, and I was kicked out at the beginning of year 11, but I did get support from the Job Centre and a college, and through an organisation called TwentyTwenty. I like myself more now.

Growing up through the financial crisis, I do worry about whether I'll have a job or a house when I'm 25, or be able to have a family, but I also feel I'm a bit too young to think about it at the moment. But other things worry me. I'm too scared to go abroad – watching the news and seeing stuff like terrorism and the rise of Isis, it does scare me.

I don't think politicians know what our lives are like, or how the changes they make affect young people in the real world. Young people are unfairly treated by lots of policies – for instance, you're only allowed working tax credits from the age of 25, even though lots of young people earn very little. There are young people who work but really get nothing for working.

*All photos posed by models

SOME ISSUES:

What issues bother you?

What would you say are the main issues young people face right now?

Do you think it is difficult worrying about global issues and studying at school?

What can we do to help young people cope with the pressures of today?

Zachary Phillips, 15, London

I want to be a professional tennis player, and I spend most of my time training for it. I'm an athlete, and I don't drink or smoke, but other people at school do.

Tennis is everything, and I'm not really thinking about doing any other jobs. If I don't become a player, I could become a coach, so that's my back-up plan. If tennis goes well, then hopefully everything will go the right way for me, financially.

I think many young people are unhappy. There's nothing for them to do. If I didn't have tennis, I don't know what I'd be doing – probably hanging around on the streets with my friends. That's the way people seem to pass their time, and you can get into trouble. My friends get stopped and searched a lot by the police, and I have been as well. It's disappointing that they would stop and search me for no reason. It's frustrating but I just get on with it.

Isaac Grinnell, 16, Leeds

There is definitely pressure at school. I've got mock exams starting soon, and school piles on the pressure to do well. That makes you feel nervous. Things like university fees worry me a lot because I don't know whether I will be able to afford to go, even though I really want to.

Stuff like alcohol hasn't been a problem for me because my parents have always brought me up thinking it wasn't appropriate for my age. But when I'm walking to school there are lots of people smoking, and I see pictures on Facebook of people drinking alcohol.

Body image affects boys too. There is pressure to look a certain way, and social media heightens it – for men, it's to be really fit and have muscles.

I feel like people my age have grown up with some serious and frightening events going on around us. It's not necessarily that I'm worried that, say, I walk into Leeds and there's going to be a terrorist attack; it's more that I'm worried about how it affects other people. After the Paris attacks, I got worried about people living in Paris, and also about migrants having to flee from their country. It all just adds to the pressure – that you're thinking about them, while also trying to do your exams.

> "After the Paris attacks, I got worried about people living in Paris, and also about migrants having to flee from their country"

> "There is so much expectation on how young women should dress, and there is too much sexualisation. But if you wear tight clothes or too much makeup, you get shamed for that as well. I live my life how I want"

Keiarnya Grant-Blissett, 20, student, Manchester

While I was growing up, my mum had a lot of control over my social media and what TV programmes I watched, so I think I was protected from some of the negative aspects, but now you go on and it's: "You need to be this if you want to be perfect." Social media isn't great at showing the diversity of people, and it does make you question yourself. There is so much expectation on how young women should dress, and there is too much sexualisation. But if you wear tight clothes or too much makeup, you get shamed for that as well. I live my life how I want.

I took a step back from social media so I could focus on studying, but I still find there is too much media around. Sometimes when I've spent too long online I think I could have read a book, or gone out exploring.

There was a lot of pressure at school – from the moment you pick your GCSEs, you feel that if you do well you'll get into college, and then you'll get into university and then you'll get a good job. But even if I do this degree, am I going to get a job? That worry is always there.

My mum has always made sure we've had anything we needed, but I've seen her struggle financially – she's a carer – and it's made me want to do well so I can give back to her and make her proud.

Willa Duggan, 15, Surrey

There can be a lot of pressure, and I feel like the decisions we make now will have a big impact on our future lives, but generally, picturing what adulthood might be like, I feel like I don't really have a lot of responsibilities right now, and so I don't really feel like it's a miserable time. I do think about things like whether I'll be able to afford a house in the future. I would need my parents' support – it's harder for people to do it on their own.

Climate change really scares me. My mum is really passionate about politics, so I learn a lot from her and I watch the news. I feel like politicians are all quite well off and have a good lifestyle, and don't really know how a lot of people live.

I spend a lot of time on social media – Facebook, Snapchat and Instagram are the main ones. I feel like it's a bit of a competition. People judge you by how many followers you have or the pictures you post. It becomes a bit of an obsession to check up on people to see what they're doing, rather than getting on with your own life. I'm pretty attached to my phone. When I'm on my phone, all my friends are messaging each other and I feel like, if I'm away from it, I'm being left out. It's hard to be the person who doesn't go on it.

The Guardian, 19 March 2016 © Guardian News & Media 2016

"Climate change really scares me"

Environment

There's a population crisis all right. But probably not the one you think

While all eyes are on human numbers, it's the rise in farm animals that is laying the planet waste

George Monbiot

This column is about the population crisis. About the breeding that's laying waste to the world's living systems. But it's probably not the population crisis you're thinking of. This is about another one, that we seem to find almost impossible to discuss.

You'll hear a lot about population in the next three weeks, as the Paris climate summit approaches. Across the airwaves and on the comment threads it will invariably be described as "the elephant in the room". When people are not using their own words, it means that they are not thinking their own thoughts. Ten thousand voices each ask why no one is talking about it. The growth in human numbers, they say, is our foremost environmental threat.

At their best, population campaigners seek to extend women's reproductive choices. Some 225 million women have an unmet need for contraception. If this need were answered, the impact on population growth would be significant, though not decisive: the annual growth rate of 83 million would be reduced to 62 million. But contraception is rarely limited only by the physical availability of contraceptives. In most cases it's about power: women are denied control of their wombs. The social transformations that they need are wider and deeper than donations from the other side of the world are likely to achieve.

At their worst, population campaigners seek to shift the blame from their own environmental impacts. Perhaps it's no coincidence that so many post-reproductive white men are obsessed with human population growth, as it's about the only environmental problem of which they can wash their hands. Nor, I believe, is it a coincidence that of all such topics this is the least tractable. When there is almost nothing to be done, there is no requirement to act.

Such is the momentum behind population growth, an analysis in the Proceedings of the National Academy of Sciences discovered, that were every government to adopt the one-child policy China has just abandoned, there would still be as many people on Earth at the end of this century as there are today. If 2 billion people were wiped out by a catastrophe mid-century, the planet would still hold a billion more by 2100 than it does now.

If we want to reduce our impacts this century, the paper concludes, it is consumption we must address. Population growth is outpaced by the growth in our consumption of almost all resources. There is enough to meet everyone's

SOME ISSUES:

Why are we not more aware of the impact of meat production on the environment?

If more people knew about the damage to the environment, would they eat less meat?

Why is meat consumption increasing faster than the rise in population?

What can individuals do to help to solve the problem?

Raising these animals already uses three-quarters of the world's agricultural land

need, even in a world of 10 billion people. There is not enough to meet everyone's greed, even in a world of 2 billion people.

So let's turn to a population crisis over which we do have some influence. I'm talking about the growth in livestock numbers. Human numbers are rising at roughly 1.2% a year, while livestock numbers are rising at around 2.4% a year. By 2050 the world's living systems will have to support about 120m tonnes of extra humans, and 400m tonnes of extra farm animals.

Raising these animals already uses three-quarters of the world's agricultural land. A third of our cereal crops are used to feed livestock: this may rise to roughly half by 2050. More people will starve as a result, because the poor rely mainly on grain for their subsistence, and diverting it to livestock raises the price. And now the grain that farm animals consume is being supplemented by oil crops, particularly soya, for which the forests and savannahs of South America are being cleared at shocking rates.

This might seem counter-intuitive, but were we to eat soya rather than meat, the clearance of natural vegetation required to supply us with the same amount of protein would decline by 94%. Producing protein from chickens requires three times as much land as protein from soybeans. Pork needs nine times, beef 32 times.

A recent paper in the journal Science of the Total Environment suggests that our consumption of meat is likely to be "the leading cause of modern species extinctions". Not only is livestock farming the major reason for habitat destruction and the killing of predators, but its waste products are overwhelming the world's capacity to absorb them. Factory farms in the US generate 13 times as much sewage as the human population does. The dairy farms in Tulare County, California, produce five times as much as New York City.

Freshwater life is being wiped out across the world by farm manure. In England the system designed to protect us from the tide of slurry has comprehensively broken down. Dead zones now extend from many coasts, as farm sewage erases ocean life across thousands of square kilometres.

Livestock farming creates around 14% of the world's greenhouse gas emissions: slightly more than the output of the world's cars, lorries, buses, trains, ships and planes. If you eat soya, your emissions per unit of protein are 20 times lower than eating pork or chicken, and 150 times lower than eating beef.

So why is hardly anyone talking about the cow, pig, sheep and chicken in the room? Why are there no government campaigns to reduce the consumption of animal products, just as they sometimes discourage our excessive use of electricity?

A survey by the Royal Institute of International Affairs found that people are not unwilling to change diets once they become aware of the problem, but that many have no idea that livestock farming damages the living world.

It's not as if eating less meat and dairy will harm us. If we did as our

Livestock farming creates more greenhouse gas emissions than the world's cars, lorries, buses, trains, ships and planes

doctors advise, our environmental impacts would decline in step with heart disease, strokes, diabetes and cancer. British people eat, on average, slightly more than their bodyweight in meat every year, while Americans consume another 50%: wildly more, in both cases, than is good for us or the rest of life on Earth.

But while plenty in the rich world are happy to discuss the dangers of brown people reproducing, the other population crisis scarcely crosses the threshold of perception. Livestock numbers present a direct moral challenge, as in this case we have agency. Hence the pregnant silence.

The Guardian,
19 November 2015
© Guardian News & Media 2015

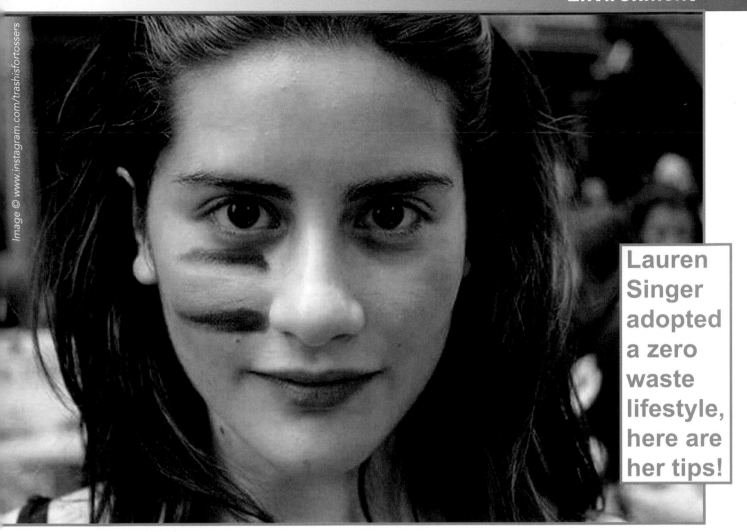

Image © www.instagram.com/trashisfortossers

Lauren Singer adopted a zero waste lifestyle, here are her tips!

Zero Waste Alternatives: The Ultimate List

Lauren Singer had always been interested in the environment, but two moments brought her to a conscious decision to live sustainably and to have a trash-free, waste-free lifestyle.

At college her professor, activist and entrepreneur Jeffrey Hollender, emphasised the importance of living your values, making her think about her own personal environmental impact. At the same time, she saw other students' everyday use of throwaway plastic bags, water bottles and containers, and thought something had to change.

When she heard about a family in California who called themselves the Zero Waste Home she decided that this was the way she could not merely claim to love the environment, but actually live like it.

She set up her blog - Trash is for Tossers - to show that leading a Zero Waste lifestyle is simple, cost-effective, timely, fun and entirely possible for everyone and anyone.

Her methods are so effective that two whole years' worth of her trash - what she throws into the bin rather than recycles or reuses - fits into one small screw-top jar.

SOME ISSUES:

Why is it important that we reduce the amount of things we throw away?

Do you recycle?

Were you aware of how many alternatives there are for things you use?

Would you consider using these alternatives?

What else can we do to reduce our waste?

This is Lauren's definition of Zero Waste:

To me, Zero Waste means that I do not produce any garbage. No sending anything to landfill, no throwing anything in a trash can, nothing. However, I do recycle and I do compost.

She offers two steps to Zero Waste

1 Evaluate: *the first step is to take a look at your daily life.*

To do this, Lauren asks the following questions:

How much garbage am I currently producing and what types?

Why am I even interested in decreasing my impact?

What do I actually use on a daily basis (what is in my daily routine) and what do I not use/need?

What products do I use that I can get more sustainable alternatives to?

Looking at your life like this and understanding what you value and why can help you to answer the biggest question of all:

How much and what do I really need to be happy? Really assess why you own and hold on to certain things.

2 Transition: *start to downsize and properly dispose of the unnecessary things:*

Bring a reusable bag and water bottle with you everywhere!

Get rid of the plastic. From Tupperware to take-away bags plastic is toxic.

Replace these products with sustainable, long-lasting alternatives. Such as organic cotton, stainless steel, wood, and glass.

Be creative. Figure out what you can use in different ways.

Make your home your sanctuary - have a few things that are really important to you.

Minimise. Ask yourself, what do I NOT need? What do I wear every day?

Think Organic, think Local, think Sustainable and BUY IN BULK.

In practical terms, Lauren proposes alternatives to everyday items that are wasteful, non recyclable, polluting and, often, expensive. But she warns:

"Please keep in mind that throwing out an old item for one of the items I have listed is not a good alternative. Use up old products, recycle, donate, give away or sell the rest! The purpose of Zero Waste is to prevent as much matter from heading to the landfill as possible!"

We all know we should no longer be using disposable plastic bags, and most people are aware of how wasteful and expensive water bought in plastic bottles is, but there are other environmentally helpful switches to think about.

As well as her Trash is for Tossers blog, Lauren has a YouTube channel, a Twitter feed, a Facebook page, an Instagram account and she is the head of The SimplyCo which creates products which they say are "Safe for our bodies, our homes and the environment".

Her efforts are enterprising, remarkable and thought-provoking. If she can achieve that much reduction in waste, couldn't we all at least achieve some?

"The purpose of Zero Waste is to prevent as much matter from heading to the landfill as possible!"

Two years of trash for Lauren Singer

Image © www.instagram.com/trashisfortossers

10 easy changes:

The wasters are:	Wasteful, non-recyclable and also ...	Waste-free alternatives
Disposable razors	Expensive	Safety razor or laser hair removal (expensive!)
Plastic toothbrushes		Bamboo compostable and sustainable toothbrushes
Disposable makeup remover wipes	Expensive, unnecessary, and often have toxic chemicals	Organic coconut oil and reusable cotton rounds
Body wash in packaging	Contains chemicals	Unwrapped bulk soap
Bleached toilet paper	Dangerous chemicals	Recycled natural unbleached toilet paper
Cotton balls	Cotton requires a lot of pesticides and water	Reusable cotton rounds
Individually portioned coffee and tea and disposable coffee filters		A cafetière - the coffee tastes better, easy to clean, no plastic, no waste!
Plastic chopping boards	These boards develop nicks which foster bacteria	Wooden chopping boards
Plastic straw		Stainless steel straw
Wrapping paper for presents		Re-use newspaper and biodegradable twine from a hardware store

"Be creative. Figure out what you can use in different ways"

Source: www.trashisfortossers.com

Art to Save the Sea

'Washed Ashore' is an organisation which turns plastic pollution from the ocean into art to bring attention to a global issue.

washedashore.org

This non-profit organisation builds and exhibits striking, powerful art to educate a global audience about plastic pollution in oceans and waterways and spark positive changes in consumer habits. Washed Ashore sculptures are constructed entirely from debris that has washed up on the shore. These giant sculptures are created by artist Angela Haseltine Pozzi with help from volunteers. They represent the sea life most affected by plastic pollution. They are part of a travelling exhibition to encourage reducing, reusing, repurposing and recycling.

SOME ISSUES:

Why do you think it is important to highlight the damaging effect of plastic on the environment?

Why are creative solutions often more successful?

What other creative ways can you think of to raise awareness of environmental problems?

What should we do to help reduce the amount of plastic we use?

© WashedAshore.org

© WashedAshore.org

Sebastian James the Puffin

Tufted Puffins are diving birds. They swim using their wings underwater to catch fish, their main food source. Like many ocean birds, puffins have been known to mistake plastic for food. This fills them up and can lead to starvation. Becoming entangled in abandoned fishing gear can also be fatal. Sebastian James the Puffin is made from:

bottle caps, flip flops, shoe soles, tyres, disposable lighters, toy truck wheels, car oil bottles

LEAVE NO TRACE!

Help preserve the environment. The next time you travel to the beach, river, or any wilderness, leave only footprints and take only photographs, memories, and trash, home.

© WashedAshore.org

Sea turtles have been swimming through the world's oceans for 100 million years. Nearly all species of sea turtle are now classified as threatened or endangered. Humans are primarily responsible for the decline in their numbers. Plastic bags, one of the most common marine debris items in global oceans, can be mistaken for jellyfish and eaten. Herman the Sea Turtle is made from:

water bottles, boots, shot gun shells, bottle caps, fake flowers, detergent bottles, brown shoe soles, shovels, plastic lighters

USE A REUSABLE

We use plastic water bottles despite the fact that our tap water is safe to drink. Use reusable water bottles to save resources and help the environment in a big way.

Herman the Sea Turtle

© WashedAshore.org

Lidia the Seal

Seals are commonly found near populated coastlines around the world, and often encounter plastic pollution. Whether they directly ingest bits of plastic, consume fish that have eaten small plastic fragments, or become entangled in packing straps or nets, the harm is real and can be deadly. Entanglement in plastic rope, rubber rings and strapping is a common threat for these curious creatures. Lidia the Seal is made from:

a variety of lids (hence the name Lidia), buoys, netting, shoes, flip flops, beach toys, wheels, toothbrushes, plastic lattice

PLASTICS ARE FOREVER
The next time you buy a plastic product, consider how long the plastic is going to last. If it cannot be recycled, find a creative way to reuse or repurpose it and avoid adding to the waste stream. Just like Washed Ashore, you can repurpose discarded plastics.

About 300 million pounds of plastic is produced globally each year and less than 10 percent of that is recycled.

Octavia the Octopus

© WashedAshore.org

Although they live an average of just four years, Giant Pacific Octopuses can grow over 20 feet in length. The octopus is one of the most intelligent species in the ocean. It has the ability to problem solve, use tools and communicate by changing colours. In order to keep these incredible creatures healthy, we need to keep their environment clean. Octavia the Octopus is made from:

disposable lighters, buoys, a plastic chair, bottle caps, a dog leash, beach toys, a plastic cooler, a plastic goose decoy

EVERY ACTION COUNTS
Say thank you to the ocean during your next visit by bringing a bag or bucket for cleaning up. If you bring something to the beach, take it with you when you leave.

Each year, sea birds, whales, seals, sea turtles and other marine life die after ingesting plastic or becoming entangled in it.

© WashedAshore.org

Marlin are some of the fastest swimmers in the world and a highly sought after sport fish. Blue marlin, the most tropical of the 10 marlin species, cruise through the open ocean often covering hundreds of miles in their migration patterns. During their travels, they pass through waters inundated with plastic pollution. Clean water is vital to keeping marlin healthy. Flash the Marlin is made from:

sunglasses, a toy fish, toothbrushes, woven beer cans, 4 fishing lures, 3 fishing poles, a toilet seat

REDUCE YOUR USE!
The best way of keeping plastic out of the ocean is reducing the amount of plastic we produce on land. Reduce your use of single use plastics:
carry a reusable water bottle
bring a reusable bag

Flash the Marlin

"We need more than 'reduce, re-use, recycle... We must also rethink, repurpose, find alternatives, and take action."

Artist, Angela Haseltine Pozzi.

Family & relationships

'I know my estranged mum loves me – even if she doesn't like me'

'I know my estranged mum loves me – even if she doesn't like me'

SOME ISSUES:

How important is it that families get along?

If families don't get along what should they do?

Is there more pressure put on mothers to get along with their children, than on fathers?

If things are difficult, is it best to cut all ties with your family and just get on with your life?

"How's your mum?" asked an old friend, innocently; standard small talk when you bump into someone at the supermarket whom you haven't seen in a decade.

"She's well," I lied, "Keeping busy..."

The truth is socially unacceptable: "I have absolutely no idea. We haven't spoken in a year. Do you mind not mentioning her name? I might start crying right here in the cereal aisle."

My relationship with my mum can at best, be called "patchy", and at worst, totally estranged.

We can go a year without a phone call, even longer without seeing each other. Our text message history comprises a series of hollow excuses, sent months apart, as to why we haven't been in touch.

It wasn't always this way. When I was growing up, I took it for granted that - unless tragedy struck - Mum would be a constant in my life. Yet I'm

not the only adult child who has a severed relationship with the woman who gave birth to them.

New research from Cambridge University and Stand Alone, a charity that offers support to adults who are estranged from their family, explored the common triggers and long-term side effects of such relationship breakdowns among 800 adults, aged 18 to 60.

The report, Hidden Voices; Estrangement in Adulthood, discovered most are predicated by emotional abuse, mismatched expectations about family roles or "clashing personalities".

Interestingly, most occur when the son or daughter is between the ages of 24 and 35 - I'm 33 years-old.

It is often thought the most turbulent years of mother-daughter relationships are the terrible teens, and that from that point on, things can only get better. But I actually got on quite well with my mum when I was an adolescent, despite the odd disagreement about boys and make-up. Our relationship didn't sour until I moved out of the family home, aged 20. There was no one incident which tore us apart. We never had a real argument, which is worse in a sense.

Instead, we drifted slowly apart like a couple who realise they have nothing in common; who still love each other but don't really like each other anymore.

At first, I'd visit once a month and call every Friday, but I frequently walked away from our interactions feeling drained, tired and despondent. Had Mum always been so negative? Had I always been so reactive?

We began to bicker in a way we never had before; first over small disagreements, such as whether I should cut my hair into a pixie bob, but then about life-shaping decisions. When I ignored her advice and decided to end a relationship with a boyfriend she wanted to become my husband, she refused to answer the phone to me for six weeks.

It seemed our dynamic had only worked while I was dependent on her - now I was an equal, we were locked in a power struggle. If we were friends, I'd say we had "outgrown" our relationship and drawn a line under it; but you can't give up on your flesh and blood.

Photo posed by model

It seemed our dynamic had only worked while I was dependent on her

It didn't help that Mum was entering the menopause. I think that's the problem with many mothers and daughters – one of you outgrows teen

Photo posed by model

Gradually, the stretches between our interactions became longer – first weeks, then months – as we both made excuses

angst, just as the other starts to battle their own hormones. I tried to be supportive by emailing links to articles about hot flush remedies, but she'd either ignore them or tell me I had no idea what she was going through.

Gradually, the stretches between our interactions became longer – first weeks, then months - as we both made excuses. One night, after texting me to say she was too busy to call, she accidentally sat on her phone and dialled my number. I listened to her watch an entire episode of Come Dine With Me with a sinking feeling in my stomach.

I decided to not phone again until she called me. In hindsight, it was a childish move, but I waited and waited, and waited.

It was 18 months before we were forced to reunite for my older brother's wedding. In the same room, surrounded by family and friends, we acted as if nothing had happened; laughing and joking like a happy family. But immediately afterwards, the silence started again.

I should point out my parents are still married, and my dad and I have a very close relationship. It hurts,

sometimes, that he doesn't step in to "fix" things with Mum, but I've never asked him to and he isn't the type to interfere.

Instead, we've adapted our own relationship to work around it; I only call when he's at work and meet up on his lunch break. We never talk about my "Mummy issues".

Every now and again, something triggers a moment of grief. It breaks my heart to think that if I ever have children they may not know their grandmother. When I see mothers and daughters shopping or chatting together, I feel a deep, aching longing for something I'm missing. But I don't let myself dwell on it, I don't know where that sadness will spiral.

When I met my boyfriend, four years ago, I explained that Mum and I have a "cyclic relationship". At the time we were, luckily, in a good patch so she got to meet him and we had the most wonderful family dinner, which I'm grateful for.

Despite everything that's gone on between us, I know Mum loves me, even if she doesn't like me. For the past few years, I've kidded myself that our estrangement works in my favour, making me a stronger, more independent woman.

So, why, as I write this, am I crying?

For support with an estranged relationship visit Standalone.org.uk

Daily Telegraph, 24 January 2016
© Telegraph Media Group
Limited 2016

Why, as I write this, am I crying?

Photos posed by models

A moment that changed me

– the death of my sister and the grief that followed

When my 32-year-old sister died of cancer the grief hit me like a freight train

Emma Dawson

SOME ISSUES:

If you knew you were going to die, what would you do with the time you had left?

Does facing death change how you feel about people?

Should we be more honest about how we feel?

Why is it important to tell those who we care about how much we love them?

In August, my younger sister Lucy died. She was only 32 years old and the light of our lives. We knew it was coming, not quite as quickly as it did, but she had advanced cancer, so her days were numbered. As soon as the cancer reached her brain, it was game over.

There is nothing that could ever have prepared me for the past weeks since she died, and while this isn't the first time someone has written about grief, and it certainly won't be the last, it is my experience first-hand, and it's very different to what I had expected.

Grief, as we all have heard, comes in waves. That's a lie. These aren't waves; these are gargantuan freight trains that ram into your very soul, from nowhere. They come as you stand in the fruit aisle of the supermarket, looking around you, wondering how the hell anyone can manage to get on with life when this terrible thing has happened and suddenly, from out of nowhere that train comes hurtling at you. It feels as if someone has sucked out everything you have – your guts, your heart, your oxygen, your whole being. Of course the Brit in you remains still and stoic as the train does its thing before pulling away, and you continue filling your trolley with Granny Smiths. But it's there, and you never know when it will run into you next. You live in fear of that.

For a little while I didn't speak to any friends on the phone, for fear of breaking down. I only spoke to my parents, my husband and to my three-year-old. Job number one was to explain to her that her beloved aunt was dead. No easy feat. I can barely remember it. I came up with a nonsensical story of her now being an angel, and a star in the sky and that whenever the sky was pink in the morning, it meant she was saying hello. Now, whenever the sky is pink, my daughter shrieks up to the sky excitedly. My husband feels uncomfortable with it; I don't ever know what to feel. But it was all I

had at the time. It's probably confused her more than I'd like to admit.

After Lucy was told she had cancer, it was the last time she and I ever looked at each other in the eye. We avoided that. I know she felt the same. We knew that if we ever locked our gaze, that the tears would never stop. So it was better that way. Now I regret that, I regret not grabbing her and looking at her, deep into her soul, and telling her how much I admired her bravery. How she was a warrior, a trouper, an inspiration, and a truly beautiful human being and of course, how much love I had for her, but I didn't, and I hate myself for that. I know she knew, but did she actually know?

My sister's two greatest fears when she was ill were 1) being forgotten; 2) leaving

behind any sadness. The first is just silly. The second not so silly. I was never one who feared death, really. I mean, I knew it would come, I just assumed it would be when I was an old lady, and I was fine with that. Now, I have a fear, in fact utter terror, not so much of death, but for what happens after death to the people who remain. The life change that happens to those people the minute they find out that their loved one is going to die. This experience for her was, I think, the worst of all of it. Her worry for her beloved fiancé, bereft at losing the only girl he ever loved, the heartbreak of our lovely parents, the confusion of her niece who thought she had "pancer", and her seeing the sheer devastation of her friends of 25 years who just couldn't believe that their best mate would no longer be around. She never wanted us to be sad. But we are – so, so utterly filled with sadness.

Actually, I can get through the days. My biggest amazement and awe in all of this is the

My sister's two greatest fears when she was ill were 1) being forgotten; 2) leaving behind any sadness.

wonder of the human brain. The kindness of it, that it allows you a few hours, sometimes three or four hours in a day or night, where you are all right. Where you laugh, smile, make a meal, play with your kid … you just are allowed to be OK sometimes and I thank the brain for that. Allowing us a little slice of time-out from the horror that surrounds us.

What haunts me, more than anything, more even, than her not being here any more, is the thought of the fear she faced alone. From 3 March 2015 until the day she died, she faced the worst thing any person could ever face. She looked death in the eye and it never let up. It was relentlessly wheedling its way into her life and she dealt with that with absolute poise and composure. How she managed to control that fear is truly beyond me. My guilt that my sister, who I was supposed to protect my whole life, would be lying there at night, while the world slept, knowing her drugs weren't working and this cancer was killing her. That destroys me. And when I see my mother sobbing like a wounded animal at her grave every Tuesday lunchtime, I know it destroys her too.

The secret stories that only we shared just evaporate, because they are too old or too weird to try to explain to anyone else. Every year we wrote the exact same thing in each other's birthday cards, and howled with laughter each time we opened them, knowing full well what it would say, but there isn't any card to write now, so that joke just disappears forever.

Sometimes I feel anger towards my loving and sensitive three-year-old, when she carelessly throws something that was a gift from my sister on the floor. I shout and she gets frightened and doesn't understand. When she does that, I find myself preferring my sister to my own child, and then I hate myself. I have a paralysing fear of losing things such as the screw top of a cheap plastic bottle that she bought my daughter at Disneyland in July, in case the bottle is no longer whole. The guarding of every solitary thing she ever gave us as gifts over the years, like a lioness with her cubs, and the blind panic and rage when one of those things is temporarily lost among the chaos of living with a three-year-old.

So it's hard. No doubt it is life-changing. And what next? Well, we've been dreading December, of course. The month we share for our birthdays, Christmas, the time of happiness and love and family and light. And yet for us there is none of that without her. We will pretend, though. We have become good at that. But we all have an underlying anxiety that while we slowly move toward 2016, desperate to see the back of the year that brought us so much sadness, we also fear entering a year not touched by her, moving further and further away from the last time we were a family, all present and correct.

We will survive, though. Unlike her, we will survive. But we will for ever live with a shade of darkness over us. A grey filter over our world for ever.

The Guardian, 3 December 2015
© Guardian News & Media 2015

I regret not grabbing her and looking at her, deep into her soul, and telling her how much I admired her bravery

We've placed motherhood on such a high pedestal we've forgotten the huge pros of being a child-free woman

You could be forgiven for thinking that women don't exist in any other form than mum or mum-in-waiting. In the film world, recent research showed 58% of roles for women revolve around their position in the home as wife or mother - Rachel Pashley

SOME ISSUES:

Do we assume that everyone wants children?

What are the pros and cons of not having children?

Why are women more closely associated with motherhood, than men are with fatherhood?

Why do you think childless women may have more opportunities yet having a child does not seem to affect a man's opportunities?

Forgive me if the beginning of this piece sounds a bit like a disaster movie, but Earth is being taken over by an alien life form: the Not-Mums. These are women of any age who, miraculously, haven't had children. Shocking, I know.

As a society we've placed motherhood on a ridiculously high pedestal, from the Virgin Mary through to the current cult of online parenting and celebrity mums. These mothers in the public eye, who are some of the most successful headline-grabbers and whose buying decisions often inspire and influence other mums-to-be, are part of an industry forecast to be worth £463million in sales by 2019 according to Euromonitor.

You could be forgiven for thinking that women don't exist in any other form than mum-in-waiting, mum and then hopeful grandmother. In the film world, recent research revealed that 58% of roles for women revolve around their position in the home as wife or mother.

And if you want an Oscar then statistically it's a sure thing in the role of 'wife', with nearly 1 in 3 Oscars awarded to women in the role of either wife or widow.

In the advertising world, our vision of womanhood is barely more diverse, with the 'Busy Working Mum' a keen creative cliché. 'Housewife With Kids' is an equally popular trope, ignoring the fact that in the 1950s working mums were the minority, and today over 70% of women with children also have a career. The idea of a woman as a full-time mum is becoming increasingly redundant.

Then, of course, there's the political favourite: the 'hardworking family', just doing the best for their offspring. So what happens when you don't fit into this paradigm? What happens when you become the Not-Mum?

...childless British and American women out-earn their male peers

In the US elections as reported by New York magazine, single unmarried women are set to wield the most decisive influence on the run for the White House. They accounted for 23% of the voting electorate in 2012, and some 40% of the African American electorate.

While in their twenties, childless British and American women out-earn their male peers, meaning they present a significant source of taxable revenue to the economy.

In 2015 the Not Mum Summit was the first landmark meeting of an organisation founded by Karen Malone Wright to promote and protect the rights of those women choosing not to have children. In a world where women who are actively childfree are admonished by Pope Francis for being 'selfish', or publicly derided for 'not having much love in them' - such was the criticism aimed at Julia Gillard in the Australian parliament by Labour Leader Mark Latham - sadly it feels like childfree women are in need of someone on their side.

While women's abilities to bring life into the world as a mother are life-changing and wonderful for many, I prefer to see ovaries in the same way as nuclear weapons: you shouldn't have to use them to be powerful.

Our strengths extend beyond our ability to bear children. And if 86% of women worldwide feel that femininity is a strength not a weakness, perhaps we should be more awakened to the idea of 'Female Capital' – the values that women bring to the world as women, not necessarily just as mothers.

Personally, I look forward to the rise of the Not-Mum: because she's here already, pulling the strings in the background, and it's high time we recognised her for the worthy social contributor that she is.

Rachel Pashley is the Global Planning Director of J. Walter Thompson London

The Independent, 7 March 2016
www.independent.co.uk

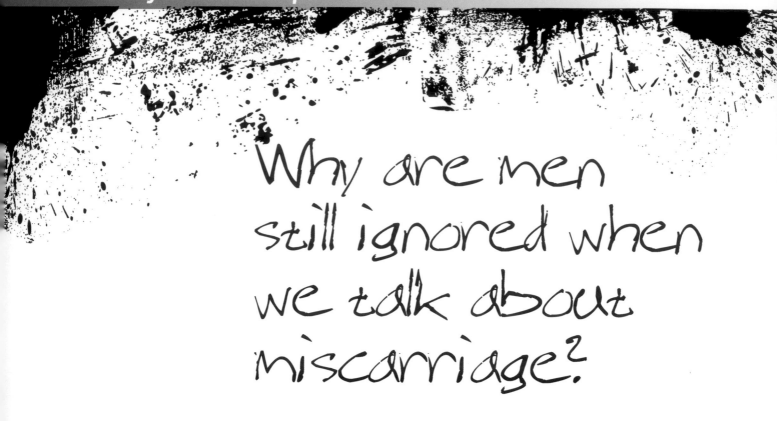

Why are men still ignored when we talk about miscarriage?

While it is couples who are "having a baby", miscarriages only happen to women. But minimising the grief of fathers is damaging

JULIA HARTLEY BREWER

"How is Julia doing?" That was the question my husband was repeatedly asked after our first miscarriage. And after our second; and third; and fourth. We had lost baby after baby, but it was my state of mind and health – the devastated mother who had lost her child – that was uppermost in the thoughts of our family and friends. Almost nobody asked my husband the other obvious question: how are you doing?

While it is couples who "are going to have a baby", miscarriages only happen to women. Yet the emotional trauma of the overwhelming sense of loss and grief affects both parents. So it was with great courage that Facebook chief Mark Zuckerberg chose to reveal, as he announced he and his wife are expecting a baby girl, that they have suffered three miscarriages. His deeply personal words will have echoed strongly with everyone who has experienced the loss of a pregnancy: "You start making plans, and then they're gone. Most people don't discuss miscarriages because you worry your problems will distance you or reflect upon you. So you struggle on your own."

SOME ISSUES:

Why do you think people are generally more concerned about the woman after a miscarriage?

How might it affect the man?

What does it say about our attitudes towards men and towards fathers?

"So you struggle on your own."

And that it precisely what many men do after losing a baby. They struggle on and bottle up their own feelings of loss to keep strong for their partners. Yet, as Mark Zuckerberg explained in a poignant Facebook post, for the couple who have miscarried, it was very much a real baby, containing all their love and hopes for the future, so the grief is very real too. And it needs to be treated like any other grief.

We, as a nation, have come a long way in learning to talk about death and loss, including after miscarriage. But men have been left far behind on that journey.

Photo posed by model

Men struggle on and bottle up their own feelings of loss to keep strong for their partners.

New research by the Miscarriage Association has found that, despite their intense feelings of sadness, anger and loss, a quarter of men whose wives or girlfriends miscarried never spoke about their grief with them because they feared upsetting her or saying the wrong thing. The sheer horror and shock of a miscarriage, and all the bleeding it can entail, can be overwhelming – an emotion that is compounded by a man's utter powerlessness to do anything to help the woman they love.

Yet – and, importantly, quite unlike women – men are simply expected to get back on with normal life straight away, with no time off to recover. They report returning to work shell-shocked but unable to talk about their loss with colleagues because the pregnancy had been kept a secret. Even when men do attempt to talk about their feelings the response can do more harm. Well-meaning but clumsy comments such as "never mind, you can try again" and "at least you aren't shooting blanks" underestimate the grief experienced.

The best way to cope with miscarriage is for men and women to talk – to their partners, to their friends, to a counsellor. After a rich, successful man like Mark Zuckerberg publicly shared his grief about his wife's miscarriages, it may make it easier for more men to finally open up about their own feelings of loss. There is nothing unnatural about grieving for the loss of your unborn child.

Julia is an ambassador for the Miscarriage Association

The Independent, 4 August 2015
www.independent.co.uk

I BELIEVED THE STEREOTYPES ABOUT DOMESTIC ABUSE - THAT'S WHAT MADE IT SO HARD TO REALISE I WAS A VICTIM

I am a proud, outgoing and political woman, with a supportive family and wonderful friends. I didn't think that abuse was something that could happen to me

Anonymous

SOME ISSUES:

What do you think the writer is referring to as the 'stereotypical' abusive or bad relationship?

Why do you think that so many people abuse their partners?

Why might people not report such abuse?

What can be done to support people in abusive relationships?

THERE ARE 7.6 MILLION VICTIMS OF ABUSE IN THE UK. I AM ONE IN THOSE MILLIONS. BUT I FOUGHT FOR A YEAR TO DENY THAT I WAS SUBJECT TO EMOTIONAL ABUSE.

When my partner fell out with my friends and blamed me, I concluded that he was just a difficult character. When he told me that I was emotionally unstable, and imagining him flirting with other women, I sought counselling in private. When I avoided certain conversational topics out of fear of him shouting at me until I had a panic attack, I would conclude that our relationship was uneasy and, at worst, different.

For a year, he taunted me, telling me repeatedly that I was ridiculous and over-sensitive. This tactic, known as 'gaslighting', is an emotionally manipulative form of abuse. My story is painful, but it isn't unique. Victims are everywhere.

As much as we have a stereotype about abusers, we also carry a stereotype of victims. Whether we see victims in terms of social status, intellectual ability, gender or sexual orientation, it can be easier to reconcile victimhood when it is kept at a distance. I, like most others, wouldn't consider myself a stereotypical victim of abuse. I am a proud, outgoing, political woman, with

COULDN'T THEY GET OUT? COULDN'T THEY HELP THEMSELVES?

I MAY BE FRAGILE GOODS, BUT I HAVE SURVIVED

a supportive family, wonderful friends and a burgeoning career.

But abuse is intelligent, insidious; it doesn't have a type. The fear in the notion of abuse is that it can happen to absolutely anyone, and the perpetrators are everywhere.

What keeps an abuser abusive is their need to control, and their insatiable thirst for power. When I found that I couldn't offer the man that I loved what he needed, I didn't see him as abusive. I saw myself entering into a category of people that not only frightened me, but which I resented. I was ashamed of my internal derision towards victims. Couldn't they get out? Couldn't they help themselves? How could I identify with that stereotype in my head of a meek girly girl who had spent years at the helm of some patriarchal breadwinner?

Just as I had to debunk the stereotypes, I would urge you to do the same. Any person can be abused. We associate violence with those from lower-income families because these are the people more likely to need a shelter's support. According to Shelter, domestic abuse is the single most quoted reason for women being homeless. Just as there is no evidence that there is a typical victim of abuse - we look at statistics and fail to rationalise that the people accessing domestic violence shelters are those who are in visible need - there is evidence that abuse has been tolerated in our society for far too long.

It is a silent killer, the lingering pause after that sentence, that squeeze of the hand, the breath as you open your mouth to try and say: "Yes, it happened to me too."

I may be fragile goods, but I have survived. I will not be joining the 150 women who died at the hands of their partner last year. It wasn't my job title that saved me, and it certainly wasn't my mind. It was nothing more important, nothing more significant, than luck.

My friends got to me at the right place, at the right time, and I was somehow able to listen. Not everyone is that lucky under the sporadic, restless nature of attack. A victim may walk away with scars, and they may walk away with their life - or they may not. When we are faced with the cold, hard facts, there isn't any point in pigeonholing or finger-pointing.

The Guardian, 9 December 2015
© Guardian News & Media 2015

Wilber C-Velasco   William C-Velasco   Carlos B-Castro   Jorge B-Castro

Screenshots from Fox News

Brotherly love

Two sets of
twins living
in the same
city make an
astonishing
discovery

SOME ISSUES:

Do you think you would feel
closer to the sibling you had
been raised with or the sibling
you were biologically related to?

How does upbringing
affect personality?

And how do genetics affect
personality?

Does our upbringing affect
what we can achieve in life?

In the summer of 2013,
William Canas Velasco, a
slight, 24 year old man
who had moved to Bogota,
the capital of Colombia,
from the countryside, was
working in a butcher's
shop. His twin brother
Wilber also worked in the
meat trade.

Although they had ended
up in the same line of
work, the twins were not
alike in appearance or in
character. William was
always teasing Wilber -
even though his brother
didn't like a joke and was
inclined to be moody.

Although they didn't have
much, they had better
prospects in Bogota than
in the dirt-poor rural
area where they had
been brought up, where
they had left school at
12 because their parents
could not afford to send
them to high school.

Another set of twins

In a nearby office, Jorge
Enrique Bernal Castro was
working as a designer for
an engineering firm. He
had been brought up in
Bogota. The family weren't
rich but they weren't poor
either. The local schools
had been good and Jorge
and his twin brother
Carlos, an accountant,
were both happy that they
had bettered themselves.

Seeing double

One Saturday that
summer, Laura Vega, a
young woman from Jorge's
office, happened to go into
a butchers shop. She was
astonished to see Jorge
behind the counter. There
was no mistaking him, she
recognised his colouring,
his high cheekbones,
his hair, his smile, his
expression, every detail
of his appearance. But
it wasn't Jorge, it was
William.

Jorge was amused by the idea of this stranger who looked so like him.

Another discovery

At work she mentioned this strange likeness to Jorge, who was amused by the idea of this stranger who looked so like him. It was a month later that a mutual friend showed Jorge a photo of William.

When Jorge saw the striking resemblance, he could not ignore it or laugh it off. He wondered whether his father had a second, unknown, family. He needed to find out more and went to William's Facebook page. There, to his astonishment, he saw a picture of William raising a glass with a man who was the image of Jorge's own twin brother Carlos.

Amused, intrigued and alarmed, Jorge showed the pictures to Carlos that evening, explaining that he had already found out that the two men came from a rural region in the north of the country and had been born in late December 1988 - just like themselves.

The next day, the friend texted photographs of Jorge and Carlos to William in the butcher's shop. Again, there was no denying the resemblance. It seemed obvious that a swap must have happened, but the two families had lived so far apart, how could such a thing have occurred?

Odd ones out

Carlos had always been aware that he was of a bigger build and did not have the delicate features of the rest of the family and had always had the sensation of being the odd one out. Everyone assumed that Carlos took after his father while the others resembled their mother. The truth was proving to be less simple!

It also began to dawn on William why he had always felt and looked different from the rest of his family, he was strong but had a more slender frame, and why he and Wilber had such different natures.

Tracing the truth

Through mutual friends William and Jorge began to communicate. They began to find out about birthdays, blood groups, where they were born. Gradually they pieced together as much of the story as they could.

Identical twins William and Jorge were born on 21st December 1988 in Bogota. Another set of identical twins, Carlos and

Carlos always had the sensation of being the odd one out.

Screenshots from Fox News

Wilber | Carlos | William | Jorge

"All that has happened is that our families have become bigger"

Wilber, were born on 22nd December in Santander. Both sets of twins were delivered early, at seven months. When Carlos became unwell he was sent to the hospital in Bogota as an emergency. It's possible that the identifying wristband had fallen off one or more of these tiny babies and been replaced on the wrong one. After, when all three babies were discharged the wrong one - William - returned to Santander and Carlos was left behind with Jorge.

First meetings
It was only after these first investigations that William broke the news to Wilber. Wilber, upset to find that the other two had learnt so much before telling him, was reluctant to go to a meet up and had to be persuaded. When he arrived, he discovered his identical brother Carlos had had exactly the same reaction and had decided to stay away. The other pair, William and Jorge, were both more relaxed about meeting. It was evidence of a resemblance that was much more than physical.

As the first meeting went on and the similarities became clear, Wilber became increasingly curious to see his own twin. They all went to the apartment that William and Carlos shared and each of the four found himself staring in amazement and some distress at a stranger who was exactly like himself and another whose appearance and body language was exactly like his 'brother'.

Separated, yet the same
Then all four began the process of finding out how nature had made them similar to their identical twin while their upbringing had made them different. They found that Jorge and William were the strongest but also the least quarrelsome, that Carlos and Wilber were better organised and also more interested in dating girls. Wilber had a speech impediment, his identical twin Carlos had overcome the same problem with speech therapy. Carlos, the accountant, had smaller, softer, more cared for hands than Wilber who had a lifetime of working in fields and butchers' shops.

What if ...
In time they would have to deal with their loss - of identity, of birth parents and siblings, of life chances and of how they saw themselves. For two of them, the mother they loved was not their 'real' mother and they had, in effect, lived someone else's life, with a very different set of possibilities. When the four visited the troubled region of Santander and the home where William and Wilber had been brought up, Carlos would have to ask himself if he could have had his career without the swap and William would wonder what he could have been if he had been brought up with his birth family. But in those first moments of meeting, Jorge set the tone for the long term, saying: "All that has happened is that our families have become bigger."

The twins have been the subject of much media interest and scientific research as they find a way to cope with their unique dilemma. Now all four of them like to meet up and travel, they have even spoken of buying a house together - no longer two mismatched twos but a harmonious four.

What is a brother?
Perhaps the most touching part of their story is that Carlos and Wilber each reacted to the first astonishing news of their lost twin in the same way: Wilber told William "I don't care who they are. You're my brother, and you'll be my brother until the day I die." Carlos, meanwhile, hugged Jorge and simply said "I want to be your brother." Brotherhood for them is not just blood but something deeper and different.

Sources: Various

Brotherhood for them is not just blood but something deeper and different.

Finance

SHARECYCLING: 'OUR FAMILY AND FRIENDS TOOK EVERYTHING WE OWNED'

Jennifer Rigby

At first people were shy, sipping tea nervously and occasionally glancing at the cupboards. Then my sister, Louise, arrived. Without putting down her bag or saying hello, she headed for the spare room, determination on her face.

"I knew she'd be the competition!" cried my friend Rose, leaping off the sofa and darting in the same direction.

This is what happens when you open your home to friends, family and colleagues, telling them they can help themselves to everything within it. Moments later, Rose and Louise re-emerged with armfuls of clothes and pot plants, and matching triumphant gleams in their eyes.

Last month, my boyfriend and I moved to Myanmar [Burma] for two years for work, each taking a single suitcase. We couldn't afford to keep our flat in London, so when it came to our possessions, drastic measures were called for.

Some of our stuff, like books and clothes, I could cope with giving away. But there was a list of things like precious paintings and my boyfriend's childhood teddy bear that we couldn't bring ourselves to let go. Those things we decided to offer up for long-term loan. It's not recycling, nor even freecycling: we're calling it 'sharecycling'.

It was our tent that swung it for me. I made the decision as I thought about the pointlessness of putting stuff into storage for two dusty years. Instead, I imagined some of the people I loved hoisting our tent on to their backs and setting out into the countryside in the summer sunshine.

SOME ISSUES:

Do you have many things you think you could easily live without?

Why do you think we tend to buy so much stuff we don't really use?

How can we work together to reduce the amount we buy?

What are the benefits of having less stuff?

I THOUGHT ABOUT THE POINTLESSNESS OF PUTTING STUFF INTO STORAGE FOR TWO DUSTY YEARS.

We were moving away, but this made it feel as though we would still, in a small way, be with our friends. And once we had planted this seed, the idea grew. The plants on the balcony. The board games. The chairs. The wicker bin in the spare room.

To shift it all, we had an open house, inviting everyone we knew to loot our belongings. We gave them cava so they would be giddy, and take more.

"This is just like supervised stealing!" said one friend, as she loaded books by the handful into a carrier bag. I became a saleswoman. I recommended novels, waved toys at babies, and brought out coats for people to try on. My parents are convinced I will never see any of it again.

Now I am sitting in a flat in Yangon as the last of the monsoon rains hurls down outside, turning the pavements into mud and sending the monks and street sellers huddling under doorways and umbrellas.

I feel very far away from London, and from my stuff. That list we made of the things we want back? I'm not sure how much we'll consult it. So far, I haven't missed any of my pictures, or that weird mouse purse I've had since I was seven. I've missed my family, my friends, and my city.

And our sharecycling plan ties us back to them. A friend took our tent to a festival. My sister's husband, a farmer in Yorkshire, has given my boyfriend's holdall a new lease of life as a farm bag. And my favourite picture, a cross-stitch strewn with choice four-letter words, now sits proudly on the walls of a pal in south London.

This is what makes me smile: the thought of all our bits and pieces in our friends' lives, a physical reminder of our ties. Perhaps it's a cop out, as if we have pressed pause on our London lives rather than stop, making the move easier.

It shows I'm not ready to wander the world forever with just a laptop. But perhaps when we do go back, we'll be less concerned with what we have, and more with where we are going – and who with.

Daily Telegraph, 13 November 2015
© Telegraph Media Group Limited 2015

"THIS IS JUST LIKE SUPERVISED STEALING!" SAID ONE FRIEND

How being poor keeps you poor

In both practical and emotional terms, being poor limits your life chances

SOME ISSUES:

Why do you think there is so much financial inequality?

What can be done to help people out of poverty?

Do equal opportunities exist?

What can our government do to help those with less achieve more?

Being poor isn't just about 'making do' or 'going without'. A lack of money dominates every part of daily life - including how you think and how you feel. There is a bitter irony in the fact that being poor means you have to think constantly about the thing that you don't have - money. And the effects are hidden from anyone who has never had to live with the constant, gnawing anxiety of watching every penny.

GOODS COST MORE

Not having spare cash takes away choice in what you buy. The cheapest option, which is the only one available to you when you lack funds, often isn't the most economical in the long run. Poor people have to buy cheap - even if that means flimsy. For household goods, such as washing machines, this means lower priced machines, built with cheaper components, which will do the job but will fail long before a sturdier, more expensive, counterpart. It also has a cumulative effect, where you have a reliable set of appliances you are less likely to have a catastrophic failure of several at once. And if you have the money, you can make a choice from a wider range of goods and seek out a bargain. If you don't have ready cash or credit you can't snap up a bargain in the sales - you have to buy at full price

When you are poor you can't save money by buying in bulk. Grocery purchases often have to be in smaller quantities, even if the price per kilo is more expensive. The budget will not stretch to economies of scale. You may have a prepaid meter for gas and electricity to avoid big bills but you will be paying more for your energy supply as you miss out on the reductions offered by paying regularly in advance by direct debit.

CASH AND CREDIT - BANKS WON'T HELP

Part of the cycle of poverty comes from the fact that financial services are very scarce for those on limited incomes. Many banks require a minimum amount to be paid or kept in an account each month - an impossibility when you are living from hand to mouth. Only those who have stable finances can benefit from premium accounts which come with money saving deals on goods and services.

Not having a bank account also means that help and advice about avoiding problems, making savings or benefitting from saving schemes is simply not available. For example, the recently introduced 'Help to Buy' ISA, where the government has pledged to add £50 to every £200 saved, is completely irrelevant to those without the ability to save.

If you need a loan, an arranged overdraft from a bank would be the best option as it would either be free or at minimum cost - but such facilities are not available on the most basic accounts. The easiest credit for people who will literally run out of money before they receive their next wage or benefit is short term, unsecured and very expensive. Credit cards are a great convenience if you can pay off all or most of your monthly debt. But if you are without enough money when the time comes, the interest merely adds to your burdens.

BEING POOR IS BAD FOR YOUR DIET

Having to scrimp and save restricts your diet to what you can afford. On a strict budget it is much more difficult to choose what is nutritious over what is economical - and choices based on ethics, animal welfare and fair trade are overruled by the lack of money. The foods that are cheap but filling are often low in nutritional value and high in 'empty calories', but when price is the priority then a comparison of content is a waste of time - value for money, how much you can get in your basket for what you have, overrides long term considerations of nutrition.

Big retailers often desert areas of poverty leaving people with little or no choice about where to buy. Shoppers may be forced to buy their small quantities from local shops which cannot offer the same discounts and loss leaders as the large supermarkets.

CUTS HIT YOU HARDEST

In big cities, higher rents keep you out of the most convenient locations. You may have to rely on increasingly expensive public transport. In rural areas, the situation can be even worse - limited local transport restricts your options in all areas of life, shopping and job opportunities are even more restricted than in towns. You are much more dependent on public provision than those who are well off - public parks instead of a private garden, public libraries instead of bookshops - so you are hit hard by measures which affect these services.

EVERYTHING TAKES LONGER

Being money poor can make you time poor too. You take longer to get to places because you use public transport. Shopping takes longer as you hunt for bargains. You spend time fixing and repairing what you might otherwise replace.

WORK CHOICES ARE LIMITED

Being poor deprives you of options. Travelling to interviews and to workplaces can be difficult. Interview clothes are an extra expense. Childcare can make a job uneconomical. Training to improve your qualifications is costly and starting a business requires the funds to take a risk.

SOCIAL ISOLATION

Very few people like to admit that they are struggling. Someone in difficult circumstances will find reasons to refuse opportunities to socialise that are going to cost money, especially where someone will suggest splitting the bill. You can't look forward to a fun event without a feeling of stress. Eventually people stop asking - either because they too are embarrassed or because they assume that you are not interested.

CONSTANT CONCERN

Always trying to work out ways to avoid spending money or to stretch it further makes every purchase full of anxiety "Is this the cheapest I can get? If I buy this will I be able to afford something else?" This affects decisions throughout the day - nothing is casual, everything is a calculation full of care about whether the decision will prove to be correct.

GUILT AND LOW SELF-ESTEEM

This cycle of poverty and lack of opportunity also has devastating mental effects: defensiveness, anxiety, depression, shame and even guilt. Sections of society will blame you for your poverty and question anything you own that does not appear to be an absolute necessity. Society demands that poor people should be visibly making sacrifices, especially if they are receiving benefits. Just as people take credit for their own success, even when it is based on a firm foundation of a privileged background, poor people can internalise the notion that they don't deserve anything better.

LACK OF CONNECTIONS

Advantages accrue to people with money - connections that can open doors, provide opportunities, offer a favour to get you started. As the practice of offering unpaid internships grows, fewer poor youngsters - whose families can't support them while they gain experience - will be able to get a foothold in professional work. National decisions are made, in general, by people who have never experienced poverty. The everyday, grinding wearisome nature of financial anxiety does not enter their considerations.

DREAMS, AMBITIONS, PLANS

It's difficult to plan for the future if you can only plan for today. You can't say that you will save for a rainy day, a holiday, or in case of any domestic disaster because there is no saving to be done. Watching every penny is exhausting and depressing. It ruins your plans, limits your horizons and curtails your dreams. Starting poor can be a life sentence!

Sources: Various

HOW NOT to spend it!

Some alternatives to splashing the cash

Our economy and even our daily life is based around buying and selling - but what if we did things differently?

Share things

How many times a week is a lawn mower used? Most households in Britain have an array of things that are used just once in a while. What if those things were available to borrow whenever you needed them? In South London a social enterprise group is setting up the Library of Things - where you can borrow items like power drills and pressure washers, and also tents, sports equipment, bikes and bike repair kits. The library will not only loan things but hold workshops on how to use them. It aims to be a real community enterprise and to spread the word throughout the country.

Meanwhile in Frome, Somerset there is already a Share Shop where items donated by the public are available for residents to use - along with the story of the item and its previous owner. This personal touch is special and it is practical. The Share Shop charges from only £1 to £4 to borrow an item for a week. The personal stories help to build up the trust that is essential if the shop is to work. The start up money for the shop was provided by Frome Town Council and Anna Francis, its energy and recycling officer explained, "Enabling people to share resources not only saves money but reduces waste and carbon too. The average electric drill is used for just 15 minutes in its lifetime and with many households feeling the pinch [this] means everyone will be able to access the items they need - from tools to cookery to camping equipment - without the expense, hassle and storage needed to buy their own."

Exchange skills

Friends often offer to help each other out - each doing the things they are good at, sharing skills, tools and time. LETS - Local Exchange Trading Systems or Schemes - take that idea, give it some structure and extend it through the community. They are systems that allow people to exchange all kinds of goods and services with one another, without the need for money. Instead they earn 'community credits' which they can then use to obtain a service from someone else within the scheme. There are lists of wants and lists of offers, someone could earn community credits doing a repair and use that credit to get some baby-sitting.

Someone could earn community credits doing a repair and use that credit to get some baby-sitting.

SOME ISSUES:

Where does the pressure to spend money in our society come from?

Is it a good thing to spend less money?

Which is the best way of saving money?

What would you do with money you saved from finding ways to spend less?

Would spending less money affect the environment and the world as a whole?

Freecycle is an international network where people give away their unwanted goods.

The babysitter might use their credits to get some transport - or choose from whatever services are on offer. As well as providing a useful exchange of skills, LETS help to draw a community together, linking people who might otherwise never have met but who can help each other in many different ways. Local groups are often quirky and they delight in giving their community credits local names - in Sheffield they are 'stones', in Derby they are 'wads' and in Reading they are 'Readies', you earn about 10 Readies for an hour's work.

Don't replace, repair

There are websites like ifixit. com dedicated to persuading people that repair is even better than recycling. It's not just our personal economy but our environment which benefits when we keep things longer, maintain them better and repair them rather than throw them away. The website provides specialist tools, parts and instructions for repairs on smartphones and also instructions on how to fix all sorts of household gadgets. It boasts information on almost 6,000 devices and more than 21,000 free repair manuals. It's also a place where other users will offer advice and guidance.

Give and take

Charity shops are a great source of bargains and a great way to dispose of stuff that is still useful - just not useful to you. But there's an even cheaper option. Freecycle is an international network of local schemes where people simply give away their unwanted

goods. It's an entirely nonprofit movement of people who will give away, and who can get, stuff for free, in their local area. It means that things can be reused and there is less stuff going into landfills. Offers can be large or small. In one Manchester group, amongst the sofa beds and desks for collection is an offer of baby wipes and nappies - all, thankfully, "brand new never used".

"Switch off from shopping and tune into life."

The slogan above is a quote from the website of buynothingday - a counter movement to the consumer madness of Black Friday. It encourages people to have 24 hours in which they simply don't spend. Every year the media show us images of people actually fighting and trampling each other in their frenzy to grab a bargain. Buynothingday suggests countering this by simply abstaining or going further by making a public statement - dressing up as a shopping zombie, clearing a space in a shopping centre in which to play games instead of

Even if we have spare money, why should we be happy to pay out needlessly?

shopping, making a conga line with empty shopping trolleys. Of course the movement would prefer people to keep this up and "make a commitment to shopping less and living more".

At one extreme of society there are people who have entirely given up the use of money - those who 'shop' from skips or even eat roadkill. At the other there are those for whom luxury shopping is part of an extravagant lifestyle. For those people the Financial Times newspaper runs a supplement called "How to Spend It", dedicated to high end purchases such as a silver and crystal jam container for £625 (jam not included). While most of us aren't at either end of the spectrum, the question remains why, even if we have spare money, should we be happy to pay out needlessly? What positive things could we do with the money we save? We could donate to charities, start great community initiatives or find ways to help others. And those of us who have fewer resources could be finding ways to get more for less and do more with less. Either way, you have to ask, why spend more, when you can spend less?

Sources: Various

A Tax on Fairness

In April 2006 there was an outcry over confidential information leaked from a law firm in Panama. These files - known as the Panama Papers - contained details of about 200,000 companies and individuals, including business people, celebrities and politicians, who tucked away money in foreign tax havens, out of reach of their own government's tax collection services. British Prime Minister David Cameron was forced to reveal details of his family's income and tax arrangements. The Icelandic Prime Minister, Sigmundur Davíð Gunnlaugsson, was forced to resign over the fact that his family had sheltered money offshore.

But why the outcry? There is nothing illegal in making sensible use of money and in protecting investments. These havens, and the 'offshore' arrangements they provide, offer somewhere safe and secret, where money is only lightly taxed or completely untaxed. Yet those very words - 'sheltering', 'haven' - reveal what people and companies are protecting their money from - the danger that they will have to pay the same tax as the rest of us who are not wealthy or privileged enough to avoid it.

Avoiding and evading - tax havens aid both

A tax haven is a country that allows foreign individuals and businesses to pay little or no tax. Tax havens also provide little or no financial information to foreign tax authorities.

Tax avoidance means finding ways to reduce your tax bill that are within the letter of the law. It uses loopholes and gaps in the way the legislation is framed to avoid tax which would otherwise be due.

Safety and secrecy make tax havens ideal for illegal transactions - dodging tax and dodging the law

Tax evasion is illegal. It means under paying or not paying tax at all by a deliberate deception such as not declaring the full amount of income.

Avoiding tax is legal - though it may be morally dubious and people are often embarrassed when their arrangements become public. Evading tax, on the other hand, is illegal. Avoiders and evaders both make use of tax havens since secrecy is part of the attraction. Safety and secrecy make tax havens ideal for illegal transactions - dodging tax and dodging the law. Tracey McDermott, acting chief executive of the Financial Conduct Authority told The Guardian after the leaks, "The reality is, it has long been known there are lots of offshore arrangements made by lots of people for lots of different reasons, many of those reasons are perfectly legal but there is scope for arrangements like that to be used for tax evasion and to hide proceeds of more serious criminality."

Companies and criminals value secrecy

Secrecy enables crime: money laundering, fraud, tax evasion, bribery and corruption. It also provides the means by which wealth can be taken away from society in general; aid intended for poor populations has been diverted into private, secret, bank accounts on a massive scale in Africa. The economies of even developed countries like Portugal and Greece have suffered because of large-scale tax evasion.

Huge multi-national companies, such as Amazon, Google and Apple, trade worldwide but choose to base themselves in tax havens. They don't need to have any buildings or assets in the low-tax country, merely to be registered there. Nicholas Shaxson, author of *Treasure Islands: Tax Havens And The Men Who Stole The World*, offered a simplified model in a Guardian article in 2015:

SOME ISSUES:

What do you think we pay tax for?

What would happen if enough people didn't pay their taxes?

Do you think there should be stronger laws about tax payment?

What could be done to make sure big companies pay their tax?

Does knowing that a company avoids paying taxes affect whether you would buy from it?

'Let's say a corporation picks and packs a container-load of bananas in Ecuador, and it costs the company $1,000. It sells them to a French supermarket for $3,000. Which country gets to tax the $2,000 profit – France, Ecuador? The answer is, "Where the multinational's accountants decide."

The multinational sets up three companies, all of which it owns: EcuadorCo, HavenCo (in a zero-tax haven) and FranceCo. EcuadorCo sells the container to HavenCo for $1,000, and HavenCo sells it on to FranceCo for $3,000. That's basically it.'

The trick here is that the first company, EcuadorCo, made no profit on the $1,000 sale. The third company, FranceCo, made no profit on the $3,000 sale. The middle company, HavenCo, made $2,000 profit but paid no tax because it is based in a tax haven. But all three companies are owned by the same corporation which has boosted its profits by avoiding tax.

This way of working - which is often seen as sound business practice or being tax efficient - does not create new wealth or allow it to 'trickle down' to the less wealthy. It simply diverts money from the countries and producers to shareholders. In the case of our example above, we could imagine the bananas grown in a developing country whose tax revenues would be desperately needed for health, education, basic necessities and even survival.

It also gives huge multinational corporations an enormous advantage over small, local businesses. The banana exporter in our example can avoid tax but the local greengrocer cannot - and perhaps does not want to.

Striving for fairness

To highlight this obvious unfairness, small traders in the Welsh town of Crickhowell drew up plans to take the whole town offshore - out of the UK tax system - using the strategies employed by the likes of Google and Starbucks. As a Crickhowell coffeeshop owner said: "I have always paid every penny of tax I owe, and I don't object to that. What I object to is paying my full tax when my big name competitors are doing the damnedest to dodge theirs." He may have been thinking of the fact that Starbucks moved money through complex deals and paid only £8.6million in corporation tax over 14 years during which its UK sales amounted to £3billion.

In theory, anyone can place their savings in a company based in a tax haven and legally receive interest tax-free (as long as they declare this to the UK tax authorities). In practice, however, you need a sizeable amount of money. The Blairmore fund which was set up by David Cameron's father, was officially open to anybody to invest in, but its prospectus made it clear that a minimum investment of £70,000 was required.

Tax havens are nearer than you might think

Even before the leak of the Panama Papers there was indignation about the way giant multinational concerns were able to avoid paying tax in the UK while doing business here, but in fact the UK and the USA are deeply involved in the system that allows this. The terms 'offshore' and 'tax havens' may make us think of small, palm-fringed island states supporting their own economies by providing a dubious service to more prosperous ones - former Business Secretary Vince Cable called them "sunny places for shady people". But the truth is rather different.

An organisation called the Tax Justice Network produces a ranking of the most important providers of financial secrecy. If territories are ranked individually then Switzerland comes top followed by Hong Kong and then the USA. The United Kingdom is 15th. However, a whole network of territories linked to Britain - places which recognise the Queen as Head of State and follow British laws - appear in the list. These are places like the Isle of Man, Guernsey, Jersey, Gibraltar, the Turks and Caicos Islands and the Cayman Islands. In all, 20 further territories with British links are included. If Britain's network was combined, then it would move to the top of the secrecy list.

Name and shame

The uproar that arose in Britain when the name of David Cameron's father was found in the list of those who had 'sheltered' their income did not compare with the thousands who demonstrated in Iceland. Nevertheless, it revealed a strong sense of injustice, that, in the face of austerity policies, wealthy people can protect themselves from making their fair contribution to society and from paying a fair rate of tax. People and companies who 'shelter' their money from tax, nevertheless benefit - directly or indirectly - from the roads, schools, hospitals and public facilities paid for by everyone else.

What can ordinary people do about this? For years some people have been boycotting Amazon - its reputation for its treatment of employees and its effect on local bookshops drew their indignation even before the tax scandal. However the company seems unstoppable. Perhaps a more effective means would be 'tax shaming' - using social media to stir up indignation and therefore harm the image and reputation of a company to make the practices so damaging that they no longer make sound business sense.

Some companies feel damaged simply by association with a corporate world which makes use of secrecy and avoidance. There is a growing Fair Tax movement, in the same spirit (and often involving the same companies) as the Fair Trade movement. Some companies are using a Fair Tax mark "For businesses that are proud to pay their fair share". In effect it is the opposite of a boycott, it encourages consumers to use companies that pay what they owe.

Anti-corruption efforts

May 2016, saw a meeting of world leaders in London on ways to tackle corruption. In the days before this, 300 economists, including a Nobel Prize winner, eminent authors and professors from Harvard, Oxford and the Sorbonne, signed a letter asking those leaders to "end the era of tax havens".

> **People and companies who 'shelter' their money from tax, benefit from the roads, schools, hospitals and public facilities paid for by everyone else.**

They wrote:
"The existence of tax havens does not add to overall global wealth or well-being; they serve no useful economic purpose. Whilst these jurisdictions undoubtedly benefit some rich individuals and multinational corporations, this benefit is at the expense of others, and they therefore serve to increase inequality.

As the Panama Papers and other recent exposés have revealed, the secrecy provided by tax havens fuels corruption and undermines countries' ability to collect their fair share of taxes. While all countries are hit by tax dodging, poor countries are proportionately the biggest losers, missing out on at least $170bn of taxes annually as a result."

The Anti-corruption summit produced a number of proposals to root out corruption by making it easier to see who was the owner of a company or a property and to make the information available to people with a legitimate need to see it, such as law enforcement agencies. Not all agreed, however, to a public register of such ownership. Some of the British Overseas Territories and American states were among those who have resisted full transparency. But 20 countries agreed to bring in laws to seize the proceeds of crime or corruption. A start has been made, but while tax havens exist they will continue to promote corruption, crime and gross inequality.

Sources: Various

Food & drink

5 Wonderful Things About Raising a Vegan Kid

Fiona Peacock
watchingyougrow.co.uk

SOME ISSUES:

How do you rate the benefits of being vegan?

Why do you think we love some animals as pets and cartoon characters and kill others for food?

Some people who have always eaten meat become vegetarians or vegans later. Do you think a child raised as a vegan would ever start to eat meat?

Would you consider eating fewer animal products?

Raising a vegan child is awesome, not only does it shock unsuspecting old people, it is a great way to teach your child compassion. This month marks my eight year vegan anniversary. When I was pregnant, I was regularly asked whether I was going to raise the baby vegan. While I understand why people wonder such things, it always seemed like quite a ridiculous question. If I think veganism is the right thing to do, and trust the health and nutritional benefits for myself, why wouldn't I want to raise my child vegan?

We live in a world where eating animal products is the norm, and deviating away from that is unusual, so I can see why people think it's strange to raise a child vegan. But, for me, veganism is normal, and eating animal products is grim. I never questioned whether I would raise my child vegan, I didn't need to give it any thought, I just always knew that I would. In the same way that I wouldn't raise her to be a racist homophobic climate sceptic, of course I wouldn't raise her to eat animals.

With three and a half years of experience tucked neatly under my belt, I can honestly say that raising vegan kids is easy. Here are five of the best things about raising a vegan kid:

#1: It teaches compassion

I want my daughter to grow up kind and considerate to others. I want her to be compassionate to others, mindful of her impact on the planet, and passionate about the causes she believes in. Veganism is the perfect starting point for this. I've been having conversations about veganism with my daughter since she first learned to talk. She knows that some people eat animals, and that we don't. She knows where different animal products come from. And, most importantly, she understands the impact that this diet has on the animals themselves. She knows cow's milk is created by mothers to feed their babies, and that people drinking it means the calves can't. She knows that animals have feelings and family connections, just as we do. I haven't sat her down and explained the ins and outs of the 'rape rack' or slaughterhouse methods, because I don't want to horrify her. But she understands veganism in an age-appropriate way. I hope that this foundation of compassion and individual action will set her in good stead for the future.

#2: It's harder to find junk food

It's not impossible, not by any stretch of the imagination. Pretty much all food can be veganised nowadays. Supermarket shelves are filled with vegan cheese slices, chocolates and sweets. So it's not difficult, but it is slightly harder. And I think that's a good thing. I don't have to endure a tantrum each time we go shopping because my daughter wants sweets. She has ice-cream sometimes when we go out for food, but not many places have dairy free ice-cream so it's not a regular part of her diet. It's great that so many products are vegan, but it makes it that little bit easier for vegans to eat crap, which I don't really think is that good a thing. Especially where my three year old is concerned.

#3: Shoes Are Way Cheaper

This one probably isn't the reason many parents choose to raise their kids vegan, but it's definitely a hidden benefit. I don't have to spend a fortune on the go-to brand for kids' shoes, because I can't. They're all made from leather. Instead, I can save a fortune by choosing shoes made from manmade materials. Bargain.

#4: I won't have to lie to her

One of the things I find pretty disturbing about modern society, is that we fill our children's lives with animal characters. We point out cows in the field,

We fill our children's lives with animal characters... and then we feed them all of these animals for dinner.

we watch Peppa Pig on tv, and we cover their bedroom walls in sheep and other animals. Oh, and then we feed them all of these animals for dinner. At some point, children make the connection between the chicken they're looking at, and the one they ate for lunch. And when that moment arises, it's only too easy for parents to dismiss their child's reaction. No kids want to eat Peppa Pig. I don't have to worry about my daughter finding out that I've been feeding her Peppa, Shaun and Nemo, because I'm not.

#5: I know how lovely my friends are

I have been surprised at how much effort my friends have made to help Ebony feel included at playdates and

parties. I always take plenty of food and expect to provide the vegan options, but so many parents have found and made vegan foods for Ebony to enjoy. This might sound ridiculous, but it's really moving to see people making such an effort to include her. Parents have provided cheese spread, chocolate buttons, biscuits and crisps specially chosen so that Ebony can have them. I know Ebony wouldn't mind if she couldn't eat the food, knowing that I'll have some for her in my bag, but she always looks so excited to find out there is special vegan food available just for her. It's so lovely, and really makes me feel grateful to have found the friends we have. It's nice to know I don't have to worry, that people get it, and that people don't want her to be left out.

www.watchingyougrow.co.uk
21 September 2015

Do Instagram's lemon-infused water "detox drinks" actually burn fat?

The truth behind the drinks splashed across social media

Kashmira Gander

When you think about it it's odd that Instagram – no more than an online photo sharing platform – has become a go-to-place for advice on healthy living. But here we are, basing our dinners on photos of kale smoothies and quinoa salads made by people who don't have any qualifications and that we'll never even meet.

Tap "#health" into Instagram, and it's not long before you stumble across a photo of what is ceremoniously called a "detox drink" consisting of a seemingly random piece of fruit, often a lemon, floating in a jug of water. A quick Google and such drinks are lauded as having "fat burning properties" and the ability to alkalise your body – whatever that means.

Putting a piece of fruit in water has no obvious benefits other than making it more refreshing. Yet such is the power of the "Juno" Instagram filter: bathing everything in an irresistible glow.

But it begs the questions: the people in the photos seem so healthy and fit and generally better at life – surely there must be something in the, er, water? Can lemon-infused water really cut through body fat?

The resounding answer from experts is no. The only way to melt away harmful fat is by creating a negative balance of energy in the body. This is achieved by burning more calories than you consume.

Professor Jimmy Bell of the Life Sciences department at the University of Westminster explains that the concept of fat burning when the body utilises fat as an energy source, instead of carbohydrates, does exist.

But he warns the concept is misused by the diet industry to convince self-conscious dieters that some compounds can attack fat. Highlighting how such claims can lead people to buy useless, and sometimes dangerous, "fat burning" products online, he stresses: "the truth is that none have been clinically proven to actually work."

Some animal and lab studies have shown that certain foods, such as chickpeas and lentils, can affect the appetite and digestion by fermenting in the colon. This could in turn encourage the body to use its fat stores.

However, such mechanisms haven't been proven in robust human trials, he explains. "Most of the research has been done in cellular systems and in

The people in the photos seem so healthy and fit and generally better at life

SOME ISSUES:

Why do you think people like to share images of their food online?

Do you think that Instagram and other social media encourage us to eat more healthily?

Is the health and fitness advice advocated online actually healthy?

What do you think constitutes a healthy lifestyle?

Where can we find genuine nutritional and healthy lifestyle advice?

"We want to eat what we want with no consequences and think that 'detox' will clear all the problems"

smaller groups studies that have been shown to take place in animal models in large quantities."

As for lemon and fruit-infused water, he says no trials have proven that it can, or can't, burn fat.

"I can't think of a mechanism where lemon water would have an effect on body fat" he says.

Dr Yvonne Jeanes RD, Senior Lecturer in the department of Life Sciences at the University of Roehampton, concurs, and cautions against the notion of "detox" foods.

"The body has its own excellent mechanisms to get rid of toxins and waste [involving] organs such as the gastro-intestinal tract, the liver and the kidneys.

Professor Bell agrees: "So-called detox foods to counterbalance a toxic diet won't work. A detox food is not like water to fire. If you want to 'detox' yourself stop eating rubbish - you don't need 'detox' food.

"We want to eat what we want with no consequences and think that 'detox' will clear all the problems, but that won't happen. Staying healthy is a lifetime struggle."

The take away message is then, that while drinking lemon or fruit-infused water isn't harmful, it won't have a significant impact on your health.

"If adding fruit and vegetables makes the water taste nicer, it could encourage people to drink more and stay hydrated. It can also add some nutrients, such as vitamin C," says Dr Sue Reeves, Principal Lecturer in the department of Life Sciences at the University of Roehampton.

"The most important thing to consider when trying to achieve or maintain a healthy body weight is to look at overall calorie intake, taking particular care in looking for hidden sugars in food, like ketchup and savoury foods, where you might not expect them," says Dr Jeanes.

"Another good example of hidden sugars is lemon-flavoured desserts, which often have extra sugar needed to sweeten them. And above all, be sure to eat adequate amounts of fruits and vegetables."

Professor Bell has some franker advice when asked whether there is any significant benefit from putting fruit in water.

"Scientifically no, but it tastes very nice. If you spend all day drinking lemon water it stops you from eating because you're doing something else, you could be chewing gum for that matter.

He adds: "You're better off going to the gym."

The Independent, 24 May 2016
www.independent.co.uk

"The body has its own excellent mechanisms to get rid of toxins and waste such as the gastro-intestinal tract, the liver and the kidneys."

Why are we wasting?

Good food is going into bins, landfill and incinerators

SOME ISSUES:

How much food do you and the people in your household waste?

What can you do to make sure you waste less food?

Why do you think that wasting food is such an important issue?

How should supermarkets change what they do?

What action should the government take on this issue?

Enough food is produced in the world so that no-one should go hungry. Rich countries like the UK and the USA have on their grocery shelves, at any one time, twice as much food as is needed. If you were to include the grain used to feed livestock, grain which would feed humans more efficiently, that figure would rise to three or four times what we need. Our problem is not under-production but our wasteful use of resources and our uneven distribution. We are guiltily aware of starvation and under-nourishment in the developing world, as well as food poverty within richer nations, yet we willingly discard good, nutritious food produced with valuable resources. So why are we wasting so much?

Starting with the soil

In developing countries most food is produced by small scale farmers. The crops are vulnerable to extreme weather (including the results of climate change), pests, poor farming methods, lack of infrastructure, poor transport and storage. The majority of spoilage and waste occurs before the produce can reach the consumer.

UK farmers share few of these problems. Our weather can be challenging but generally they can produce food in quantity, store it correctly and transport it easily. For our farmers, the problem comes with retailers and consumers, not in the soil but the shops.

Big supermarkets are convinced that we, as consumers, like to see perfect produce. They will reject a whole crop of vegetables because of blemishes or because the individual items are not

Waste is part of our way of life.

a standard size. These cosmetic demands can result in tons of edible food being scrapped. The cut-throat price wars between supermarkets also mean that they drive down farm gate prices and will make last minute demands or changes which simply cannot be accommodated. TV chef Hugh Fearnley-Whittingstall wrote about watching 20 tonnes of parsnips sent to the rubbish heap: 'They "failed" the "cosmetic standards". They weren't wonky, or forked, or bruised or even "ugly". They just departed, sometimes by a matter of millimetres, from some bizarre set of specifications that defines, with apparent omniscience, what it is that we, the customers, demand our parsnips to be. Not that anyone's asked us.' And the failure and waste can also mean disaster for the farmers' livelihood.

Supermarkets as super villains

Once the near-perfect produce reaches the supermarket it is piled into enticing displays, offered at low prices or combined in BOGOF deals or bundles to persuade us to buy and buy more. Those tempting, abundant piles of goods appeal to our primitive need to stock up in times of plenty, ready for the periods of want. But in our modern, western society we seldom experience anything worse than a rumour that Prosecco is in short supply.

Scandalously, leftover food is placed in locked bins or has bleach poured over it so that it cannot be re-used. Supermarkets find it cheaper to send food to incinerators than to redistribute it to charities or recycling. They say they arc afraid of legal action if someone becomes ill after stealing food from one of their dumpsters (people have actually been charged with the offence of 'stealing' food which has been thrown away).

Buy one, throw one away

But if supermarkets are the villains, household are at least accomplices. Almost 50% of food wasted in the UK comes straight from our homes. Waste is part of our way of life. Supermarkets may tempt us, but they can't force us to buy more than we need. The bargains we spot, buy one get one free, multipacks, supersize, all contribute to both excess consumption and to waste. And our over-buying feeds back into a food chain dedicated to over-supply. Our way of shopping - in one weekly binge - can lead us to false economies and overestimating our needs.

Fussy eaters

Along with changed shopping habits come changed eating habits. We throw more away because we buy more food in packages and have also lost confidence in our ability to judge when food is actually 'off'. We rely on sell-by and use-by dates which err very strongly on the side of caution - it is, after all, in the suppliers' interests for us to throw something away and buy it again. With fresh food, we are put off by small bruises and bumps that we could easily cut out, we are simply prepared to see unused food go into a bin and then into landfill because there is always more.

We are consuming more calories through larger portion size. Our food is richer, more varied and at the same time cheaper than ever before - and we are throwing it away.

Our changing consumption habits are causing unseen waste too. Take this example from Tristram Stuart in his TED talk *The Global Food Waste Scandal*: he counted 13,000 slices of bread in a factory skip. This was fresh bread, baked that day. They were there because they were crusts and those aren't used for packaged sandwiches. 13,000 every day!

Humans aren't the only ones whose eating habits have changed. In the past, pigs were routinely fed on scraps left over from human meals. They efficiently converted that unwanted food into delicious pork in a traditional virtuous circle. However, since the outbreak of foot and mouth disease, this is no longer allowed in Europe and instead expensive soya has to be imported so that we can continue to enjoy a bacon butty.

What's the problem?

The fact that we can produce more food than we eat is actually a human success story. The fact that we aren't all living at a subsistence level is a triumph of human development and has allowed more progress to

We should only buy what we need and use all of what we buy.

take place. You can hardly imagine the development of art, science and technology if we were all obliged to scrape a bare living from the soil. A stable supply of sufficient food is the key to human progress and creativity. But that surplus exists only in part of our world. And the need to maintain it places demands on land, water and fuel which are actually destroying essential elements of our eco-system such as forests and underground reservoirs.

And now ..

There's something of a fightback. Hugh Fearnley-Whittingstall has fronted BBC programmes about waste, particularly of vegetables and fish. In February 2016 France brought in a law to force supermarkets to donate unsold food to charities and food banks, a move which, it is hoped, will spread throughout the European Union. In the UK there is a voluntary agreement between the government and the big supermarkets. In March 2016 Tesco announced that it would donate all its unsold food to charity via the FareShare organisation. Morrisons had announced its own distribution scheme the previous year.

In the UK organisations such as FareShare and FoodCycle use surplus food to eliminate waste and to create meals for people, promoting, as FoodCycle says, "the simple idea that food waste and food poverty should not coexist." Another organisation, Feedback, combines campaigning, research and advice to reduce waste throughout the food system. One of its projects, the Gleaning Network, works at farm level doing the traditional job of collecting produce left behind in the fields.

There are also people who aim to live entirely without contributing to the food production system. Freegans use 'urban foraging', sometimes called dumpster diving, to provide for all their needs from what others discard. Most of us don't need to go that far but we can contribute to a more rational use of food resources. There is a simple way that we can contribute to the solution for the sake of our health, our environment and our humanity: we should only buy what we need and use all of what we buy.

Sources: Various

13,000 slices of bread in a factory skip. This was fresh bread, baked that day.

It's time to wean ourselves off the fairytale version of farming

George Monbiot

SOME ISSUES:

Do you think children should know more about where their food comes from?

Do you know how the animals you eat are raised and slaughtered?

Would you consider eating less meat?

Should food companies be allowed to advertise using children's books?

How can we find out more about where our food comes from?

The way that meat, eggs and milk are produced is surrounded by one of our great silences, in which most people collaborate. We don't want to know, because knowing would force anyone with a capacity for empathy to change their diet.

You break this silence at your peril. After I published an article on chicken farming last week, I had to re-read it to check that I hadn't actually proposed the slaughter of the firstborn by terrorist devil worshippers – so outraged and vicious were some of the responses. And that was just the consumers.

The producers didn't like it much either, though their trade associations responded in more measured tones. In letters to the Guardian on Saturday, the National Farmers' Union (NFU) and the British Poultry Council (BPC) angrily defended the industry. The NFU wrote:

"In the UK 90% of all chicken is produced to Red Tractor standards and this demonstrates that the chicken has met production standards developed by experts on animal welfare, safety, hygiene and the environment. Farmers take the welfare of their birds extremely seriously, and therefore to accuse the sector of cruelty is absolutely unfounded."

The BPC maintained that chicken "provides a wholesome, nutritious, sustainable and affordable source of protein, produced by an industry unsubsidised by government."

Let's spend a moment examining these claims, before raising the issue of how they get away with it.

In my view, the Red Tractor standard is a classic example of an almost meaningless label, whose purpose is to reassure customers in

This stocking density gives each bird an area the size of a piece of A4 paper.

a vague and fuzzy way while holding producers to standards that scarcely rise above the legal minimum. That's a long-winded way of saying bullshit.

Take the key welfare issue, stocking density. Here's what the government recommendations say: "The maximum stocking density for chickens kept to produce meat for the table should be 34kg/m2, which should not be exceeded at any time during the growing period."

But the standard for broiler chickens set by the Red Tractor scheme is actually worse: "Planned stocking densities must not exceed 38kg/m2 for broilers". Incidentally, this stocking density – 38kg/m2 – gives each bird an area the size of a piece of A4 paper.

This meets the legal requirement only because the UK uses a cruel derogation from European law, permitting a maximum stocking density of 39kg/m2. So much for the NFU's statement about taking the welfare of chickens extremely seriously.

On almost every welfare indicator, and across all the main farm animals, including chickens, Red Tractor scored worse than any other certification scheme evaluated by the charity Compassion in World Farming. Amazingly, the Red Tractor label imposes no restrictions on the growth rates of chickens: it allows the most overbred varieties to be stuffed with high-protein feed, with the result that the birds often suffer from painful and crippling health problems, as their hearts, lungs and legs are overloaded.

As for the BPC's sustainability claims, if chickens fed on soya – as the great majority in this country are – are sustainable, what does unsustainable look like? Soya production is one of the major agents of the destruction of rainforests, the Cerrado and other threatened habitats in South America. The environmental impacts of chickenfeed are, well, anything but chickenfeed. The mass production of chickens has major consequences at the other end of the bird too: the

mountains of excrement cause both water and air pollution.

Nor is the claim that this industry is unsubsidised correct. Many chicken growers barely break even on the sale of birds, and survive only as a result of the government's renewable heat incentive (RHI). This is a remarkably generous scheme whose ostensible purpose is to reduce carbon emissions, but which functions as another subsidy for businesses, especially farms. Most new chicken units use biomass boilers subsidised by the RHI, and it is immensely profitable.

So now to the real question: how do they get away with it? How is it that we, who regard ourselves as a nation of animal lovers, accept such terrible standards of meat production? If dogs and cats were treated as pigs and chickens are, there would be a deafening outcry: in fact there are plenty of people in Britain who campaign against the raising of dogs and cats for food in Asia. But what's the difference? Why is it acceptable to treat some animals – even creatures as intelligent and capable of suffering as pigs – so brutally, but not others?

In part, this reflects the deep disavowal in which we tend to engage when we eat meat. But I also believe that a major part of the problem is the fairytale view of farming implanted in our minds from the very onset of consciousness.

Many of the books produced for very young children are about farms; and most tell broadly the same story. The animals – generally just one or two of each species – live in perfect harmony with the rosy-cheeked farmer, roaming around freely and talking to each other, almost as if they were members of the farmer's family. Understandably enough, none of the uncomfortable issues – slaughter, butchery, castration, tusking, separation, battery production, farrowing crates – ever feature.

So deeply embedded is this image that I believe many people go through life unable to dismiss it from their minds. It is not easy to unlearn what we are taught when we're very young, and even the grim realities of industrial farming cannot displace the storybook images from our minds. At a deep, subconscious level, the farm remains a place of harmony and kindness – and this suits us very well if we want to keep eating meat.

This book exploits children's natural sympathy with animals.

Perhaps the starkest example of this myth-making I've come across is a children's book distributed with Saturday's Guardian called *The Tale of City Sue*. It tells the story of a herd of cows on an Irish farm.

"This friendly, Friesian family
Were free to roam and browse
And eat the freshest, greenest grass
Which made them happy cows.
They belonged to farmer Finn
Who called them by their names
And when it was their birthday
He brought party hats and games.
He played his violin for them
Inside the milking shed,
And sung them soothing lullabies
When it was time for bed."

Only after I had unthinkingly read it to my three-year-old then turned the back cover, did I discover that it wasn't a book at all, but an extended advertisement for Kerrygold butter.

It wasn't billed as such. The Guardian's website marketed this publication as "A tale from the meadow of imagination: children's author Jeanne Willis's latest book captures the idyllic atmosphere of rural Ireland." Following my questions to the Guardian, this has now been changed to make its provenance clearer.

I find disguised marketing of any kind objectionable, and disguised marketing to children even worse. I feel that this book misleads children about the nature of farming and milk production and sanitises the relationship between farmers and their animals, on behalf of a large corporation (Kerrygold's parent company, Adams Foods). It exploits children's credulity and natural sympathy with animals for corporate profits.

From what I can glean, Kerrygold's marketing seems to rely on the public perception that Irish dairy farms are small and mostly grass-fed. But they are changing fast.

Last summer, 3,000 dairy farmers visited the biggest dairy operation in the country (which has 820 milking animals) to discover how to increase the scale of their operations. This farm has made a major investment in indoor facilities, and supplements the grass they are fed with maize, barley and soya.

According to the former chair of the Irish Farmers' Association, "scale must go up. ... The dairy farm of the future is going to have to be bigger."

Could the current Kerrygold marketing blitz be an attempt to embed in our minds a bucolic, superannuated image of an industry that is now changing beyond recognition? If so, it might be an effective way of pre-empting criticism about the changing nature of its suppliers.

Dairy cows, like chickens and pigs, also get a rough deal, while the effluent from dairy farms creates major environmental problems. Imagine the response if children were exposed to such blatant sanitisation of a harsh and polluting industry in any other sector. But so prevalent is this mythologised view of farming, and so wilfully unaware do we remain of the realities of industrial agriculture, that it passes almost without challenge. My guess is that the Guardian made this error – a serious one in my view – partly because the themes Jeanne Willis and Kerrygold exploited are so familiar that they are almost background noise.

Isn't it time that children's authors showed a little more imagination and stopped repeatedly churning out the same basic story, even when they are not doing it on behalf of a large corporation?

Is it not time that adults weaned themselves off the fairytale version of farming and began to judge it by the same standards as we would judge other industries?

And is it not time for all of us to become a little more curious about where meat, milk and eggs come from, and how they are produced?

Monbiot.com
The Guardian, 29 May 2015
© Guardian News & Media 2015

Gender

Parenting a transgender child: 'The day my four-year-old son told me he was a girl'

Eleanor Tucker

SOME ISSUES:

Why is gender identity important?

How can we make sure that people feel comfortable exploring their gender and support those going through a transition?

How would you react if a friend or family member said they were transgender?

Is there a right age to make a decision about gender?

Watching the Powell family in the park, there's nothing unusual about them. Parents Kathryn and Mark chat, keeping a close eye on Jack, nine, and Ruby, seven. But although Ruby – in a Hello Kitty T-shirt, clutching a doll – looks like any seven-year-old girl, two years ago the same scene would have shown Rudy, a five-year-old boy.

Thanks to the likes of Caitlyn Jenner and *Orange is the New Black* star Laverne Cox, the term transgender has recently moved into the mainstream. But they are adults. What's it like for a mother whose child makes it clear they don't feel they were born with the 'right' body?

For Kathryn, it was obvious early on that Rudy was not like his elder brother. 'Jack was naturally boyish. So when Rudy preferred playing with my jewellery to toy cars as a toddler, I thought, "He's just a different kind of boy. Maybe he'll be gay."' As soon as he was able to decide, Rudy would quietly show a preference for playing with girls, and for girls' clothes.

Kathryn began researching online and found videos of transgender children in America, like Jazz Jennings, the teenage YouTube personality who transitioned to female aged five. 'It was all very familiar,' she says.

Susie Green, chair of Mermaids UK, a charity that supports transgender children and teens, explains that gender is something you come to terms with between the ages of three and five. 'Gender dysphoria applies to someone like Rudy who is unhappy with their biological sex and wishes to belongs to the other one. It's a medical issue – it's not about sexuality or even mental health.'

Although Rudy's GP called it a 'phase', Kathryn was determined to be referred to an NHS gender identity clinic. 'I was frightened of influencing Rudy and initially I didn't want him exposed to the idea that he could transition.

For Kathryn, it was obvious early on that Rudy was not like his elder brother.

'I was frightened of influencing Rudy and initially I didn't want him exposed to the idea that he could transition'

But by this point, aged four and a half, he'd stopped saying he wished he was a girl, and was now saying that he was one. I'd read that children with gender dysphoria had a "consistent, persistent and insistent" sense of being the other gender, and Rudy definitely ticked this box.'

The clinic advised that Rudy should start to make his own choices and, specifically, recommended that he was allowed to pick an item of clothing. 'He chose a Disney princess nightie and skipped around the house in it, laughing,' recalls Kathryn. 'In the meantime, I talked to my friends: I wanted to prepare a support network. But I still hoped he'd grow out of it because I was frightened of what lay ahead for him.'

Barbara Hutchings knows exactly how difficult it can be for a transgender teen. Her son Tom, 17, is female-to-male transgender. 'Tom felt different from an early age but it came to prominence at puberty. When he told us, we were shocked but we accepted it quickly. His thought processes were very mature and he'd been repressing his true gender for years.'

Green explains that if children come out as teenagers, like Tom, it's because existing feelings come to the fore. 'There's an added sense of urgency: they don't want to become an adult with a gender they don't identify as. And as puberty progresses, the harder it is to "go back": body and face shapes alter, Adam's apples and breasts appear – these changes make it more likely that transgender adults are stigmatised.'

Hormone blockers are a low risk, reversible treatment that stop puberty and allow a child space to consider their options. But in this country, NHS waiting times to get them are long, leading many parents to get help privately either in the UK, which costs hundreds of pounds, or abroad, which costs thousands.

Cross-sex hormones, either testosterone or oestrogen, which start the process of changing the body into one that is more male or female, can only be used once a child is 16. Surgery is only possible after 18, and when the person has lived as their preferred gender full-time for at least a year.

Green is campaigning for a review of legislation for transgender people and wants to see an improvement in support and therapy services for vulnerable teens. UK law contains no provisions for trans people under the age of 18 to gain legal recognition, and options for gender treatment are vastly limited until people are over 16.

'In puberty, every day feels like a lifetime when unwanted changes are happening. That's why the UK rates of suicide and self-harm are so high among transgender teens, compared to countries like the US and Germany.' The Equalities and Human Rights Commission did a survey of 10,000 people in 2012 that found that 1 in 100 people has issues with their gender, whether they have done anything about it or not.

And a study last year by mental health organisation PACE revealed that nearly half of the 2,000 transgender young people polled in the UK had attempted suicide, and that 59 per cent had self-harmed, compared to nine per cent of all of that age group. Meanwhile, one clinic has reported that referrals are increasing by 50 per cent every year.

'There's an outdated view that children can't "know" if they are transgender,' says Green. 'Yes, there might be one in 1,000 who changes their mind, but what about the other 999?'

By the time Tom got to the gender identity clinic at 15, he was suicidal. 'He needed hormone blockers desperately, but was refused them, so we sought care, counselling and cross-sex hormones outside the UK,' says Barbara. 'Very quickly he was – and is – so much happier. We're lucky we could help him but for those who can't afford it, it's a desperate situation.'

Kathryn's experiences have been more positive. 'I couldn't fault our NHS care – but then hormone treatments are a long way off for us.' Towards the end of Year 1 at school, Rudy started wearing girls' clothes at home. 'I showed pictures to his teacher,' Kathryn says. 'I wanted the school to know what might be coming, and they were really understanding'. That summer, on holiday in Spain,

Photo posed by model

'Part of me went through a kind of mourning for the child I thought I had

Kathryn and Mark decided to let the then six-year-old Rudy wear what he wanted.

'Of course, he chose to dress as a girl. I watched him at the disco, chatting to girls, wearing a pink glittery dress. That was a turning point. "This is actually happening," I thought, and it was a really emotional mix of happiness that he was so happy, and worry about what lay ahead.'

Back home, Rudy chose a girl's school uniform for the new term and asked to be called Ruby.

'That worked – we called him Ru anyway,' explains Kathryn. 'At school, he told the class he was now a girl. I knew the kids would be telling their parents so I sent an email around, explaining, with links to articles I thought might help. Everyone was brilliant, including the children.'

'Rudy was now Ruby and he – now she – was so happy. Although that was what I wanted, part of me went through a kind of mourning for the child I thought I had. But that passes.

Sadly, some close family members have struggled to understand and accept our approach, but our friends have been wonderful. And if we ever ask Ruby if she might ever want to be a boy again, she just says, "No way!" There's never been any doubt in her mind that she is a girl.'

Tom's school, on the other hand, struggled with his transition.

'Some schools are great,' says Green. 'But some aren't, and what we need from the Government is blanket guidance in line with the Equality Act.' Tom left that school and had private tuition for a while, and is now at a sixth form elsewhere.

'I was in a very sad place for some years, but there's hope – if you can get help quickly,' he says. 'I'm now growing up just like any other teenage boy, thanks to my mum and dad's acceptance, and being permitted to medically transition.'

Medical transition for Ruby will only start at puberty and in the meantime she's seen regularly by the clinic as she grows up. 'I worry about bullying, which is common for transgender children,' says Kathryn. 'However, we haven't experienced it yet, and the good thing is that people are becoming more aware. If all this had happened just five years ago, it would have been much more difficult.'

Daily Telegraph, 15 November 2015
© Telegraph Media Group Ltd 2015

Allowing people to be who and what they are, without fear of prejudice, is the hallmark of a civilised society

Colette Douglas Home

If you have never given your gender much thought, count yourself lucky. If that tick in the box on almost every form requires no more effort than a flick of the wrist, be aware that for many people gender is not so straightforward.

For an estimated 600,000 people across the UK (one in every 100), gender remains a dominant and troublesome factor. If you imagine their troubles don't affect you, think again. Surely the way we treat the most vulnerable in our society holds a mirror to who we are.

Those who come under the umbrella term transgender are definitely vulnerable. They include people who were registered as male or female at birth but who feel themselves to be members of the opposite sex.

Transgender also describes people whose gender is non-binary. If male is at one end of a spectrum and female at another, they see themselves as somewhere in between.

That's the way life is for them. It's how they were born or how they developed. But in Scotland, as in the UK, it doesn't half make their lives difficult.

In other cultures such as in India, Nepal and Pakistan those who are transgender have long been accepted and recognised. They are a fact of life. It's no big deal; not here. Here they suffer bullying and discrimination. Often they live in the shadows.

Here the decision formally to register as a member of the opposite sex to the one you were designated at birth is complicated. It requires evidence from a psychiatrist and proof that, for two years, the applicant has been living in that gender identity. The decision is then made by a judge-led panel.

Some people have surgery just to improve their chances. Last year we communally hung our heads in shame when the film *The Imitation Game* showed how an ignorant state chemically castrated Alan Turing for being homosexual. This year in *The Danish Girl*, the story of a transgender man set in 1920s, we will see how little we have developed in our acceptance of another minority group.

Why should a judge and a psychiatrist be required to corroborate what nature has already decreed? I'm not the only one who wonders.

Maria Miller MP, chairwoman of the women and equalities committee at Westminster, headed a three-year inquiry into the subject. Its proposals, which will be published this month, will include a recommendation that people over 18

SOME ISSUES:

Does it matter what gender a person is?

How can gender limit people's lives and personal expression?

What do we expect from people of different genders?

How can we help support transgender people?

How can we help society be more understanding and accepting?

Society discriminates against those who are different.

should be able to choose their own legal gender simply by filling in a form.

Last week Ms Miller also asked why gender needs to be defined on passports or driving licences. Why indeed?

Australia and Bangladesh haven't had this requirement since 2011. New Zealand joined them in 2012. India doesn't require it on the electoral role and Nepal hasn't had it on the census since 2007.

Last year Ireland introduced a law allowing adults to choose their gender simply by filling in a form. It followed the example of Malta, Argentina and Denmark.

Meanwhile in Leeds last November, 21 year old Vikki Thompson committed suicide in a man's prison following a failed attempt to be admitted to a woman's jail. Vikki was born male but in her mid-teens identified herself as a woman. She had not undergone surgery.

Half of young "trans" people and one third of adults try to take their own life. The number of under-10s seeking treatment on the NHS quadrupled in the past five years.

So is one's gender a private matter or should society retain the right to decide? Gender identity is a subject that expands on closer inspection.

I have always been aware of people who have the body of a man but feel themselves to be a woman and vice versa. Their situation is described by the former Olympic athlete Caitlyn Jenner. She said: "The uncomfortableness of being me never leaves me all day long."

That discomfort is exacerbated by the way society discriminates against those who are different.

When Germaine Greer called trans women "ghastly parodies" attempts were made to uninvite her from a speaking engagement at Cardiff University. The younger generation may have sinned against free speech but didn't Greer also abuse it by taking a black and white, uncompassionate view of a complex issue? Was this an example of wilful blindness to gender subtleties?

We claim to be a free society, in an age of tolerance and with an emphasis on equal rights for all, so why can't everyone be given their place.

James Morton of The Scottish Transgender Alliance is keen that any change in the law should benefit those who fall between genders. They must, he feels, be able to opt out of being defined as a man or a woman; to be permitted to be identified legally simply as human beings.

Vic, who is in this category, tried to explain how it feels. "Navigating a world which always expects you to fit neatly into two boxes 'man' or 'woman' can be incredibly difficult and distressing when

these words and the expectations around them do not fit who you are." (Our language too is binary so just writing that paragraph without using he or she was a minor challenge.)

Many of those who share Vic's experience want to change the gender designation on their birth certificate and hope to have a third category to choose on official forms such as passport applications.

Ms Miller argues that we should go further and scrap the requirement to identify gender on job applications except when absolutely essential.

Most names are so gender specific it might not make a huge amount of difference. Applications could ask for first names as initials only. They could be submitted as a number. It would be interesting to see how much it also affected the current debate about discrimination between men and women candidates.

What matters most to James Morton is that the committee's recommendations, once aired in detail, are not then lost in the long grass. He says that proposals won't transform lives; legislation could.

I believe that the proposals will help, even if they go no further. They will help in the way that Caitlyn Jenner helped. They raise the profile of this issue just as the film *The Danish Girl* will do. Every time we look and listen and read we understand better and are less likely to judge.

Vic says: "Almost all of my interactions with new people start with them making a split-second decision based on my appearance on whether I am a man or a woman; and if these are the only options people are aware of, then this means that unfortunately they always guess wrong."

I feel for Vic. I also feel for the people Vic meets. As I struggle again to avoid gender-specific pronouns I can see that compassion and understanding need to flow two ways.

That way the debate can open up and a new way forward established. It is an issue for us all because allowing people to be who and what they are – without fear of prejudice – is surely the hallmark of a civilised society.

Source: This article was first published 5 January 2016 in The Herald Scotland © The Herald, heraldscotland.com

"Navigating a world which always expects you to fit neatly into two boxes 'man' or 'woman' can be incredibly difficult and distressing."

Lad culture is a symptom of misogyny, not the cause

Siddharth Venkataramakrishnan

The business secretary, Sajid Javid's statement that he wanted to "investigate" so-called 'lad culture' at British universities came out in September.

This was impressive stuff in many ways: here was the Government recognising that there was a problem in university culture: that rugby clubs telling members to "pick" a fresher and spike her drink with "a substance of [their] choice" on a night out was unacceptable.

Yet at its heart, lad culture is a symptom of wider problems rather than a cause.

That's not to say that misogyny isn't a problem at a university level; just that the image of beer-swilling, cat-calling lads as the only issue is painfully myopic.

For a start, there's the failure of educational establishments to support victims of sexual harassment – or even to have formal policies for these issues. This, fortunately, has come under fire of late, and perhaps change will come of it.

But it's hardly as if boys leave school as model believers in equality, and are inducted into the cult of misogyny via alcohol and leaving home.

Perhaps it's wrong to generalise the experiences of a school where girls only entered in sixth form, but I don't think I'm alone in seeing an environment so charged with testosterone as giving rise to some bad habits.

Even though the majority of 'lads' I knew were about as hard as chalk, they still proved themselves via acts of 'masculinity', or perhaps more accurately, idiocy.

I can remember seeing one of the class 'jokers' showing off by pretending to grind on a girl – fortunately she turned around quickly. She didn't find it quite so amusing.

It's experiences like this which make me wonder if a study of lad culture will effectively lead to change, when so many students will already have their opinions set from seven years of education.

There's a tendency to write sexism at schools off with a nonchalant 'boys will be boys'; that it's just a part of growing up. That was the response which recent proposals to avoid language like 'sissy' and 'man up' received.

And then, there's the Internet. The moment I say that, I feel like an awful Luddite and that's just not true. I love the Internet (I've certainly spent too many hours hitting 'Random Article' not to love it), and it is a brilliant resource for outing and outmanoeuvring traditional sexism.

Projects like Everyday Sexism are a grim but effective way of showing off the myriad cases of sexual harassment and assault which are culturally normalised; others, like the brilliant Wehuntedthemammoth.com, track and mock misogyny with a mixture of common-sense and comedy.

SOME ISSUES:

Do we expect different behaviour from boys and girls, and do we judge their behaviour differently?

What would you define as 'laddish' behaviour?

Do different expectations of boys and girls have any impact on their later behaviour?

The majority of 'lads' I knew were about as hard as chalk, they still proved themselves via acts of 'masculinity', or perhaps more accurately, idiocy.

The Internet is a bigger issue to tackle than lad culture.

Yet at the same time, it's hard not to see the Internet as a bigger issue to tackle than lad culture. You can take your pick of social movements and websites, each peddling their own take on why women/feminists/ anybody who doesn't agree with them is wrong.

There's the mob mentality of #GamerGate and #meninism, the pseudo-macho cyber-libertarian world of Reddit, and the home of Bizarro logic, Return of Kings (RoK). Only they could work out that Elliot Rodgers, the murderer who sought 'revenge' on women for not giving him sex and other men for having said sex, was somehow a feminist.

More insidious than the blatant woman haters are the Men's Right Activists, whose MO is portraying themselves as victims of a patriarchal system – whilst publishing articles like 'Nice Guys Commit Rape Too'.

There's something more tragic about them, which is perhaps where their appeal lies: they acknowledge the flaws of the 'manliest man' ideology of RoK and its ilk, but fall into a pit of self-pity, which invariably blames women for all the evils of the world.

As part of a generation of digital natives, Javid's plan to focus on 'lad culture' alone feels almost quaint. It's already acted as a lightning rod for the free-speech brigade, who view the ability to shout drunkenly at women as a God-given right.

If the task force finds evidence of the negative effects of lad culture, I imagine it will recommend that consent workshops are adopted more widely. There will be a great wailing and gnashing of teeth from those who find that their 'liberties' are being infringed upon (courtesy, again, of Bizarro logic) – and nothing will change.

The Reddits and RoKs will pour scorn on the establishment for its infiltration by feminazis; Men's Right Activists will continue whining about their victimisation, and the root of misogyny will be strengthened, not hacked away.

Daily Telegraph, 6 November 2015
© Telegraph Media Group Limited 2015

You can take your pick of social movements and websites, each peddling their own take on why anybody who doesn't agree with them is wrong.

Laura Munoz

To Men I Love, About Men Who Scare Me

SOME ISSUES:

How prevalent do you think harassment by men of women is in our society?

What can we do to stop it from happening?

A number of countries have made street harassment and verbal abuse a criminal offence. Should the UK do the same?

What can you do in your school or college to highlight the issue?

I got a promotion a few days ago, so I decided to stop for a drink on my way home - just me and my sense of accomplishment. I ended up alone in bar, running defence against a bouncer who held my ID hostage while he commented on my ass (among other things), and asked me vaguely threatening questions about my sex life.

This is not a Yelp review. It's not an angry rant, and it's definitely not something women need to be reminded of. As far as I can tell there is only one good lesson to pull out of this otherwise all-too-familiar interaction, which is that in my experience, a lot of thoroughly decent men are still having trouble understanding it.

I have a friend who once joked that it was all right for him to catcall women because he's good looking. I had another ask me in faux-outrage why it was okay for me to describe a cupcake (as in an actual chocolate baked good) as a "seven", but not okay for him to rank women the same way. I was recently at a house party where a

They will still insist I be polite and cheerful, even while they make me feel uncomfortable and afraid

Photos © openDemocracy

group of guys referred to a soundproofed recording studio in the basement as "the rape room", like forty-five times. Some of these jokes were a little funny; some of them really weren't. But they were all endemic of something more sinister, and I honestly don't think the men in question even realise it.

So to the generally well-intentioned men in my life, please consider this: no matter what I accomplish or how self assured I am feeling, the aforementioned moronic bouncers of the world will still believe they have a right to demand my time and attention, even when I want to be alone. They will still insist I be polite and cheerful, even while they make me uncomfortable and afraid. They will still comment about my body and allude to sexual violence, and then berate me for being "stuck up" if I don't receive it with a sense of humour. They will still choose to reinforce their dominance with a reminder that they could hurt me if they wanted to, and that I should somehow be grateful if they don't. This has made me defensive. It has put me more on my guard than I would like to be.

Decent male humans, this is not your fault, but it also does not have nothing to do with you. If a woman is frosty or standoffish or doesn't laugh at your joke, consider the notion that maybe she is not an uptight, humourless bitch, but rather has had experiences that are outside your realm of understanding, and have adversely coloured her perception of the world. Consider that while you're just joking around, a woman might actually be doing some quick mental maths to see if she's going to have to hide in a bathroom stall and call someone to come help her, like I did three days ago.

Please adjust your mindset and your words accordingly.

Laura Munoz is a writer living in Los Angeles

Every year people across the world take to the streets and join in the Reclaim the Night marches, against sexual violence and for gender equality

A lot of thoroughly decent men are still having trouble understanding this

To tackle male suicide, we have to change what it means to be a man

Daniel Morris, Communications & Project Officer for the It Gets Brighter campaign and Experimental Psychology student at the University of Oxford.

In the UK, every two hours a man kills himself. We all have a duty to change this, yet tackling the biggest killer of men under the age of 45 is no small feat. The factors that contribute to this tragic loss of life are almost inextricably tied up in our notions of what it is to be a man. These notions permeate the way men think, feel and behave towards themselves and others.

Young men of our generation are in a challenging position: the last forty years have seen a tremendous shift in the role of men in society, and being a young man in 2015 involves a complex dance between embracing these

SOME ISSUES:

How do we usually expect boys and men to behave?

Are we harder on men who are upset, than on women who are upset?

Why do we treat different genders in different ways?

How might this be damaging for people?

What can we do to encourage people to express themselves, regardless of gender?

changes and conforming to the unreconstructed remnants of traditional gender roles. All too often men are berated for their poor emotional intelligence, or condemned for supposedly unfounded fears of talking about their feelings. Yet the fact that men aren't talking about mental health should not come as a surprise. Growing up, many young men will have been fed on a diet of gender-bound expectations: a 'boys-don't-cry' mentality that prioritises perceived strength above all else: the athletic over the expressive, and stoicism over emotional honesty. This is not to say that masculinity as a whole should be branded as pathological, but that we all carry harmful notions, conditioned from the day of our birth, of what it is to be a man. Paradoxically, calls for men to be more vulnerable co-occur with notions of what is considered attractive: reputation, fortitude and confidence are synonymous with sex appeal. These mixed messages lead men to perform a difficult tight-rope balancing act between masculinity and vulnerability. It makes sense that many men feel the need to wear a mask.

The impact of this has become increasingly apparent in my welfare role at university. It is both wonderful and saddening to see a person who has been alive for twenty years share thoughts and feelings that have been caged in their minds for most of their

life. I have supported two men who, by all appearances, were the closest of friends: they faced similar emotional struggles, and yet had never considered confiding in each other. A male friend told me that he only realised that he had lived with depression for much of his life after finding support which allowed him to express his feelings. Emotional support, to him, was not just something he was reluctant to receive - it was an "unknown concept". My own experience was similar: when I first sat in the office of a therapist at the age of 17, I believed I was incapable of crying. I was depressed, and yet questioned the value of attempting to verbalise feelings that I thought I knew well enough: I experienced them every minute of the day, and believed they were a fundamental part of my character. Yet the moment I opened my mouth and said the words 'I feel so overwhelmed' I shed a year's worth of tears, and, slowly, things got better.

Without fail, when a male peer I'm supporting breaks into tears, he apologises. This is an unsurprising consequence of men being taught to believe that this entirely natural behaviour is shameful. When a man is told to stop crying, what he hears is: 'there is a part of you that makes me uncomfortable, because it doesn't fit in with what I know and expect of your gender. In order to

Photo posed by model

When a man is told to stop crying, what he hears is: 'there is a part of you that makes me uncomfortable, because it doesn't fit in with what I know and expect of your gender.'

belong to that gender, you must act in line with these expectations. Therefore you must deny a part of yourself.' The consequences of this should not be underestimated. Regardless of our gender, emotions are fundamental to our human experience. It should come as no surprise that when we teach young men to conceal their negative feelings, the results can be catastrophic. Toxic masculinity might silence the despairing voices of men, but it won't silence their thoughts. This is why so many men take the only step that they feel they can to silence those thoughts.

The problems of gender cannot fully account for the male mental health crisis. Young men are also subject to the onslaught of pressures that our increasingly visual world creates. They are expected to conform to a definition of attractiveness that is becoming more and more narrow; the rise of muscle dysmorphia (less formally called bigorexia) shows that the pressure on men to be perceived as strong includes not only emotional suppression, but also physical aesthetics. Men are also subject to the issues that all young people face - the

relentless push for unattainable perfection in academics and extra-curriculars, and the need to create a flawless social media presence. At the same time, we see a considerable disparity between men and women in the likelihood of them receiving help for the toll that these pressures take. The first step towards remedying this is acknowledging the crisis that we face, both at an individual level and at the level of government.

This is of course not to say that progress has not been made: many of the male friends that I spoke to before writing this were aware of the scale of mental illness and suicide among men, shared similar ideas for its causes, and praised the mental health services available at our university. While this is promising, it might also suggest that among some men there is a disconnect between what they know and what they do. It has been said that we need to talk more about men's mental health. This is true: raising awareness and tackling stigma is fundamental to breaking down the barriers that prevent those suffering from getting help. But we don't just need more rhetoric about the tragedy of men's mental illness and suicide. What we need is more research, more funding, better interventions, compulsory mental health training for educators, and more preventative measures that seek to address the negative consequences of unreconstructed masculinity. We have a duty to help both the current and future generations of young men, and that duty entails not only talking, but also action. Men need to be taught to prioritise wellbeing over perceived strength, and this teaching needs to begin from the first day of their lives, not after a failed suicide attempt.

This blog first appeared on www.huffingtonpost.co.uk 1 December 2015

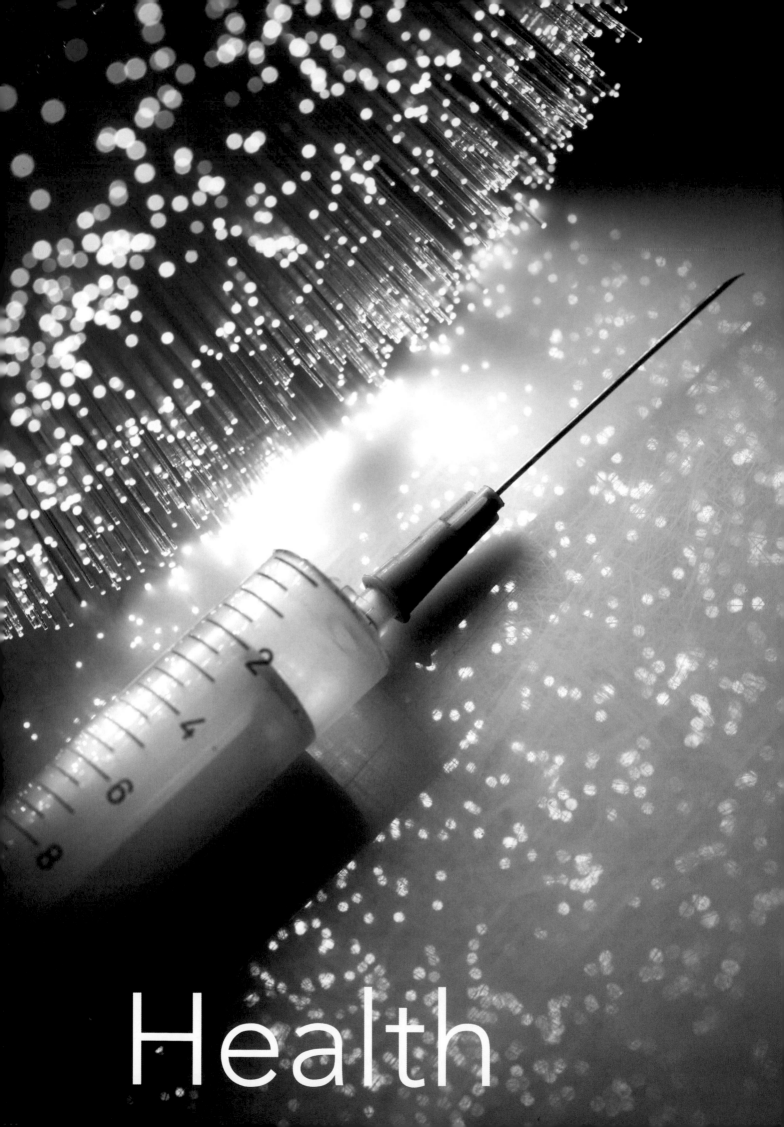

Health

The deviousness of dementia

When memory disappears, something more than memory gets LOST. This is how a world begins to UNRAVEL – and how caregivers unwittingly become part of the CHAOS

Dasha Kiper

In November 2010, when I was 25 years old, I moved in with a man who was 98. This man, whom I'll call Mr Schecter, wasn't a friend or relation or anyone I knew. He was a Holocaust survivor in the first stages of dementia, and I'd been hired to look after him. Although my background was in clinical psychology, I was by no means a professional caregiver. I was employed because Mr Schecter's son – I'll call him Sam – had seriously underestimated his father's condition. Sam's mistake was understandable. The most obvious paradox of dementia is the victim's frequent inability to recognise it, and Mr Schecter went about his life as though burdened by the normal aches and pains of aging rather than by an irrevocable and debilitating illness. If he put the laundry detergent in the oven or forgot which floor he lived on, he'd shake his head and sigh, *'Mayn kop arbet nisht'* ("my head doesn't work"). But it was a lament, not a diagnosis. And this denial, both clinical and profoundly human, led Sam to misjudge the illness as well.

For a man nearing 100, he was amazingly spry. Short, solidly built, with a firm handshake, Mr Schecter exhibited at our first meeting all the hallmarks of dementia. He repeated himself, his mind wandered, and he asked the same questions over and over.

When I learned that Mr Schecter, like my maternal grandfather, had been interned in a Soviet labour camp during the second world war, I naively thought I could protect him, that I could somehow compensate for the resilience that had sustained him in the past.

But I had another reason as well. I saw Mr Schecter as an opportunity to observe how a person fights to preserve his sense of self, even as a neurological disease is eroding it.

When someone loses an arm or a leg, we know exactly what's missing; but with the loss of memory, something greater than memory is at stake. Memory isn't just about remembering, and memory loss isn't just about forgetting. Memory is responsible for creating continuity, meaning, and coherence both for ourselves and for those around us.

Dementia not only affects the minds of its victims; it also creates a world so fragmented, so skewed and redundant – so indifferent to normal rules of behaviour – that caregivers unwittingly become part of the madness - it's not only his or her world that begins to unravel, but the caregiver's as well.

"So where are you from?" Mr Schecter asked as soon as I put down my bags. "Where did you go to school? Where do your parents live?"

"Russia," I told him, adding that my family had moved to San Francisco in 1992 and that I'd gone to the University of California at Davis, then Columbia for graduate school.

He digested this for about 30 seconds and then looked me in the eye. "So where were you born? Where did you go to school? Where do your parents live?" He didn't ask these questions every day for a year. He asked them five or six times a day, every day, for a year.

The more Mr Schecter tried to fill in the gaps of his memory, the more automatic his behaviour became. Every time I heard him wind his mechanical wristwatch, check his pockets for keys, or relentlessly pace the hallway at night, my body would tense up, unnerved by his anxiety and my own helplessness.

SOME ISSUES:

What do you think would be the most difficult challenges in caring for someone like Mr Schechter?

How good a job do you think Dasha did?

What other illnesses can affect those around them?

What can we do to help people suffering from dementia, and also their carers?

My own healthy brain was as incapable of adjusting to him as his brain was to me

But I knew I had to endure it. Because for those stricken by dementia, repetition is not merely a symptom but also a refuge, a coping mechanism that attempts to counter memory loss. That was what kept the chaos at bay.

I was a comforting presence, someone who made him tea and the occasional dinner, someone he could talk to – and how the man liked to talk!

This incessant repetition became the basis of our relationship. He relied on me to assure him of the status quo, and I, in turn, relied on his dependence, taking it as proof of our closeness.

Although dementia often makes its victims uncharacteristically open, I couldn't help but feel that he was confiding in me because of me, and not because of his illness. Why else did we sit every day in his living room, not two feet apart, as he spoke in the emotional register one reserves for a dear friend?

[But] when the phone rang, jarring us apart, it broke more than just the silence. Mr Schecter would trundle off to the desk in the hall while I went to my room to give him some privacy. After a minute of conversation, I could almost hear Sam say over the wire, "How is Dasha?" To which Mr Schecter invariably replied, "How should I know? She's sleeping, the door to her room is closed, the light is off." (The door was never fully closed, and the light was always on.)

These disruptions, when I abruptly disappeared from his consciousness, never failed to shock me. Only gradually did I begin to comprehend that my own healthy brain was as incapable of adjusting to him as his brain was to me.

Even when we know that dementia is mercilessly erasing experiences, we still feel that its victims are capable of keeping emotional tabs on their relationships, since those bonds were formed gradually over time.

He began to fixate on things he could control. Aside from repeatedly calling his son, he channelled his energy into rearranging the food in the fridge or fiddling with the electric fixtures and lamps.

To Sam, his father's behaviour was consistent with his usual inability to acknowledge or adapt to change.

Sam: Stop trying to fix the lamp in your room. It's dangerous.

Mr Schecter: I don't touch the lamp. I don't know what you want from me.

Sam: You mess around with the lamp and the wiring. That's how you cut your hand.

Mr Schecter: (agitated): I never touch the wires. What wires have I touched?

Sam: Don't argue with me! Just do as I say. It's for your own good.

Mr Schecter: When do I argue with you?

Sam: You always argue with me. You're always giving me trouble!

Mr Schecter: No one ever said I give anyone trouble.

Sam: You're giving me trouble right now!

Mr Schecter: How? How am I giving you trouble?

Sam: You don't listen to me. And if you keep arguing and contradicting me, I swear I'll stop coming to see you.

Mr Schecter: (worried): I promise. I promise I will listen to you 100%.

Sam: OK. Now promise me you'll stop touching the lamp in the bedroom. Repeat it to yourself - "I will not touch the lamp!"

Mr Schecter: (indignant): I never touch the lamp. What lamp?

Sam: Goddammit, stop arguing with me!

Mr Schecter: When do I ever argue with you?

To help Sam over this hurdle, I showed him pictures of the dementia brain, with the hippocampus pitifully shrunken to half its normal size. Staring at the coloured images of the healthy versus the diseased brain, Sam looked appropriately sombre. Yet only an hour after Sam had viewed these photographs, he and his father were shouting at each other again.

Such is the deviousness of dementia: its ability to keep hope alive while its symptoms signify only futility. As long as his father seemed like himself, Sam could continue to argue with him. As long as they kept fighting and as long as Sam clung to that familiar futility, it felt as though nothing had changed.

One evening, perhaps seven or eight months into my stay, Mr Schecter decided to change the battery in the smoke detector, which was in the hall, near the ceiling. Ignoring my warnings, he retrieved a chair from the kitchen and put it under the alarm. When I tried to stop him, he retorted that he was "the boss" and knew what he was doing.

"Forget about the alarm," I said firmly. "It's too dangerous to stand on the chair."

"You don't know what you're doing!" I shouted. "You haven't been to work in over a year! You don't do a damn thing alone!"

He paused, and I continued to berate him. My words both startled and amused him. "You are crazy," he told me with the superior air one reserves for spoiled children.

And now this 99-year-old man was about to climb on a chair and perhaps kill himself in the bargain.

It was too much, and I accused him of being impossibly stubborn, of being both needy and domineering, and finally, shamefully, I called him "a burden". That stopped him. For a moment he glared at me and then shuffled off to his bedroom.

Appalled by what I'd done, I carried the chair back to the kitchen and collapsed on the linoleum floor. I was angry at him for the perpetual stress. But mostly I was angry at myself for being cruel. As I sat sulking and reprimanding myself, he returned to the kitchen. He wanted a snack, but finding me on the floor, he stopped and broke into his wide, sweet smile. Then he noticed my tearful face and was dumbfounded and genuinely moved.

"Are you alright?" he asked. "Who should I punish for upsetting you?"

Memory and language are bundled together. We're fooled into thinking that people remember the words we utter. Even those who ought to know better – the caregivers who deal with dementia on a daily basis – often fail to remember that their patients forget. In this way, language instils hope and makes fools of us all.

And we go on, because decency requires it, because we cannot abandon those we love, and because the momentum of language, with its implicit hopes and promises, continues to carry us along.

• *This is an edited version of an article that first appeared in the autumn edition of The American Scholar.*

Such is the deviousness of dementia: its ability to keep hope alive while its symptoms signify only futility.

Photo posed by model

Why we need to
talk about OCD

By Kimberley Giles

SOME ISSUES:

Before reading this, did you know what OCD was?

What positive things could arise from more people speaking openly about their problems and mental health issues?

How can we help to support people who are suffering from mental health issues?

For too long, a vast majority of people in society have considered obsessive compulsive disorder (OCD) to be all about hand-washing. It's time we talked more about OCD and spoke about the debilitating torment this illness can have and how hand-washing is in fact just one part of it all.

I've had OCD since the age of seven, but it was left undiagnosed and untreated until I turned 22.

For years prior I had lived a secret life of ritualised hand-washing, hair pulling, counting syllables and trying to maintain a balance between good and bad.

I can only describe the 'OCD part of my brain' as noisy, and it is this noise that us who suffer with OCD can be scared to talk about. This might be through fear of what someone may say to us or through not wanting to

I had lived a secret life of ritualised hand-washing, hair pulling, counting syllables

admit there's even a problem. That was the case for me – the noise I had in my head, which I know better now as intrusive thoughts, was unbearable, yet admitting that they were a problem was something I was afraid to do for years of my adolescent life. I would lay in bed, night after night, going over each and every situation that I had encountered throughout the past day, frustrated at where I hadn't followed my rituals of hand-washing, moving a certain way, or punishing myself for things that had gone wrong. The torment was awful. If things hadn't gone how I'd planned for them to, I'd punish myself in any way I could, just to 'get the balance right.'

As I grew older, my OCD symptoms were exacerbated by general life experiences, and I found my fear of contamination became stronger by the day. I wash my hands so vigorously and so frequently that they are now dry, cracked and very sore some days. I rely heavily on hand sanitisers which dry my hands out even more. I now also pull the hair from my eyebrows and eyelashes, and I'm left with noticeable gaps (thank goodness for make up!). Furthermore, I count syllables during conversations with my fingers – as you can imagine, this can be incredibly annoying and I often don't seem as though I'm listening or that I've 'zoned out' when in fact I am repeating the sentences that have been said to me over and over in order to count the syllables correctly.

In terms of intrusive thoughts, these have changed and adapted also as I have become older. Some thoughts I still can't bear to share with anyone, but they make me feel like the most awful person in the world. Sometimes they are strong images, so vivid in my mind that I fear they will truly happen at any moment. On many occasions I have had to sit on the floor, shutting my eyes and turning my music up loud, in the hope I can drown them out. I suffer from severe panic attacks because of these thoughts, or if I haven't followed out my rituals as I need to. They leave me exhausted and drained.

There is still so much stigma around OCD. A lot of individuals consider it to only be about germs and being tidy, yet this is so far from the truth. In fact, I can be a very untidy person, just ask my partner! And these misconceptions anger me, for they do not represent what it is truly like living day-in, day-out with this illness. Yes, my hands look as though they belong to someone three times my age at times, but this is only one segment of the chaos in my mind that is OCD.

Now that I have come to terms with my diagnosis and have learnt more about this illness, I have decided I want to talk about it more. I want to work towards breaking down the myths surrounding OCD in the hope that individuals who speak out about having OCD are treated with the same respect as they would a

physical illness. Treatment for OCD can be difficult enough without adding stigma into the mix. Thankfully, I am now about to start some intensive therapy that will work out where my OCD originated and start to change my thought processes in the hope of easing symptoms.

If you suffer with OCD, I urge you to speak out and seek treatment. There are options out there including medication and talking therapies. Some things will work for you, and others won't. But I still have hope that one day I will be able to live alongside my OCD rather than it live my life for me. The stigma in society is a big enough issue in itself, but by not talking about the true reality of OCD, we are adding to the stigma too. So speak out, be proud, and believe that things will one day be better.

Kimberley Giles blogs regularly at musingsofananxiousgirl.blogspot.co.uk, and you can reach her on Twitter @LittleKimmyJane

I want to work towards breaking down the myths surrounding OCD

The first step to getting better is accepting that you need help - a young man's experience with depression

You're not alone

Tobias Berchtold

SOME ISSUES:

Why do you think that people tend not to speak openly about depression?

How can we encourage more sufferers to speak openly and feel supported?

What benefits are there to speaking out about our problems and health concerns?

Why is this account important?

Where can you go for help with depression?

I wrote this ages ago, but I feel like I can share this now that I'm feeling better (and I've built up enough courage to do so). This has probably been the most difficult year of my life, so I just wanted to write something to try to put it behind me. This may seem a bit sappy but writing this is cathartic for me. It gives me the opportunity to look back and see how far I've come (even though I still have a long way to go).

Depression is shit. There's no other way to put it, it's absolutely shit. From the outside it looks like a bad day here or there, but on the inside it means living with the fear that any day people will find out how you actually feel. It's not just about feeling down or being unmotivated, the main problem is the fact that it's almost like being terrified of feeling nothing at all. The fact that it can be invisible to those around you makes it just that bit harder to deal with.

I've been seeking help for my depression since Easter but if I think about it it's probably been affecting me since the start of university last year. The worst feeling about it is that I blamed myself - I had no reason at all to be unhappy. I got into my first choice university for medicine and had a good group of friends around me but still something didn't feel right. Then I fell into a cycle of guilt and shame as I felt that the fact that I was unhappy was my own fault, and that I was undoing all of my own hard work by not pulling myself together. I felt like I was an impostor, like I didn't belong. I was scared to pursue treatment because to me it felt like failure. I didn't want to open up to people and tell them the truth, so I invested massive amounts of energy in covering it up to people. To this day, people are still surprised when I tell them that I've been depressed for close to a year now which shows how much I felt like I had to hide it. That led to near-constant exhaustion and meant that I made those people that I felt like I could open up to unhappy, and for that I am still sorry.

Depression makes you constantly alone, regardless of how many people are there to support you. Even when I was out with a group of my closest friends I felt like I didn't fit in, so I had to try incredibly hard to feel normal. The amount of extra effort that it took for me to achieve that feeling of normality meant that it was no longer enjoyable for me to spend time with people. I withdrew and stayed in my room when all of my friends were out having a great time and this served to make me feel even worse about missing out, yet I couldn't for the life of me bring myself to join in. I lost my appetite, and would hardly ever cook for myself any more when previously it was one of my favourite pastimes. Once it had taken over everything that I enjoyed, life became so ridiculously difficult that I wondered what the point of it was at all.

About two months ago I took several weeks off university because I realised that my situation wasn't sustainable. I started focusing more on my mental health and began attending counselling sessions and started practising mindfulness (through an app called Headspace - which I would thoroughly recommend to anyone, with mental health problems or without), and since then I feel like I've been on a steady upward trajectory. There was a point a few months ago where I honestly couldn't see myself making it to Christmas, as several personal things cropped up amongst which was losing a close relative for the first time in my life. When that happened I didn't see a way past it and was pretty sure that I wouldn't be able to recover. I'm so grateful that I've been lucky enough to have a good support network around me to help me - I have my family (and Patch, our border collie), the counselling and my mates to thank for getting me through probably the most challenging phase of my life so far.

The taboo about being open with regards to mental health is something that I think needs to change for any progress to be made. You wouldn't hide a cold or another disease from people out of shame, so that shouldn't be the case for depression. Mental health problems are so prevalent within society that it should be more openly acknowledged. As a young male, it's pretty clear to me how uncomfortable a lot of my peers are talking about mental health. Suicide is the

> **The taboo about being open with regards to mental health needs to change.**

> **You wouldn't hide a cold or another disease from people out of shame, so that shouldn't be the case for depression.**

most common cause of death for males under the age of 40, and the lack of knowledge about mental health is frustrating to see. In the UK, 1 in 4 people in any given year will experience some form of mental illness, be that depression or something else. The more the stigma is broken down, the easier it will be for every party involved. I'm not sure if I actually ever was stigmatised because of my mental health, but the problem with depression in particular is that it creates a perceived stigma - you feel like people will treat you differently, even if they don't. Spreading the word and improving education about mental health will only serve to reduce this feeling, and hopefully at some point people won't be afraid of seeking help.

I guess what I'm trying to do by writing this is to tell anyone that feels the same way that I did to not be afraid of going to seek help. Depression is a real illness, even if it may not look like it from the outside. It hijacks every facet of life and takes over everything that you used to enjoy. Getting help, whether that's through medication or counselling is the best thing that you can do to prevent it becoming a problem. It is frustrating to me to see how poorly mental health is taught and explained to people, and it seems like the only people that really understand what it's like are those that have experienced it or those that have been close to someone who has. That needs to change.

A YouTube video *I had a black dog, and his name was depression* is probably the best way of relating to depression from the outside, and it even helped me translate it into a tangible thing I could show or explain to people so that they could understand how it feels.

If anyone reading this feels even remotely like this could apply to them then please go and talk to your parents or your GP, the biggest aid to getting better is taking that first step and noticing that something isn't right.

Being depressed isn't a normal way of life, so don't be afraid of letting people know. The more people around you that know the easier it becomes to open up and to come to accept the fact that something can be done to help you.

Tobias Berchtold is about to enter his third year as a medical student. He posted this account of his depression on his Facebook page in December 2015.

Photos posed by model

Social anxiety at school: the best actor in the world's worst play

by Sarah

SOME ISSUES:

Why do you think people hide their anxieties and problems?

If someone is suffering with anxiety, how can you help?

Should someone - a teacher, a parent or another student - have seen what Sarah was going through?

Sarah doesn't say what help she got from her GP. What sort of help do you think would be available?

I never thought of myself as a good liar but when I eventually faced up to my problems I realised that's what I had been doing constantly, for 3 years, to my family, my friends and even myself. I've been described as 'the best actor in the world's worst play', which I think is appropriate. I acted like everything was perfect when it felt like the world was crashing around me.

I can't identify a moment in time when everything got difficult for me. I can't even remember a time when I was truly happy or carefree. The one thing I know for sure is that I've never been happy with myself. Even when I was very young I knew I wasn't 'normal' (whatever that is supposed to mean). The fact I was different had never really bothered me until it developed into what I later found out to be a social anxiety disorder along with an eating disorder.

I was 13 and had never had a set group of friends. Everyone else had been with their friends throughout middle school and were set in their ways. I was the slightly larger side of normal for a 13 year old girl with a different taste in music

I acted like everything was perfect when it felt like the world was crashing around me.

No one knew I would cry myself to sleep every night. No one knew I was starving myself

The next issue revolved around my anxiety based compulsions that started when I was 14.

and clothes to everyone else. I spent my time drifting from one group to another because I would convince myself that as much as they smiled and talked to me, they didn't want me there and I was embarrassing them with how I looked and annoying them with my likes. So I moved on.

Throughout the constant movement of groups, no one knew what was really going on. The smile that was almost constantly painted on my face didn't indicate any problems so no one thought there were any. No one knew I would cry myself to sleep every night. No one knew I was starving myself to lose the weight that I thought was keeping me from having normal friendships and relationships.

The next issue revolved around my anxiety-based compulsions that started when I was 14. In an attempt to be 'normal' I started straightening my hair every morning but whenever I finished I didn't trust myself to unplug the straightener. I forced myself to take pictures on my phone of the plug out of the wall before I could leave the house without being convinced something bad would happen. This developed into me not being able to trust myself with basic tasks that any other 'normal' teenager could do with no hassle: like locking the door when leaving the house. I would take pictures of my hand on the door handle to signify it being locked.

No one knew how much I was suffering. The smile stayed and I was determined to keep it that way. I became incredibly possessive about where my phone was because, if anyone got hold of it and looked at the pictures I'd been taking to keep my peace of mind, my life would unravel and the part I'd been playing for so long would crash. I didn't want them thinking I was weak. That wasn't an option, the phone stayed with me at all times. I never went anywhere without it.

These behaviours carried on unnoticed until one day when I was 16. I was sat talking to my only real friend

and I don't remember why but I crumbled. The strength that I had worked so hard to hold on to was gone. The smile was washed off by the tears that I had never cried. Once I had eventually calmed down, I told him he could go if I was freaking him out and that I was just being stupid and I would be back to normal the next day. That wasn't going to happen, he told me I shouldn't have done it alone, that I wasn't any more and he would help me through this. He suggested I get an appointment with my GP and it was the best thing to ever happen to me.

I'm now 18 and I know the worst is over. I'm not perfect but I don't have to be, I'm happy and I am finally at a place where I am not afraid to talk about what I went through. I still have difficulties everyday but don't find them as difficult to handle.

I didn't tell anyone about anything because I didn't know enough about mental health to identify my problems and I thought people would judge me as weak. I built up this appearance of being strong and being able to defeat anything that came my way but the strongest I've ever felt was the point when I realised it's OK to ask for help.

Time to Change, www.time-to-change.org.uk

I realised it's OK to ask for help.

By the end of my first year as a doctor, I was ready to kill myself

Doctor suicide is the medical profession's grubby secret – but it's unclear why some of those dedicated to preserving life silently plot their own deaths

Anonymous junior doctor

SOME ISSUES:

What do you think might contribute towards the stressful conditions of junior doctors?

Why do you think so many doctors keep their stress a secret?

What can be done to help support doctors suffering from stress?

Why are there more patients than staff can cope with?

On my morning drives to the hospital, the tears fell like rain. The prospect of the next 14 hours – 8am to 10pm with not a second's respite from the nurses' bleeps, or the overwhelming needs of too many sick patients – was almost too much to bear. But on the late-night trips back home, I'd feel nothing at all. Deadbeat, punch-drunk, it was utter indifference that nearly killed me. Every night, on an empty dual carriageway, I had to fight with myself to keep my hands on the steering wheel. The temptation to let go – of the wheel, the patients, my miserable life – was almost irresistible. Then I'd never have to haul myself through another unfeasible day at the hospital.

By the time I neared the end of my first year as a doctor, I'd chosen the spot where I intended to kill myself. I'd bought everything I needed to do it. All my youthful enthusiasm for healing, big dreams of saving lives and of making a difference, had soured and I felt an astronomic emptiness. Made monumentally selfish by depression, I'd ceased even to care what my husband would

think of me, or that my little boy would grow up without his mother.

Doctor suicide is the medical profession's grubby little secret. Female doctors are twice as likely as the general population to take our own lives. A US study shows our suicide rate appears higher than that of other professional groups, with young doctors at the beginning of their training being particularly vulnerable. As I wrestled silently with the urge to kill myself, another house officer in my trust went right on and did it. To me, that monstrous waste of young life seemed entirely logical. The constant, haunting fear of hurting my patients, coupled with relentless rotas at work, had rendered me incapable of reason.

Though we know large numbers of doctors kill themselves, what is less clear are the reasons why, when dedicated to preserving human life, some doctors silently plot their own deaths. A 2006 study at the University of Pennsylvania identified that during their first year as doctors, young physicians experienced

> I was entrenched in a hospital system that brutalised young doctors. Working on my hospital's surgical emergency unit, there were simply too few of us to cope with the daily onslaught of patients.

skyrocketing rates of burnout, with symptoms of emotional exhaustion, depersonalisation, and reduced sense of personal accomplishment soaring from 4% to 55%.

For me, the explanation ran deeper. I was entrenched in a hospital system that brutalised young doctors. Working on my hospital's surgical emergency unit, there were simply too few of us to cope with the daily onslaught of patients. Officially eight or 10-hour days ran routinely into 13, 14 or 15 hours as we house officers worked at fever pitch to provide what was, at best, a mediocre service for our patients. Run ragged, we fought to keep our patients safe, but their numbers outstripped ours 20 or 30 to one, and the efforts this took were superhuman. The nurses knew, the consultants knew, even the hospital management knew, yet no one seemed to give a damn.

It wasn't just exhaustion that drove me into depression. Plenty of jobs are busy. But there is something uniquely traumatic about being responsible for patients' lives, while being crushed under a workload so punitive it gives neither the time nor space for safe assessment of those patients. Days were bad enough, but nights on call were terrifying. I remember running from the bed of one patient, still haemorrhaging blood from her surgical wound, to another whose heart rate had plummeted to 20, perilously close to a cardiac arrest. Two stricken patients, but only one doctor, wracked with the knowledge that if something went wrong, the guilt would be hers alone.

I was lucky. I was pushed by the colleague in whom I finally confided into seeking professional help. It took anti-depressants, therapy and a narrowly-avoided psychiatric inpatient admission to bring me back to the land of the living.

Now, on the cusp of junior doctors' first national strike in 40 years*, I'm astounded the health secretary persists in ignoring unanimous condemnation of his new contract from juniors and medical leaders alike. If he gets his way, [Health Secretary] Jeremy Hunt will make it easier for hospitals to abuse their juniors, by stripping away the safeguards that stop hospitals overworking us. Under his new contract, our hours will become even longer, even more antisocial – at a time when we simply have nothing more to give. And as we are pushed to treat more and more patients, faster and faster, fatigue and psychological distress will dull our competence: your lives will be less safe in our hands. And our own? Take it from someone who's been there. Watch the suicide rate climb.

The Guardian, 5 January 2016
© Guardian News & Media 2016

*Junior doctors took industrial action in 2016 as part of their campaign against new contracts imposed by the Health Secretary

Big Pharma's worst nightmare

Sarah Boseley

Jamie Love has spent years battling global drug companies, in the belief that even the world's poorest people should have access to life-saving medicines. Is it time that our own government listened to him?

SOME ISSUES:

Who do you think should own the rights to life saving medication?

Should there be laws in place to make medication affordable?

What is the problem with big businesses controlling medication prices?

How would you feel if you or someone you loved needed this medication?

If money is limited in a system like the NHS, how can someone choose who should receive drugs and who should not?

In the year 2000, the number of people living with HIV/AIDS worldwide had topped 34 million, many of them in the developing world. An Indian billionaire drug manufacturer, Yusuf Hamied, was looking for a way to break the monopoly held by pharmaceutical companies on AIDS drugs, in order to make the costly life-saving medicines available to those who could not pay.

Hamied had a secret meeting with Jamie Love, head of the Consumer Project on Technology, a not-for-profit organisation. Jamie Love has never worked in healthcare. His crusade for access to medicines developed

out of an early recognition that the drive for profit of big corporations was harming the poor. Love specialised in challenging intellectual property and patent rules. For five years, he had been leading high-profile campaigners from organisations such as Médecins Sans Frontières in a battle to demolish patent protection.

Patents grant protection on inventions, guaranteeing those who hold them a period of monopoly to recoup costs – in the case of drug companies, this can be as much as 20 years. With no competition, pharma companies can charge whatever

The drive for profit of big corporations was harming the poor

AIDS activists in the US and in Europe accused the companies of having blood on their hands.

they want. Love, an economist and self-confessed patent nerd, had taken on politicians, civil servants and corporate lawyers, arguing against unfair monopolies on products from software to stationery. His overwhelming concern at that point was the many millions of lives cut short for want of affordable medicines.

The meeting between Love and Hamied was confidential, because their targets were the wealthy and powerful multinational pharmaceutical companies who were fierce in defence of their patents. For four years, a three-drug cocktail costing between $10,000 and $15,000 per year had been available to treat people with HIV in the US, and other affluent countries. But in Africa, a diagnosis remained a death sentence. In 2000, more than 24.5 million people in sub-Saharan Africa had HIV. Many of them were young, many also had children and could not afford life-saving treatment.

Love had a question for Yusuf Hamied. How much, he asked, does it cost to make AIDS drugs? Hamied had been making the antiretrovirals that hold HIV at bay for a while. In India, drug patents granted in the US or Europe did not apply. The cost of manufacturing a drug, Hamied told Love, is barely more than the cost of the raw materials.

A plan was hatched. Hamied would make Triomune, a cheap, once-daily pill combining the three AIDS drugs sold by different manufacturers for such huge sums in the US and Europe, and sell it in Africa and Asia for a fraction of the cost.

By 1998, a powerful alliance had already begun to form against Big Pharma. In South Africa, by the end of that year, more people were dying of AIDS than in any other country. Yet at that critical moment, some 40 drug companies brought a joint legal action to block the South African government from buying cheaper medicines from abroad. Over three years, they spent millions preparing a case that would deny treatment to the poor in the interests of profit.

Finally, in response to an international outcry, the drug companies abandoned the case, but not before the action had done lasting damage to their public image. AIDS activists in the US and in Europe accused the companies of having blood on their hands. In this turbulent atmosphere, it was clear to Love that if campaigners wanted affordable medicines of all sorts for the poor, they should be focusing their energies on AIDS drugs – public opinion was on their side and millions of lives were at stake. Over the previous few years, Love became known for his formidable grasp of intellectual property rules. "I'd been following AIDS but only really on the periphery of it and not very involved," Love recalled. "I felt like, oh my God, I'm actually going to be able to do something about this."

Trials had shown that the three-drug cocktail of very expensive antiretroviral drugs could not only keep people with HIV alive but healthy enough to live and work normally. The cost, around $15,000 a year per patient, was out of the question in sub-Saharan Africa. The way to drive the price down, Love believed, was through compulsory licensing. The patent owner would get compensation, but not the enormous profits they might have expected.

At first, his idea met with strong resistance. It might be illegal and it would certainly outrage Big Pharma, whose lawyers would fight it. Love did not care. He was more than willing to take Big Pharma on.

When Yusuf Hamied met Love and others in August 2000, Hamied said he was already manufacturing the individual drugs needed to treat people with HIV. He was prepared to make the drugs available at low cost, but he needed a guaranteed market.

The following month, at a meeting of the European Commission, Hamied publicly offered to make this three-drug AIDS cocktail for $800 a year. His company, Cipla, would also help other countries make their own AIDS drugs, he announced, and give away

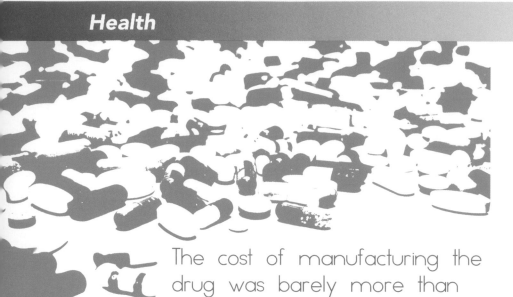

The cost of manufacturing the drug was barely more than the cost of the raw materials.

the single drug, nevirapine, that prevented mothers from passing HIV to their babies in childbirth.

Hamied waited for his phone to start ringing – but the calls he expected from HIV-hit governments or donor organisations asking to buy Triomune did not come. "And one bright day, on 6 February 2001," said Hamied, "when I was absolutely despondent that nothing was happening, Jamie rings me up from America and says, I've been thinking as to what we should do. Is it possible for you to reduce the price of the drugs to below $1 a day? That was Jamie's idea."

Hamied agreed to offer the cocktail to Médecins Sans Frontières for Africa at $1 a day. AIDS drugs would now be affordable for developing countries or donors willing to help them.

Fifteen years on, it is no longer just the poor who cannot afford the drugs they need. New medicines for lethal diseases such as hepatitis C and cancer have been launched on the global market at such high prices that the richest countries in the world are having to find ways to ration them. And Jamie Love is back in the fray.

In 2010, the cause Jamie Love has fought for all his life suddenly became intensely personal. His wife and colleague, Manon Ress, was diagnosed with stage-four breast cancer. Within days of her diagnosis, Ress started chemotherapy, but since both her mother and her sister had suffered from cancer, it was possible she had an inherited genetic propensity to the disease that could affect which treatment she should be given. There were delays in getting the necessary test – probably, Love believes, because it was patented.

"It took weeks before we got the result back and I was so angry," said Love. "The test is very cheap to perform but very expensive because of the patent. This is sort of crazy."

Ress's aggressive cancer responded to the drug Herceptin for a time. When that stopped working, Ress was prescribed T-DM1, marketed by the Swiss pharmaceutical giant Roche as Kadcyla. The drug was originally listed in the UK at £90,000 per patient per year, making it the most expensive breast cancer drug ever sold.

Kadcyla worked straight away. While Ress could – through

her insurers – buy extra years of life, she and Love were outraged that other women, even in rich countries, did not have the same opportunity.

Big Pharma has a simple justification for charging high prices for drugs: it costs a lot of money to invent a medicine and bring it to the market, so the prices have to be high or the companies will be unable to afford to continue their important research and development (R&D). The figures drug companies usually cite are from the Tufts Center for the Study of Drug Development in Boston, Massachusetts, which describes itself as an independent academic institution, despite the fact that it receives 40% of its funding from industry. In 2000, it put the cost of bringing a drug to market at $1bn. By 2014, that had risen to $2.6bn.

But those figures have been contested by Love and other campaigners. Many drugs begin as a gleam in the eye of a university researcher: somebody in academia has a bright idea and pursues it in the lab. Much medical research is funded by grants from public bodies, such as the US National Institutes of Health, or, in the UK, the Medical Research Council. When the basic research looks promising, the compound is sold, often to a small biotech firm.

Over the years the biggest drug companies have increasingly gained new drugs by buying smaller biotech firms with promising compounds on their books. Campaigners argue that the actual R&D carried out by the big profit-making companies – and the cost – is much less than they claim.

Even where a company has invented and developed the drug itself, there are other factors that push up the price. The cost of developing the many drugs that have been through trials and failed to work are factored in – more controversially, so is advertising and marketing.

After Ress's cancer diagnosis, the cost of medicines became very personal. Love started to ask generic firms whether they could make a version of Kadcyla, or T-DM1. Biological drugs such as T-DM1 are made from living organisms such as sugars or proteins and are complicated to manufacture. To make a biosimilar – a copy of a biological drug – some research and testing is required.

available at a cheap price in an affluent country and set a precedent for access to affordable medicines for the entire world.

On 1 October, the health secretary Jeremy Hunt received a letter from a group put together by Love and Ress, involving doctors, patients and campaigners in the US, Europe and UK. It proposed that Hunt should tear up the patent on Kadcyla, allowing either the manufacture or the importation of a cheap copycat version. The government could legally set aside Roche's patent and issue a compulsory licence, provided it gave the company "affordable compensation". Love had found a loophole and invited the British government to use it.

Chris Redd of the Peninsula College of Medicine and Dentistry in Plymouth, one of the signatories, felt the proposal would allow the British public to hold the government to account. "There are 1,500 UK citizens living with breast cancer right now, who could be kept alive by this medication. The solutions are all there in the document. The only question that remains is whether our government is more interested in protecting its citizens or the shareholders of a multinational drug company," he said.

Audaciously, Love proposed that the UK government could invest in the research funding, which would give it a financial stake in the drug and ensure it got it at cost price. The UK could even sell it to other countries afterwards and make a profit.

On 4 November 2015, NHS England announced that Kadcyla would stay on the Cancer Drugs Fund list, after Roche agreed, following lengthy negotiations, to lower the price – although it declined to say by how much. Within days, however, Nice announced its final decision on the drug. It was still too costly for general NHS use. So while the fund would provide the money to pay for patients in England to get it, those in other parts of the UK could lose out.

The British government is still pondering Love's proposal.

Source: This is an edited version of an article which appeared in The Guardian, 26 January 2016 © Guardian News & Media

There are 1,500 UK citizens living with breast cancer right now, who could be kept alive by this medication.

The Swiss pharmaceutical giant Roche launched Kadcyla onto the UK market in February 2014. Trials had shown the drug extends life for women with incurable breast cancer by at least six months, but in April 2014, the government's National Institute for Health and Care Excellence (Nice), which decides whether drugs are sufficiently cost-effective to be used in the NHS, turned it down. The Cancer Drugs Fund, set up by the government in 2010 to provide funding when life-extending drugs were judged unaffordable, covered the cost of treatments until April 2015, when NHS England, which runs the fund, declared it would be dropping Kadcyla from the list.

At this point, Love saw an opportunity to make the drug

It was a bold, unprecedented move, challenging a first-world government to take on Big Pharma. Yet there was an undeniable logic to it. The government could not afford to treat all the women who needed the drug at the price Roche wanted. And if Love could persuade the government to embrace his scheme by issuing a compulsory licence for T-DM1, it would set an important precedent – one that could change the cosy relationship between rich countries and Big Pharma for ever.

The only question that remains is whether our government is more interested in protecting its citizens or the shareholders of a multinational drug company.

Check Your Nuts - It Might Save Your Life

Phillip Krynski

The year was 2005. I was 15 and in my 10th year of schooling. This was the year I threw up for the first time from tequila shots, first awkwardly kissed a girl at a house party, and I was diagnosed with testicular cancer.

We used to have family dinners where we would have interesting conversations inspired by my step-father's profession. As a GP, he had some interesting stories on a variety of topics, including uncomfortable prostate exams with embarrassed middle-aged men and drug addicts requesting pain medication for their "constant migraines". One particular night, we had a discussion about testicular cancer. He explained how important it is to self-examine your testicles to make sure there are no lumps. My brothers and I cringed and begged him to change the topic. Regardless, the conversation stuck with me.

Some months later, I was fondling myself as any male teenager does, and I noticed that something seemed different. There was a tiny speck the size of a grain of salt on my right testicle. I disregarded it, thinking that it must have always been there without me noticing. More time passed and it became a growing concern of mine. I started to wonder if it really had always been there. I considered going to a doctor, but I didn't want to tell my family because as everyone knows, it's extremely uncomfortable as a teenager to talk to your parents about anything sexually-related. Anyone who's been given the 'condom talk' knows this. I let it slip to the back of my mind.

At the end of that year, my school had a program to travel overseas for an eight-week tour. All the students had to undergo a medical examination before being accepted for insurance purposes. In the doctor's office, all I could think about

SOME ISSUES:

Why is it important to be aware of all illnesses, even 'embarrassing' ones?

Does it surprise you how old the person in this article was when he realised he had testicular cancer?

Why do you think we have certain preconceptions about different illnesses?

How can we raise awareness of all the different types of cancer, and how to check for them?

I didn't want to tell my family because as everyone knows, it's extremely uncomfortable as a teenager to talk to your parents about anything sexually-related.

Photo posed by model

A few days later I received a call to come in to the hospital.

was the opportunity I was now given to enquire about my concern. The appointment dragged on with the standard "breathe in deeply and hold" etc. My head was screaming "TELL HER". The session came to an end, I thanked her and headed to the door. My hand clasped the cold metal handle and I paused. I turned around and apprehensively told the doctor that there was one more thing I would like her to check. She told me to lie down on the examining table and remove my pants. She was the first woman to see my penis since hitting puberty. Embarrassment sunk in; my whole face went red as I sat there with my bits out. She had a feel and couldn't tell if anything was wrong, so she wrote out a form for me to have an ultrasound. I left the office, and in the car I told my mum. She wondered why I hadn't mentioned it sooner. It's not that simple when you are a teenager.

The ultrasound technician had just rubbed cold sticky goo onto my testicle and was examining the region on a screen. Before going in, I had thought there was definitely a sexual undertone to rubbing goo on someone's testicles. The overweight elderly lady technician put a stop to any of those thoughts and it became strictly a medical procedure. I kept asking if she could see anything, but she didn't have an answer. She just kept saying that the doctors would have a look at it after the examination.

A few days later I received a call to come in to the hospital. I found out that the results had come back inconclusive, and they would have to do invasive surgery to tell for sure. The one question they asked me was, if it turned out to be cancer and they needed to remove the offending testicle, would I like a replacement? Having 'balls' is seen as such an important representation of being a man. I couldn't imagine being different from other 'men'. I decided I would take the prosthetic if it became necessary. That

way, I could still technically say that I had balls. No one had to know that one was a silicone insert.

Surgery day arrived. My mother drove me to the hospital and I went into the ward to have a final chat with the surgeon. Before he arrived, I had been feeling so calm that I leaned against the wall and activated an alarm button. Three panicking nurses rushed to respond to the blue alarm. Apparently that's the highest level of emergency in the hospital. Oops. They left, happy to know that it was just an accident. The surgeon then arrived and explained that they would examine me under general anaesthetic and if it was cancer, I would wake up with a new fake testicle. I then got changed into the hospital gown and an orderly wheeled me to the operating theatre. As the anaesthetist put the mask over my face, I joked about

I couldn't imagine being different from other 'men'. I decided I would take the prosthetic if it became necessary.

When you get diagnosed with cancer at 15, other things seem much less important. Movies, parties, soccer games – they all literally become child's play

how there was no way the drugs would be able to put me to....... I woke up some hours later to find my mum in the room reading a book in the corner. At first I didn't know what was going on - standard operation side-effects. She then explained that they had found a malignant tumour in my right testicle and it had been removed.

When you get diagnosed with cancer at 15, other things seem much less important. Movies, parties, soccer games - they all literally become child's play as you are faced with the reality of your own mortality. At that age, dying usually isn't even a factor in your thinking. The average life span is around 80, and as kids, we just assume that we'll make it to near there. Now I had to deal with cancer.

I had an appointment with an oncologist during which we discussed the options. I was told that it had been caught in the earliest possible stage. Lance Armstrong* had waited till his testicle turned the size of a "grapefruit" before even mentioning it to his doctor. Luckily, I had caught it before it had the chance to cause real damage. The doctor informed me that the cancer had not spread,

but there was still a chance that it could. Option One was to commence chemotherapy to make sure the cancer cells had been completely eradicated. I immediately froze at the thought. I had been growing my hair for the past year and it was a beautiful length. I wanted to be known as the guy with the long hair, not the bald guy undergoing chemo. Option Two was to monitor my body regularly for five years. This was to include CAT scans, PET scans and regular blood screens. I got to the point where I was so used to them that I would happily watch the needle piercing my skin, to the confusion of the nurses. All I could think about was losing my hair, so I essentially based my decision around that. Never mind the devastating effects to my immune system and overall health, I was concerned about no longer looking like Jesus. The doctor thought it was a good option, considering the cancer had been caught so early and there was a low risk of it spreading.

Now I had to deal with outsiders.

I had informed all my immediate family members and received plenty of support, but I decided that it would be best to keep it a secret outside of that. I didn't want to be treated differently. I didn't want pity and I certainly didn't want people to think I was weaker. Most of all, I didn't want to be teased for having one testicle. I told the kids at school that I'd had a hernia operation and I would be home for two weeks. Upon returning to school, it felt weird at the start. I'd had a significant life experience and had decided not to tell even

my closest friends. Everything back at school was so normal; the world always continues spinning no matter what. People asked if I was okay in the first week, but interest obviously died down quickly as a hernia isn't too serious. The regular tests continued and would consistently come back negative. After the pain died down, I guess you could say I had mild discomfort for the next few years. I was always very aware that I hadn't been born with one of my testicles. After finishing school, my friends were shocked as I told them one by one, some only finding out years later.

When five years had passed, the oncologist gave me the all clear. This meant that I was as likely to have cancer again as anyone else. I like to say that it's like chicken pox; you can only get cancer once. People don't always know that I'm taking the piss.

These days, the ordeal is just another chapter of my life that could have ended badly if I hadn't turned around and decided to speak up at the doctor's office that day. Instead, I now have a cool party trick that when the lights are off I can shine a torch behind my fake nut and it glows like an orb. Seriously cool. All the discomfort disappeared years ago and I have the same sperm count as any other healthy 26 year old. So guys, check your nuts and speak up, it might save your life.

*Professional cyclist who recovered from testicular cancer and went on to have a spectacular series of wins before being exposed as a drugs cheat.

11 October 2015
Read more from this author here:
huffingtonpost.co.uk/phillip-krynski/
and follow his progress on twitter:
@phillipklionel.

Internet
& media

I am ashamed to call myself a journalist

by John Darvall

John Darvall is a presenter for BBC Radio Bristol and is engaged to the MP for Bristol, Charlotte Leslie. When his daughter was killed in a car crash, the fact he was well known distorted the reporting of the incident - giving the role of 'Dad' to him, instead of Simon, the man who had looked after her since she was three. Darvell was particularly disturbed that his own employer, the BBC, failed to use the correct information supplied by the family and instead caused more distress.

SOME ISSUES:

What should have happened in this case?

What sort of damaging effects can journalism have on people's lives?

Who decides how matters are reported?

Should the media be made to be more responsible for how it treats people?

How do you think you would feel if the newspapers wrote something incorrect about you?

When something is reported incorrectly, what should be done?

On Saturday 31st October, at 1.30am, my 22-year-old eldest daughter Polly was killed when she lost control of the car she was driving and hit a tree. She was alone in her VW Beetle, no one else was hurt and, I am told, it was instant.

I can tell you that having lost my father as a child, other close family members along the timeline of life and having said many times 'on air' that losing a child must be the worst thing of all, it is. It really is. It's not a grief 'competition' it just is. Losing a child is the worst thing of all.

Polly's mother Sarah and her dad Simon, who brought Polly up from the age of 3 and did such a brilliant job, are broken by this, as are all our families. My eldest son, Polly's brother Oliver, is broken too but one of the few comforts I am taking at the moment is what a fine, brave, courageous man he has become. Again his mother Sarah and dad Simon deserve all the credit.

It is Simon, Polly's dad, who has prompted me to write this blog. I am Polly and Oliver's father, Simon is their dad. That is always the language we use, though Ollie and Polly always call me dad when we are together. Language is vital if we are to understand who we are and what we do.

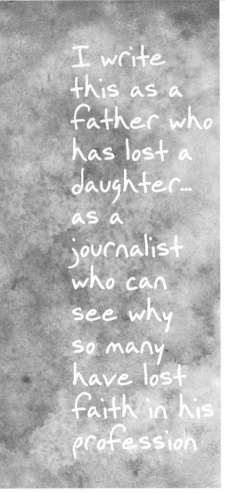

I write this as a father who has lost a daughter... as a journalist who can see why so many have lost faith in his profession

The news of my daughter's death, because of the nature of the work I used to do (I know I will never be the same again) and who I am engaged to means that there is some media interest in me with the local and national newspapers and TV. Those who know me well will know that I never, ever wanted to be the story, just to tell or share the story, as a journalist, correctly. I have never wanted to be on TV, I don't want to be known, perhaps just be known of, to do my job well and to help people if I can and to get to the truth for others.

As all the family came together on Monday morning to start the process of making arrangements for Polly, I was contacted by the BBC for a quote about her. There has been quite a reaction to the news, because of me, with many kind words paid in tribute to my daughter and kindness shown towards me from those who listen and maybe even enjoy what I do daily on the radio. I gave the BBC 'the line', agreeing it while on the phone to them with Polly's mother Sarah and Polly's dad Simon hearing me do this. I wanted the quote, the tribute to come from Sarah, Polly's mum, who did such a brilliant job in bringing our daughter up with Simon. The name order was also agreed to be 'Sarah, her husband Simon Bosworth and John Darvall'. I was clear.

On Monday night, on Points West, the local BBC News for the West, none of this happened in their broadcast about Polly. Simon was called Polly's 'stepdad', a phrase we have NEVER used. Simon, Polly's dad was straight on the phone to me. He was rightly furious and more. This journalistic failure significantly added to his pain, and to mine. To hear Polly's dad rage at you about your profession, about the things you have clearly agreed whilst standing in his family home just hours before when our daughter has been killed...words fail me.

This poor piece of journalism made Tuesday probably the worst day of this whole episode so far. This includes seeing our dead daughter in a hospital mortuary just 12 hours after she was killed.

Newspapers have contacted me and provided appallingly written articles, which I have had to change, 'polish' or make actual sense of. Other papers have published articles using my personal relationship as 'the in line', when this is NOT the story but, at best, just a very small part of the story. This has hurt many who are in the throes of grief. Other papers have just published without checking and have got facts wrong. One paper spliced a year off my age. I will take that!

The way we all consume news is changing. The way we share news has changed and will continue to change at a faster pace. This week TV and newspapers have proven to me why they are not the future of news. If they can't even get their facts right, be trusted with clear information and then report it accurately is it any wonder that we are all turning to Facebook, Twitter and other internet sources for our news and information? The internet allows us to come to our own conclusions by checking our own facts. We really can't trust the traditional outlets to do it right or properly.

I write this as a father who has lost a daughter. I write this as a journalist who loved his work but can now clearly see why so many have lost faith in his profession and traditional media. They, we and I have brought this on ourselves.

I also write this to set the record straight for Polly's mother Sarah and Polly's dad Simon. I am ashamed to call myself a journalist and I am truly sorry to have added to your grief. I have spoken to Simon and he knows I have written this.

Two bits of advice for you reading this, if I may:

Trust nothing you read or watch. Check it, at least twice, as it's more than likely wrong from just a single source.

Love your children and loved ones. Properly love them. Tell them every day, make sure they know that you love them regardless of what might be happening. Nothing is more important than that.

johndarvallblog.com
5th November 2015

Social media is harming the mental health of teenagers. The state has to act

The pressure to be perfect and always 'on' is overwhelming many of us, as studies show, but the government will not step in. Statutory PSHE lessons would be a start

June Eric-Udorie

SOME ISSUES:

Why do you think people find social media so addictive?

Is social media good or bad for people and relationships?

In what ways might social media affect your mental health?

What can be done to make sure people have a healthy relationship with social media?

The digital landscape has put increased pressure on teenagers today, and we feel it. There are so many social media channels: Facebook, Twitter, Instagram, Snapchat, Tumblr, you name it. I made a conscious decision to avoid Snapchat and Instagram because of the social pressure I saw them putting on my 14-year-old little sister. If my mum turned off the WiFi at 11pm, my sister would beg me to turn my phone into a hotspot. She always needed to load her Snapchat stories one more time, or to reply to a message that had come in two minutes ago because she didn't want her friend to feel ignored. If I refused, saying she could respond in the morning, I'd get the "You're ruining my social life" speech. Even as a teenager as well, I sometimes find this craze a little baffling.

Anxiety & depression

A new study has found that teenagers who engage with social media during the night could be damaging their sleep and increasing their risk of anxiety and depression. Teenagers spoke about the pressure they felt to make themselves available 24/7, and the resulting anxiety if they did not respond immediately to texts or posts. Teens are so emotionally invested in social media that a fifth of secondary school pupils will wake up at night and log on, just to make sure they don't miss out.

Perhaps the worst thing about this is that teenagers need more sleep than adults do, so night-time social media use could be detrimental to their health. Research has shown that teenagers need 9.5 hours of sleep each night but on average only get 7.5 hours. A lack of sleep can make teenagers tired, irritable, depressed and more likely to catch colds, flu and gastroenteritis. These days, I am always tired at school, and I'm not one to stay up until 2am chatting with a boy. Homework and the pressure to have the perfect set of grades mean I'm up late working. And it seems that at school, most of my mates are exhausted too.

Lost phone

During the summer holidays, I lost my phone. And for the week that I was phoneless, it felt like a disaster. I love my phone. It gives me quick access to information and allows me to be constantly looped in with my friends, to know exactly what is going on in their lives. So when I didn't have my phone for a week, I felt a slight sense of Fomo, or if you're not up to speed with the lingo, fear of missing out. By the end of the week, I'd got used to not having a phone and

Photo posed by model

When I didn't have my phone for a week, I felt a slight sense of Fomo

I'd quite enjoyed the break from social media. But there was still a lingering sense of sadness at the back of my mind that there would be conversations I had missed, messages that had been sent, funny videos shared and night-time chats that I would probably never get to see.

Comfort

A separate study by the National Citizen Service found that, rather than talking to their parents, girls seek comfort on social media when they are worried. The survey also suggests that girls are likely to experience stress more often than boys – an average of twice a week.

It's becoming more and more obvious how the pressures of social media disproportionately affect teenage girls. I can see it all around me. Pressure to be perfect. To look perfect, act perfect, have the perfect body, have the perfect group of friends, the perfect amount of likes on Instagram. Perfect, perfect, perfect. And if you don't meet these ridiculously high standards, then the self-loathing and bullying begins.

What is really worrying is that time and time again, these studies pop up and demonstrate that the mental health of teenagers, especially teenage girls, is on the line. We know this. We know the perils of the internet, we've heard about online bullying and the dangers of Ask.fm, we know the slut-shaming that goes on in our schools. We know these things. We know that these studies demonstrate that we have to make personal, social and health education (PSHE) statutory in schools and ensure it covers a range of issues from healthy eating and sleeping to consent. And yet, [Education Secretary] Nicky Morgan and the government refuse to act. So I ask: what are we waiting for? Inaction on these issues is harming the physical and emotional wellbeing of young people in this country. What has to happen before we do something?

The Guardian, 16 November 2015
© Guardian News & Media 2015

The citizen reporters

Covering ground professional journalists cannot tread

'Citizen journalism' is a term often associated with misinformation and bias, but as Robin Yapp **discovers, new digital technology is enabling volunteer journalists around the world to uncover significant stories of political injustice and corruption**

SOME ISSUES:

We have a "free press", so why don't people always trust the main newspapers and news sites?

Should more citizen journalism be encouraged?

Why is it important to know about what is happening in the world?

How else can mobile technology be used to influence events?

"All journalists are citizens but not all citizens are journalists," says Afghanistan's Paiwandgah website, a platform served by more than 750 citizen journalists throughout the country.

Interest in reporting by civilians is growing as internet connections and mobile phones proliferate in all corners of the world. At the same time the very notion of what constitutes citizen journalism and how reliable it is remain matters of debate.

Jay Rosen, who teaches journalism at New York University, has defined citizen journalism as "the people formerly known as the audience employ[ing] the press tools they have in their possession to inform one another".

Paiwandgah defines it as "original reporting of local events and opinions from citizens on the ground" and says it matters "because journalists cannot be everywhere at once".

It also matters because of the profound risks many exponents take; 139 citizen journalists have been killed in Syria alone since March 2011, according to freedom of speech non-profit organisation Reporters Without Borders.

As the digital revolution breaks down borders, technology looks certain to ensure that citizen journalism in its widest sense is here to stay. Everyone from disempowered urbanites clutching camera phones to bloggers using open source methods to probe distant conflicts are having their say. Public interest stories in remote or dangerous locations that newspapers and TV stations rarely cover are now more likely to come to light.

In Brazil a group called Papo Reto (meaning 'Straight Talk') is highlighting the plight of residents in Rio's Complexo do Alemão cluster of favelas, where police brutality often leaves innocent people dead.

"Facebook in Afghanistan is a serious discussion forum"

"The digital revolution breaks down borders"

Recent victims include a 72-year-old grandmother and a 10-year-old boy.

Brazilian police kill around 2,000 people each year according to official statistics, but human rights group WITNESS says the true figure could be far higher.

Papo Reto's members use smartphones, tablets and the WhatsApp messaging service to gather photos, videos and audio evidence of police raids and their impact on the community, which they post on Facebook and YouTube. But the collective could itself face serious dangers from police impunity or shoot-outs between officers and drug dealers.

WITNESS has partnered with Papo Reto to offer equipment and equally vital advice on how to minimise danger, maintain their right to film and securely upload footage to cloud storage or Dropbox.

Priscila Neri, who oversees WITNESS' work in Latin America, cited a study of police violence in Rio that found prosecutors dismissed 99.2 percent of cases. Video evidence was often a powerful factor in the few exceptions, she said. Yet harsh reality means her group's first rule is that citizens should not film unless they feel safe to do so.

In Afghanistan, Paiwandgah – meaning 'a place to connect' – is capitalising on the fact that around 70 percent of Afghans are thought to have mobile phones and 1.3 million use social media. Citizens can submit stories in English, Dari or Pashto via phone, SMS, a web form, email, Facebook or Twitter.

Executive editor Jean MacKenzie, a former GlobalPost correspondent, said smartphones have "helped Afghans get in touch with the world".

"Facebook in Afghanistan is a serious discussion forum, in part because of smartphones and other technologies that allow users to share on the spot," she said.

She admits verifying stories and the "danger of disinformation" pose challenges but sees offering journalism training as one way to mitigate this by keeping unpaid volunteers committed to their task.

Singapore was ranked 153rd in the 2015 World Press Freedom Index, putting it 31 places below Afghanistan. But The Online Citizen's volunteer reporters, photographers and videographers have been stimulating more open debate in the city-state for almost a decade.

Terry Xu, the website's interim chief editor, agrees that smartphones are vital but also mentions forging links with academics and government insiders who can help verify stories. He said

Photo posed by model

"It's a challenge to make sure that the information is reliable"

this becomes easier once you have committed volunteers and can convince the public of the need for independent news reported "from the perspective of citizens".

Some citizen journalists have broken stories through a painstaking process of analysing what others have captured on film or camera.

Eliot Higgins scours hundreds of Syrian YouTube channels from his home in Leicester to piece together clues about the weapons being used by various groups. The conclusions he publishes in his Brown Moses blog have been widely reported in mainstream media: he helped expose the Syrian regime's use of cluster bombs and detected Croatian weapons in the hands of rebels.

Higgins talks of a "growing global community of open

source investigators" whose methodologies can be used in many investigations "even if it's not in their own backyard". He is especially excited by online Russian language communities using such tactics to examine the Ukraine conflict and Russia's bombing of Syria.

But with all the information reaching the public via citizen journalists, can we trust their reports as much as those from established media organisations?

Tom Felle, acting director of interactive and newspaper journalism at City University London, sees a risk of confusing citizen advocates or activists with citizen journalists.

"We've seen an awful lot that has been biased or even fabricated – in Syria all sides are seeking to exaggerate or 'sex up' stories," he says. "We now need a much more questioning and dispassionate look at what citizen journalism is and who is doing it."

In Neri's view we should move on from the "never-ending debate" about what citizen journalism is to concentrate on the real world implications of stories being exposed.

"How do we make sure this sort of media is created and shared in a safe and ethical way when we think about graphic imagery or interviews that could put lives at risk?" she asks. "How do we ensure it has an impact on policies infringing the rights of people taking risks to make these videos?"

A free mobile app launched in June by legal group the International Bar Association could help address such issues by enabling witnesses to store evidence of atrocities in encrypted form with a time-stamp and GPS-fixed location.

MacKenzie from Paiwandgah, who has worked in Afghanistan for nearly a decade as a correspondent and journalism trainer, is philosophical about the complications of the job.

"The future of citizen journalism is still to be determined," she said. "It's a boon to have multiple sources in places the professional media cannot penetrate, but it's a challenge to make sure that the information is reliable."

Xu argues that in places such as Singapore, some bias in citizen journalism is actually desirable – in favour of freedom of information and more rights for citizens, for example. "We are not balanced," he states. "We are the balance."

Positive News, 4 December 2015
positivenews.org.uk

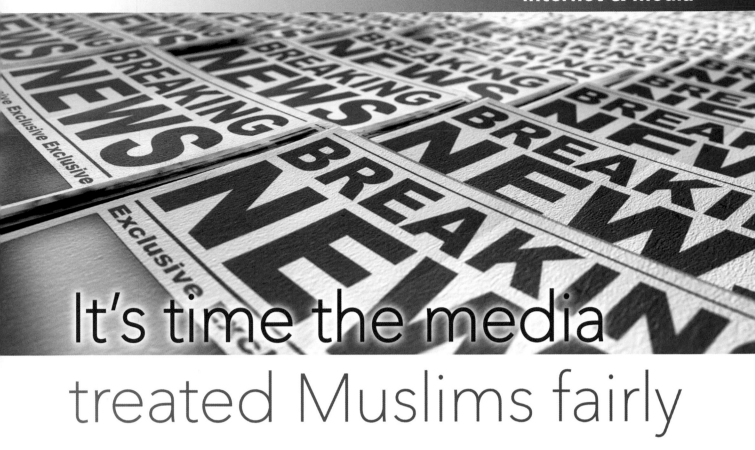

It's time the media treated Muslims fairly

When a study finds that nearly all stories about Muslims are negative it's clear this is the last acceptable form of bigotry – and it's tearing society apart

Miqdaad Versi

SOME ISSUES:

How much does the media affect people's opinions and how they view others?

How can people know whether what they read in newspapers is true?

What sort of news stories would encourage understanding and integration?

Hats off to the *Mail on Sunday* for finally apologising for its incendiary headline: "Muslim gang slashes tyres of immigration-raid van". In the piece in question, an attack on an immigration enforcement van in east London was blamed on the "Muslim community" and "Muslim youths" – even though the faith of the perpetrators was not known, nor relevant. This fact has now been acknowledged by the paper, and it has rewritten the story and issued a correction both online and in print.

In the media, using Islam or Muslims as descriptive terms when referring to criminals remains all too common, even in cases where faith has little or nothing to do with the crime. The Times ran a front-page story in March with the provocative headline "Call for national debate on Muslim sex grooming". There is nothing in Islam that could justify such heinous acts, and none of those involved in this particular crime cited Islam as their motive. So why was this story headlined in this way when articles about other cases of paedophilia made no mention of the perpetrators' faith or ethnicity?

Using Islam or Muslims as descriptive terms when referring to criminals remains all too common, even in cases where faith has little or nothing to do with the crime.

The media plays a key role in the development of anti-Muslim hatred

When tens of innocent pilgrims tragically lost their lives in Saudi Arabia earlier this month, the *Mail Online* linked their deaths to Osama bin Laden and 9/11 in its headline: "At least 87 people killed … after giant crane 'operated by Bin Laden firm' collapses … on anniversary of 9/11 attacks", references that mimicked a plethora of rightwing bigots on Twitter. The newspaper did eventually remove the 9/11 reference, and later the Bin Laden link. But the damage was done: the odious headline had already spread across the internet like wildfire.

Should Muslims – and society more broadly – just accept this bigotry? We know sensationalism sells, especially online, where news sources use clickbait headlines and copy to attract readers in a crowded marketplace. And what better way to get people to read an article than by linking it to the far-right narrative that Islam is evil, and that its adherents need to be civilised to become "good Muslims"? It's a narrative that many Muslims feel is often reflected in government rhetoric as well.

According to an Islamophobia Roundtable in Stockholm, held in June last year, and featuring world-renowned experts on the topic, the regular association of Islam and Muslims with crime and terror in the media and on the internet is vital to the spread of Islamophobic rhetoric.

The real-world consequences of the spread of one of the last acceptable forms of bigotry affects the very cohesiveness of our society. According to the largest survey of its kind in the UK, over a quarter of children aged between 10 and 16 believe Islam encourages terrorism, and almost a third believe Muslims are taking over the country. In addition, 37% of British people who were surveyed admitted they would support policies to reduce the

This "othering" of Muslims has also manifested itself in a growth in hate crime.

number of Muslims in the country. Is it any wonder that more and more Muslims feel alienated?

This "othering" of Muslims has also manifested itself in a growth in hate crime: a 70% rise in the past year according to the Metropolitan police. We now live in a country where most Muslims know someone who has suffered from Islamophobic hate or abuse.

Of course, the media should not be held responsible for violence against Muslims – that is the liability of the attackers. But with over 90% of reports about Muslims taking a negative angle and playing up faith, even when irrelevant, it is not reasonable to deny that the media plays a key role in the development of anti-Muslim hatred.

So what can be done?

First, build awareness. According to research presented at the Muslim News' Conference on "Reporting Islam and Muslims in Britain" last week, there have been improvements in the language that is being used, but religious illiteracy remains rife within parts of our newspaper elite. Until recently, a managing editor of a major national newspaper did not know that "jihad" had multiple meanings, and that "fatwa" did not just mean a death warrant. The lack of comprehension on a topic that is part of the bread and butter of newspapers today is deeply distressing and its role in editorial decision-making cannot be understated. I would like to think that this is due to sheer ignorance rather than pure malice, which is much harder to tackle.

We now live in a country where most Muslims know someone who has suffered from Islamophobic hate or abuse.

Second, diversity. There is an under-representation of all minority groups, but particularly Muslims, within the media – especially within senior positions – and greater diversity will improve coverage and help combat misreporting. This requires greater outreach on the part of media organisations to bring in talent from all backgrounds through diversity programmes, paid internships and fast-track schemes to proactively close this gap.

The final piece in the jigsaw is regulation. Clause 12 of the Editors' Code of Practice

Avoiding daily smears, group libel and the violent consequences is not too much to ask of the nation's editors.

says: "Details of an individual's race, colour, religion … must be avoided unless genuinely relevant to the story." The problem is that this protection only extends to individuals and not to groups, which is why Katie Hopkins was able to get away with her infamous comments comparing refugees to "cockroaches". The arguments about censorship and free speech are complex – but Jonathan Heawood of the Impress Project, an independent monitor of the press, believes the Editors' Code should incorporate Lord Leveson's suggestion that this clause is broadened to include groups. This would allow representative groups to hold the media to account for using "Islam" or "Muslims" where it was not "genuinely relevant" to the story.

We are equal members of society and demand fairness, not favours. Avoiding daily smears, group libel and the violent consequences is not too much to ask of the nation's editors.

The Guardian, 23 September 2015
© Guardian News & Media 2015

Sexual
issues

Not gay, not straight: Meet the young people who refuse to define their sexuality

New figures show that half of millenials don't feel they fall into any particular sexual category.

VICKI NOTARO

SOME ISSUES:

Do you think that younger people are more open minded about sexuality than the older generation?

Why do you think people seem to want to define their sexuality?

What might be the benefit of not defining your sexuality?

How does this affect gender and relationships?

For 19-year-old psychology student Greta Warren, the question of whether she defines herself as gay or straight is a meaningless one.

Both terms, she believes, are just labels. And who needs labels? "I've tried imposing labels like bisexual and pansexual on myself but I just don't feel comfortable with them," she says.

Greta, from Galway but studying at Trinity College Dublin, has had relationships with both men and women and feels comfortable romantically and sexually with both genders, but sees her sexuality as something fluid, and not something she can easily categorise.

"It's something I found frustrating during the marriage referendum with everyone commenting on and celebrating the gay and lesbian right to marriage, with little to no reference to everyone else on the sexuality spectrum," she says.

It might sound unusual, but in fact Greta's viewpoint is one that more and more of her contemporaries share. A poll published in the UK last week by YouGov showed that just 46% of 18 to 24-year-olds considered themselves to be exclusively straight, but only 6% classed themselves as homosexual. Almost half - 48% - said they wouldn't choose either label.

This week, a study of over 10,000 22 to 28-year-olds conducted by Notre Dame University in the United States showed that women are three times more likely to have sexual experiences with both men and other women than their male peers.

These figures show that increasingly, younger people feel free to experiment with their sexuality in a way that previous generations didn't. No doubt society's more liberal attitude towards same-sex relationships has played a role in this development, as has celebrity culture. Singer Miley Cyrus had had high-profile relationships with both men and women, and

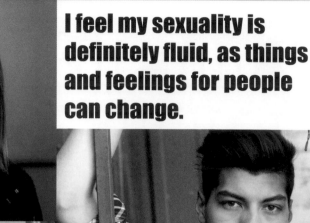

I feel my sexuality is definitely fluid, as things and feelings for people can change.

Photos posed by models

is currently believed to be dating Victoria's Secret model Stella Maxwell. But Cyrus has rejected the notion of classifying her love life - or even her gender.

She told Out magazine that she didn't relate to what defines a boy or girl, and that in terms of sexuality she wants to be nothing at all.

When labelled "gender-queer" by the media, she reacted by Instagramming the quote and declaring herself "free to be everything."

Actress Kristen Stewart's relationships are much discussed and analysed in the media and online, but the Twilight actress refuses to even discuss it. "Google me, I'm not hiding," was her response to Nylon magazine when asked about her sexuality.

"If you feel like you really want to define yourself, and you have the ability to articulate those parameters and that in itself defines you, then do it... I live in the f-king ambiguity of this life and I love it. I don't feel like it would be true for me to be like, 'I'm coming out!'".

Just this week, Lily Rose-Depp, the teenage daughter of Johnny and Vanessa Paradis, lent her face to the Self-Evident Truth project, a celebration of the sexuality spectrum that wants to acknowledge those who identify as anything other than 100% straight.

The notion of fluid sexuality isn't new. In 1948, Alfred Kinsey developed his now infamous scale designed to show the spectrum of human sexual desire at a certain point in time. Those who rated a zero were deemed exclusively heterosexual, while the people who rated a six exclusively homosexual.

According to Kinsey, we all fall somewhere in between in terms of experience, desire or both, although he also acknowledged those who are now known as asexual, or not having socio-sexual reactions.

Kinsey believed that this can change across the course of a person's life, leading many to believe that as we get older, we're more likely to go one way or the other. Is it that millenials are more at ease with not defining their sexuality at all, and seeing it as a fluid thing throughout their lives?

However, as Greta points out, it's not as simple as defining themselves as bisexual either.

"It's too narrow for me, and makes me feel like I have to be half one way and half the other," says a 28-year-old man who didn't wish to be named. "I'm neither gay nor straight, not a little of both."

"For me, to date, the commonly used terms haven't quite summed me up," says 27-year-old Dubliner Kasey Daye. "I feel my sexuality is definitely fluid, as things and feelings for people can change. Not everyone is locked into a label or a sexuality, nor should they be.

"I wouldn't say that I'm negatively reluctant to label my sexuality, I just consider 'labelling' another process we use to develop preconceptions of people."

Kasey, an events coordinator, says that growing up, she felt that other people focused more on the physical aspect of sexuality. "Nobody cared about feelings, self-expression or self-confidence.

"It's not an easy experience, not having an explanation for yourself, let alone other people. I will never forget the depths of depression I faced when I felt like I didn't fit 'gay or straight'. Sexuality does not, and should not totally define anyone."

For Kasey, "bisexual" is just another label. "I don't think there is anything wrong with the term. I know a lot of people don't favour it and I've found people to be less tolerant of it, only factoring in the 'sex' aspect. They forget that it's more about people having the capacity to love or have attraction to different genders."

Kasey says it's all about being happy and confident. "It might be as simple as wearing suit pants and Converse to an event rather than a dress and heels, but I'm empowered by these little things. Rather than labels, it's these little things that make me more comfortable and that little bit closer with myself."

Emma Kelly, a 25-year-old journalist from Dublin, also rejects the bisexual label. "I'm reluctant to label my sexuality because I don't have a clear idea what I identify with. I have always questioned my sexuality, but I don't feel like I'm bisexual in that it's 50/50. I'd just say somewhere on the queer spectrum."

For Emma, the term bisexual is fine if that's how you identify. She just doesn't feel like that's a label that applies to her, even though it relates to attraction to both sexes.

"I may have only had relationships and romantic feelings towards men, but have had sexual feelings towards women. If someone asked, I'd probably say heterosexual, but I have had an experience with a girl recently in a group setting, and want to explore it more."

Emma says she'd be open to relationships with either men or women, "if I developed romantic feelings."

Emma credits celebrities coming out as bisexual in a casual way, or refusing to label their sexuality, as making it easier for young people who feel similarly. "It makes people believe that it's okay to say that about themselves, and with queer nightlife it's easier to meet more likeminded people too."

Not everyone is locked into a label or a sexuality, nor should they be.

"Sexuality and identity are absolutely inextricably linked. In my experience, not wanting to see your sexuality in one particular way can be a sign of an internal struggle," says Eithne Bacuzzi, a psychosexual therapist with Relationships Ireland.

"There are a lot of people who don't just experience difficulty with coming out to their family and friends, but also to themselves, because it might mean having a different life than expected."

However she acknowledges that for some people, experimentation is part of the quest for self-discovery. But is it possible perhaps that a lot of young people feel under pressure to experiment sexually these days?

"I don't think there's a pressure to experiment, but I do think there's a pressure to be who you truly are, and for some people that can be incredibly difficult," says Eithne.

"A lot of young people are more comfortable to not identify in any one strict category," says Oisin McKenna of youth website SpunOut.ie. "But it's true that they might also identify a unique kind of discrimination, and even rejection from gay or straight people. There can be an urge among people to want others to identify as strictly one way."

Luke Keating is 25 and a designer. "I refuse to label both my sexuality and gender because I believe that they're fluid and on a spectrum, but also because I don't believe the language and vocabulary we have today accurately describes or allows for the actual diversity that exists within people. I believe it desperately needs to be reexamined and reevaluated."

The UK poll, says Keating, is "one of the first pieces of research I've seen that is honest and brings new ways of looking at things to light - it's quite revolutionary.

"Our brains have been sadly trained into traditional patriarchal ways of thinking, and in order to change this for the better we need to empower ourselves and reject labels, follow our hearts and be honest to ourselves and others."

Perhaps this is nothing new, and young people have always been experimenting, a natural part of growing in to adulthood. It could be that today's youth are just far more open about what was previously kept quiet. Either way, it seems that for the youth of today, not wearing a label is better than wearing the wrong one.

Independent.ie, 27 August 2015
© Irish Independent

Sophie & Samantha

Pioneering website RUComingOut inspires, supports and unites those who are living their lives either completely, or partially in the closet. It provides a platform for LGBT+ people to share their experiences. Here Sophie gives us her personal account of coming out, and shares her good news.

Sophie | Training Officer | Hampshire, England

I could finally be myself

SOME ISSUES:

Why do you think we presume people are straight unless they tell us otherwise?

Why do you think it is so difficult for people to come out?

What can we do to make sure that the world is safe and fair for people regardless of their sexuality?

I guess I always knew that I wasn't the same as all my other friends, although it didn't stop me acting like them. I had boyfriends all the way through school and, to be honest, I over compensated. I went out with my last boyfriend, Andrew, until I joined the army at 16. I really liked Andrew and cried when we spilt up but I knew deep down that it was for the best, because I had a secret: I was in love with my best friend. I did whatever I could to spend as much time

as I possibly could with her. I knew that she was straight but I didn't care I just wanted to be with her. We spent every hour of every day together. I felt like I could talk to her about anything and everything - well, everything apart from the most important thing.

I wrote in my diary every night about what we had done that day and how I was jealous about the way her boyfriend kissed her and how I wished it was me. I hid my

Their baby daughter Aria

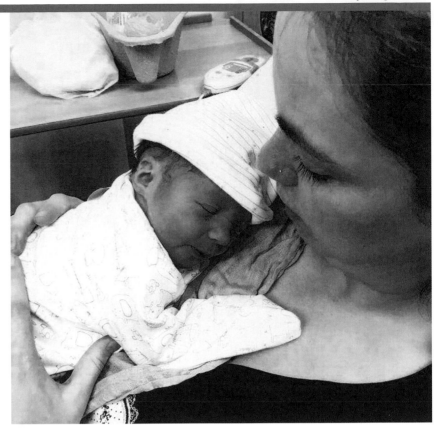

OMG!
What had they read?
What did they know?
What would they say?

diary under my book case in my room and NEVER left it out EVER just in case my mum and dad came in and found it. I wasn't ready for that. I came home one night and got a drink from the fridge to find my diary on top of the microwave I was in a sheer panic - OMG! What had they read? What did they know? What would they say?

I grabbed my diary off the side and ran upstairs, slammed my bedroom door and didn't come out till the next morning. When I woke up I panicked - what were they going to say to me? I got dressed, went down stairs and not a word was said, everything was like normal: "How are you babe? What you up to today anything nice?". I breathed I sigh of relief, thank god my secret wasn't out.

Looking back I know that my mum must have read that diary but chose to pretend she never did. I guess she must have known that I wasn't ready. To be honest, I don't think she was ready either.

I joined the army at 16 and knew straight away that I loved it. I could finally be myself. I had my first proper girlfriend when I was 17 and knew it was time that I told the truth to the people that I loved. I chose to ring my sister and before she had chance to speak I said "I'M GAY". I knew that she wouldn't be able to keep her big mouth shut so it was a cop out really.

I've been in a civil partnership for almost ten years and I gave birth to our beautiful daughter 12 weeks ago.

About 3 minutes later I had a call - it was mum. It was a weird conversation. It started with her saying she always knew that I was gay and then that it might be just a phase. Whatever she said didn't really matter to me - I'd done it, I'd told the truth and it was a weight lifted off my shoulders.

I'm out of the army now and have been in a civil partnership for almost ten years with Samantha. We have just had IVF treatment and I gave birth to our beautiful daughter, Aria, 12 weeks ago.

My mum and dad love Sam and their granddaughter and my sexuality isn't an issue to them which makes me beam with pride.

Me and my best friend lost touch. I wasn't sure whether it was because I was in the army or because I told her I was gay. I hope it's not the latter but whatever the reason I will always be thankful to her and will never forget my first love.

Follow Sophie on Twitter @Sophie_843
www.rucomingout.com

My mum and dad love Sam and their granddaughter and my sexuality isn't an issue to them which makes me beam with pride.

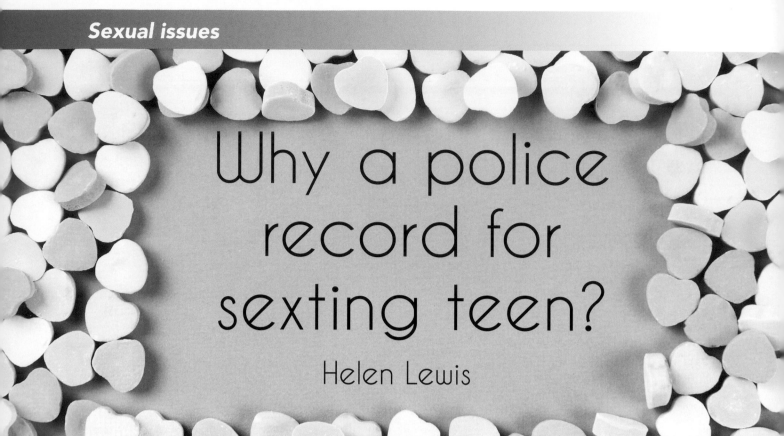

Why a police record for sexting teen?

Helen Lewis

The young need to be educated, not censured, on relationships and social media

SOME ISSUES:

Do you think the police were right to act as they did?

How should other people - the school, the people who received the photo, parents - have acted?

Do you agree that the boy is a victim and others have got off lightly?

Would the incident have been different if the roles had been reversed - if a girl had sent a revealing photo?

How can young people protect themselves against this sort of incident?

Here's a modern morality tale. One night at home, a 14-year-old boy called Simon* sends a naked picture to a classmate. Instead of deleting the picture, his love interest sends it on to other pupils at their school, where it is passed around from phone to phone. Simon ends up feeling humiliated, eating lunch in the library alone to avoid his peers.

At this point, it is usual to sigh, perhaps whistle through your teeth, and reflect soberly on the perils of mixing lust-filled teenagers and new technology. Poor kid. Bet he won't send another naked selfie. Still, I hope he's getting the support he needs.

Unfortunately, in the internet headline writer's favourite phrase, what happened next will surprise you. When the school found out about Simon's sexting, the police were informed. And because the incident was classed as a sexual offence, the officer had no choice but to record it on the police database, where it could be disclosed to employers for the next 10 years.

When the Today programme revealed Simon's story last week, it provoked strong feelings. Of course it did. This is a case made for moralising. It has everything – scarce facts, lusty teenagers and new technology – and as a bonus it involves sexual behaviour that wasn't possible when anyone over 30 was growing up. (You couldn't sext on a Nokia 5110, the cult teenage phone of the 1990s. We had to get our thrills by writing 55378008 on a calculator and turning it upside down.)

But don't listen to anyone who comes to a glib conclusion about what happened to Simon, because not everything is a moral panic or a howling injustice. The lessons to be learned from his unfortunate experience are surprisingly small and simple.

First, let's untangle why the police acted as they did. There are two possible interpretations of Simon's actions and we've only heard his side of the story. What if he sent the picture unsolicited? In that case, what happened is more like flashing than flirting – and early sexual offences are a big red flag for escalation into more serious

Digital technology and social media have made it easier to reinforce a sexual double standard where boys are legends and girls are sluts for enjoying the same things.

crimes. There are good reasons for the police to have a policy of recording every underage sexual offence reported to them by a school.

But let's take the facts at face value – Simon was flirting with a girl and she made it clear that she would not be averse to seeing him naked. That shakes the kaleidoscope. Oddly, his age then counts against him. If he were an adult, sharing his nude selfies without his consent would be distributing "revenge porn". And under a new offence introduced in April this year, it could be punishable by up to two years in prison.

Yet the girl in this case seems to have been treated very leniently, as have the other sniggering teenagers at the school. "I've not seen the image since, but I know that some people still have it," Simon told the BBC. "It bugs me, because they say how bad it is to distribute images, but now everyone's got them, they don't do anything about it." That is unfair. While it seems disproportionate to prosecute teenagers for sharing the photos, they should be punished by the school – and Simon should not be denied the status of victim. A wrong was done to him, and because he is male, it is not being properly acknowledged.

But before I mount my high horse on his behalf, I have to acknowledge this springs from understandable foundations. The majority of revenge porn victims are women and there is no obvious male equivalent of the widespread "slut shaming" of teenage girls. The famous case in Steubenville** was not a one-off. In 2012, 15-year-old Californian Audrie Pott killed herself after pictures of her being sexually assaulted at a party were shared around school; a year later, 17-year-old Canadian Rehtaeh Parsons did the same. Also in 2013, an Irish 17-year-old took an overdose and ended up in a coma after she was photographed performing oral sex on a boy at an Eminem concert.

Digital technology and social media have made it easier to reinforce a sexual double standard where boys are legends and girls are sluts for enjoying the same things. The social theorist Danah Boyd, who has studied teenagers and technology for more than a decade, has an explanation. "Boys will share pictures of girls with other boys; girls will share pictures of boys with other girls; and girls will also share pictures of girls with other girls; but boys will never share pictures of boys with other boys out of fear of being seen as gay," she said in 2011. "We live in a homophobic society, regardless of what Glee might try to convey. Thus, it's usually the pictures of girls that spread further and faster."

Yet there is no reason male victims should suffer because they are rarer. It is perfectly possible to reconcile the feminist observation that sexting gone wrong falls more heavily on girls and do right by the minority of male victims.

The way to do that is to focus not on the action itself, but its effects. The police are already encouraged to do this in other crimes involving new technology: for example, in "trolling" cases, the CPS guidelines set a high bar to prosecute messages that are offensive or unpleasant. At the same time, stalking charities are educating the police and public that an insidious drip-drip of low-level incidents can cause serious psychological harm. I've heard Labour MP Stella Creasy, who has consistently spoken out against Twitter abuse, give a useful analogy: imagine being sent a bunch of flowers. How lovely! Except if they are from your ex, and you have a restraining order out against him, and that bunch of flowers is his way of saying: I know where you live.

If you apply that logic to Simon's case, the wronged party becomes clear. He is the one eating lunch in the library because of bullies, not the girl who received his selfies. Once that is acknowledged, the lessons are clear. The young need a better understanding of consent – making sex and relationships education compulsory in all schools would be an obvious first step – and for victims of bullying to get proper support. We can't stop teenagers sexting, but we can help them practise safe sext.

* Not his real name

** In the small town of Steubenville, Ohio, a teenage girl who drank too much at a party and became unconscious was sexually assaulted by other teenagers who circulated pictures of the prolonged assault.

The Guardian, 6 September 2015 © Guardian News & Media 2015

Sport

The girl who played boys' football:

I almost liked the jokes and sexist comments. They got me really fired up

As a 12-year-old girl playing boys' football Niamh McKevitt was unique – and targeted. The defender recalls her rude awakening in this extract from her book

SOME ISSUES:

What are the advantages and disadvantages of boys and girls playing on the same team?

In the early 20th century, women's football drew big crowds but the FA banned female matches (the ban was lifted in the 1970s). What do you think were the reasons for a ban and the consequences of it?

What could encourage more female players?

What parts of Niamh's story and attitude stand out for you?

Unfortunately, the most memorable thing about my first game for Millhouses had nothing to do with football. As well as the pace, the other big difference was the amount of what Dad calls "sledging". Boys' football is a lot more vocal than the girls' version. Quite a few girls' matches I've been involved in have been played in total silence. Boys are much more likely to talk to each other, and not just to members of their own team either. I discovered mind games are a big part of football.

The sledging usually starts during the pre-match handshake, which is supposedly a goodwill gesture initiated by the FA to promote sportsmanship – but that's really all it is: a gesture.

My brother says he once played in an under-eights match when the biggest player from the other team whispered "F*** you!" every time he shook hands with someone.

For me it's usually something like, "Ooh! Hello darling!" or, "Which one's your boyfriend?" or maybe a lame joke like, "Hey, I didn't know we were playing netball!" Sometimes I can't tell what they've said, but I hear them laughing about me after I've gone past. And I get wolf-whistled quite a lot.

I just pretend I haven't heard. I don't let it bother me.

If they say something directly to me, I just roll my eyes, but if they say something to one of their mates, I just pretend I haven't heard. I don't let it bother me. I think sexist comments are inevitable, sadly.

Sometimes, when we line up for the kick-off and I'm on the side of the pitch near the spectators, I can hear the opposition parents also making jokes about me. Usually nothing too mean, but I guess they just think it's funny that a girl is playing.

Perhaps they'll say, "Make sure you get her number as you go past her" or, "Don't get distracted by the full-back."

I pretend to ignore this, but I find it really helps to get the adrenaline pumping. I'd almost go as far as to say that I like it when it happens because it gets me really fired up, especially if it's freezing cold or I'm not really in the mood for the match for some reason.

I usually go up for corners to mark the goalkeeper and I try to distract them. There was one team we played and, as I ran into the area, they all started singing, "Bird in the box! Bird in the box!" I think they were trying to put me off, but we still scored. You do get used to it and you just have to learn how to cope. Another time I went up for a free-kick and one lad said, "Why have I got to mark the girl?" We were winning so I was feeling quite bold and said, "And why do I have to mark the dick?" That got quite a few laughs – even from his own team-mates.

It's not all one-way though. If I flatten someone in a tackle then I always help them up, ask them if they're OK and apologise for hurting them. But really what I'm doing is making them feel worse, confirming that, yes, you really were just decked by a girl!

However, there is a point where sledging stops and abuse starts. I've never been threatened directly, but I've been called a "slag" a few times and I've played in matches where I've heard people threaten to break someone's legs: "if you try to go past me again …" or something similar. Some teams have a reputation for trying to intimidate the opposition and it's sad to say that, in my experience, they often end up succeeding.

When you're playing those kinds of teams you might find that some of your own players go missing. It's little things like they stop making runs or stop calling for the ball. And when they do get it they give it away as quickly as possible.

In games like these you need leaders who'll show that they aren't scared, won't pull out of a tackle and don't really care what the other team is saying. I always try to be one of those players, as if to give the impression: "Hey lads, if the girl isn't scared, then we don't need to be."

Just two days after our first game against Thorncliffe Colts, we were away at Darfield in Barnsley for an evening kick-off.

I was a bit concerned about the referee, who seemed to be the same age as us and was, rather disconcertingly, on first-name terms with all the Darfield players. Again I started the match, but we went two goals down fairly quickly. About half an hour into the game, I went in for a header and got kicked in the face. My first instinct was to think, "For God's sake, don't cry!" My second was to think, "Ouch, that really, really hurts."

Instead of a free-kick to us the referee awarded a throw-in to them. Overwhelmed by the injustice of it all and the pain, I burst into tears and had to come off. While most of the time it feels like I'm just one of the lads, it does occasionally feel like I'm not just one of the lads. This was the first of those times. If Chris or Bilal got kicked in the face and cried, it was because they got kicked in the face and it really hurt. But if I got kicked in the face and cried, it was because I'm a girl. If Dan or Sheriyar screwed up, or tried to do something and it failed to come off, it was because they weren't good enough; if I screwed up, it was because girls aren't good enough to play football. I didn't want Iain and Dave to think, "We've made a mistake signing Niamh, this league's too tough for her," so I had a drink and told them I was ready to go back on.

It was an agonising wait through the rest of the half and half-time, but with 25 minutes to go I did go back on. I was absolutely determined to show everybody that I was tough enough to play at this level, and most of all to show the winger who had kicked me in the face (and on purpose, I had decided). Within five minutes I got my

If I screwed up, it was because girls aren't good enough

chance. A 50-50 ball. I threw everything into the tackle. Sometimes, you know what's going to happen before it happens and this just felt right. I took the ball cleanly, the player went flying, and I kicked it up the pitch to Bilal who did his thing of running at 90mph past two defenders and scoring.

We ended up losing, but Iain said it was the best game I'd played.

"Perhaps we should get someone to kick you in the face before every match Niamh," he said.

It hadn't been a perfect start, but I now felt ready to take on whatever boys' football threw at me.

Playing With the Boys by Niamh McKevitt is published by Vision Sports Publishing, RRP £12.99

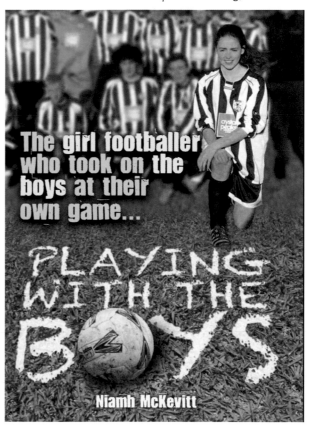

Image © Andrew Brownbill / AP/Press Association Images

SPORTING POWER VERSUS SELLING POWER

SOME ISSUES:

Why was Sharapova chosen by so many brands?

Does the sponsorship difference between these players represent racism within our society?

What image do you think stronger woman have in our society?

Should earnings match sporting achievement?

Serena Williams is a tennis phenomenon. She is currently ranked world number one in women's singles tennis - nearly 2000 ranking points ahead of her nearest rival. She has won four Olympic Gold Medals, she holds numerous tennis records for the most titles won, the most Grand Slams and is formidable in singles and both sorts of doubles. No less an expert than John McEnroe recently described her as "the greatest player, I think, that ever lived."

Naturally, Serena is one of the highest paid athletes in the world. In 2015, she earned $36 million in prize money and was said to have a net wealth of $145 million. She was one of only two women in the 2015 Forbes list of the world's highest paid athletes, however she was only ranked at number 47 with total earnings of $24.6 million, lower and less than the other female athlete!

The only other woman was Maria Sharapova who earned $29.7 million dollars in 2015, making her then the 26th highest paid athlete in the world despite being five places lower than Serena in the world rankings, achieving only about a third of Serena's ranking points and earning only $6.7 million in prize money.

The fact that Sharapova and Williams were, and in 2016 still are, the only two women in the top 100 is interesting in itself, but the discrepancy between their earnings seems inexplicable if it is judged in terms of tennis achievements.

THE DISCREPANCY BETWEEN THEIR EARNINGS SEEMS INEXPLICABLE IN TERMS OF TENNIS RESULTS.

The gap in earnings was down to endorsements, the money players earn for advertising or simply using certain products. Sharapova earned $10 million more than Serena from these sources in 2015.

While Sharapova is undoubtedly a great player, her achievements don't equal those of Williams, who has outmatched Sharapova on every occasion that they have met. The score in the London Olympics final in 2012, for example, was 6-0, 6-1 to Williams. Yet Sharapova was the most bankable star in women's tennis.

So why did Sharapova earn more? Clearly tennis rankings don't directly translate into earnings from endorsements. Sharapova has the reputation of being an astute business woman but she also has the advantage of being tall, white, slender and blonde. It is a look that fits the convention of what a young woman 'should' look like.

Serena, on the other hand, with her evident strength and musculature, her ebony skin and an air of being capable, challenging and even fierce, does not necessarily fit the conventional advertising template.

It is not only that she is black - black male athletes receive plenty of endorsements. It isn't only that she is in a sport not traditionally associated with black athletes - Tiger Woods earned a great deal from golf (and still was ninth highest earner in 2015 despite his poorer form and troubled personal life).

Earnings from endorsements are about lending your name to a product - and your name is valuable because it will sell things. When Chinese tennis player Li Na became number 2 in the world in 2014 she received more endorsements than Serena because being associated with Li Na was an opportunity for brands to enter the lucrative and growing Asian market.

Sharapova earned more than Williams because companies believed she would shift more goods.

It's not about who is the better athlete but who is the better sales proposition. The worldwide audience for tennis has a majority of high earners. The sport has some of the aura of glamour and wealth that is also associated with sports such as golf or sailing. When luxury car brand Porsche wanted to expand its appeal to women (85% of its customers are men) it signed a deal with Sharapova.

All of this changed in 2016. At the quarter-finals of the Australian Open in January 2016, Sharapova lost, as so often before, to Serena Williams and was then tested for drugs. She was found to have been using Meldonium, a substance which has the ability to increase oxygen uptake and endurance and which had been banned from January 1st of that year. Sharapova claimed that it was an honest mistake, she had been taking the drug

Image © PA-26599384

SERENA IS LESS SALEABLE. IT REPRESENTS ISSUES THAT OUR SOCIETY HAS WITH THE IMAGE OF A STRONG, BLACK WOMAN

for 10 years while it was not banned and that she had failed to open the relevant email about the ban (and presumably, all previous ones). Porsche and two other sponsors, Nike and luxury watch makers Tag Heuer, immediately suspended their relationships with her. In June 2016 she received a two year ban from competing in Tennis.

The size of her potential loss of earnings is even more shocking than the fact that she is banned. By the time the Forbes list of highest earning athletes for 2016 was published, Sharapova had dropped to 88th in those rankings and she had lost nearly $30 million in endorsement payments. Her earnings will plummet still more under the ban as she will not be able to play the minimum number of matches that are stipulated in her contracts.

Serena Williams herself maintains a cool and distant attitude to the difference in earnings. She said in an interview in The New York Times in August 2015:

"If they want to market someone who is white and blonde, that's their choice. I have a lot of partners who are very happy to work with me. I can't sit here and say I should be higher on the list because I have won more. I'm happy for her, because she worked hard, too. There is enough at the table for everyone. We have to be thankful, and we also have to be positive about it so the next black person can be number one on that list."

But that difference must raise bigger questions. In the widest sense it isn't fair that Serena is less saleable, it represents issues that our society has with the image of a strong, black woman. It isn't fair that there are only two women in the top 100 earners. But, in the business of sport, fairness isn't what counts - it's profits.

In 2014, BT sport ran a survey of British female athletes. 80% said that felt pressure to conform to a certain body type - and that pressure had influenced diet and training in more than 70% of cases. Sport England surveys show that one of the barriers to more women taking part in sport is their fear of being judged on their appearance. Endorsement does not just mean money - it means support, backing, approval and encouragement. If advertisers are reflecting and reinforcing a view of female athletes that values and promotes only one body type, only one set of characteristics, and primarily, only one race, they are playing a part in persuading other females that sport is not for them.

Sources: Various

In July 2016 Serena Williams won her 7th Wimbledon title and equalled the record for Grand Slam (major tournament) wins.

CHEATING IN SPORT IS BECOMING EVER HARDER TO JUDGE

Maria Sharapova's drugs ban throws into sharp relief the issues surrounding today's transgender athletes

Catherine Bennett

SOME ISSUES:

Do you think it is important for sports to have rules about who can participate?

How might such rules affect inclusion and opportunity?

Why do hormones and gender matter when it comes to participating in sport?

Can high-level sport ever be really fair?

Is it really 'the taking part that counts'?

Four years ago, Oscar Pistorius, still a hero rather than a murderer, was about to compete in the London Olympics against enabled athletes, running on his carbon-fibre blades. Not everyone was happy about this. The German team, for instance, said his Flex-Foot Cheetahs used 25% less energy and were unfair to natural runners. How was it fair to ban all doping, then allow one athlete to use special technology? It was against fair play, the spirit of the Games.

Pistorius's supporters were incredulous that anyone could accuse an awe-inspiring double amputee of having an unfair advantage. That was definitely against the spirit of the games.

In the event, after Pistorius failed to qualify for the men's 400m final, it was he who complained most bitterly, after being beaten at the Paralympics by Brazil's Alan Fonteles Cardoso Oliveira. The winner's blades were too long, Pistorius said. He wanted an official investigation. "I believe in fairness in sport," he said, "and I believe in running on the right length."

With Pistorius and his blades out of the way, suspicions about sporting unfairness have returned to doping, whose detection is now practically a sport in itself, albeit a little on the slow side. Details are still emerging, thanks in part to whistleblowers, of the substantial contribution made by banned performance-enhancing drugs to the excitement at Sochi 2014. In its 2015 report, the World Anti-Doping Agency (Wada) said a cheating Russian team had effectively "sabotaged" the London Games, assisted by official inaction, and called for Russia to be barred from international athletics. *[In June 2016, Russia's track and field team was barred from competing in the Olympic Games].*

Definitely absent from sport for the next two years will be their compatriot, Maria Sharapova, the tennis star and the world's

© Abdeljalil Bounhar / AP/Press Association Images

Caster Semenya from South Africa crosses the finish line to win the women's 800-metres at the International Mohammed VI track and field meeting in Rabat, Morocco, Sunday, May 22, 2016.

HOW WAS IT FAIR TO BAN ALL DOPING, THEN ALLOW ONE ATHLETE TO USE SPECIAL TECHNOLOGY?

highest paid female athlete for 11 consecutive years. She has benefited, it emerges, from a fantastic sounding drug called meldonium, which is said to improve stamina and even, not unlike PG Wodehouse's fabled Buck-U-Uppo, give the user "mental focus" and a "sharper edge".

Alas, thanks to Sharapova, the online price has reportedly soared, from £15 to £27 for 40 tablets, the athlete's personal endorsement evidently carrying more weight than official warnings about the danger of unlicensed drugs and, indeed, meldonium's designation, by Wada, as against "the spirit of sport". One of Wada's purposes, its director general has explained, is to discourage the use of performance-enhancing drugs at the amateur as well as elite level, where it also constitutes

a "challenge to the values of sport and its integrity". Those values, he specified, included "ethics, honesty, respect for rules, self-respect and respect for others, fair play and healthy competition".

If those don't already sound quaint, given the colossal investment that rich countries consider a fair price for one medal, Wada may want to consider how sporting values accord with the IOC's recent decisions on competition between individuals whose biology is so different that, some predict, fair play in certain women's events could become impossible.

The former Olympic champion Sonia O'Sullivan has drawn attention to the latest triumphs of Caster Semenya, the South African sprinter who is now predicted to win a gold medal in Brazil. She won a silver medal in London, then faltered, not even qualifying for the 2014 Commonwealth Games. The reason usually advanced for Semenya's impressive return to form is the Court of Arbitration for Sport's (CAS) decision to suspend an earlier ruling by the IAAF that put an upper limit on testosterone for intersex athletes competing in women's events. It

FAIR PLAY IN CERTAIN WOMEN'S EVENTS COULD BECOME IMPOSSIBLE

was designed to ensure – at some cost to the dignity of intersex women athletes – fairness for the majority, who have much lower testosterone levels. Last year, the ruling was the subject of a legal challenge by the Indian sprinter Dutee Chand, arguing her right to compete without taking testosterone-suppressing drugs.

The CAS duly suspended the regulations and asked for more evidence that high levels of testosterone confer a performance benefit. "To me, that CAS decision seems ludicrous," O'Sullivan writes. "That's the one marker that created the imbalance in performance and which has long been known."

Adding yet more interest to future women's events is the IOC's decision to allow people who self-identify as women to participate in the 2016 Games, including, for the first time, women who have not physically transitioned. The contestants must, however, have kept their testosterone levels below 10 nanomoles per litre for a year. Women usually have fewer than three nmol/L.

If the potentially arresting consequences seem to have been subjected, as yet, to relatively little public examination, it probably, as with Pistorius's blades, seems more in the spirit of the Games to welcome a landmark triumph over exclusion and discrimination for athletes who have as much right to compete as anyone.

The question is, when athletes are routinely segregated, in the interests of fairness, according to sex, often weight, who should they compete against? Only the Games themselves will show if the cost of fairness for transgender and intersex women will be its loss – contrary to the spirit of the Games –for cis* women athletes.

Then again, there's nothing particularly fair about the Olympics, unless athletes from wealthy and powerful countries are just naturally better than athletes from everywhere else. Why shouldn't intersex athletes enjoy their victories? But Joanna Harper, a physicist, athlete and trans woman, who is an adviser on gender issues to the IOC, says of the suspension of testosterone limits: "Allowing these [intersex] athletes to compete in women's sport with their serious testosterone-based advantage threatens the very fabric of women's sport."

The IOC's declared emphasis in Rio, on protecting "clean athletes" from the dopers, may only add to the indignation of some women competitors, held back by average hormone levels.

One solution, if testosterone is not all the help it's cracked up to be, would be to remove it from the banned list of pharmaceuticals, to allow for individual topping up. And if that led to demands, from people who don't fancy the side-effects, for testosterone alternatives, there is surely a place for niche tonics such as Sharapova's Buck-U-Uppo or Lance Armstrong's preferred androstenone, the active ingredient in – really – Boarmate.

As well as sparing athletes the incessant testing that never, anyway, keeps up with cheating's finest, the freedom to take any safe, performance-enhancing drug would guarantee, for the audience, Olympics that are genuinely, as advertised, ever faster, higher and stronger.

It would be a shame if any sudden leap forward in Brazil were restricted to women's events, courtesy of newly validated contestants.

If, however, the overriding sporting objective of fair competition dictates that pharmacological advances continue to be excluded from the range of athletics-enhancing innovations – from competitive swimsuits to the "secret tech" promised by British cyclists – the IOC might be advised to remind women in certain events of the importance of being a good loser. It's the taking part that counts, right?

The Observer, 12 June 2016
© Guardian News & Media 2016

Cisgender: someone whose self-identity matches their biological sex; not transgender.

It is good news that 23 athletes at London 2012 have failed drugs tests as it means we are exposing cheats for what they are

Denise Lewis

SOME ISSUES:

Why do you think sports people feel the need to cheat?

What can be done to make competing fairer?

Where does the pressure to win come from?

What amount of pressure is healthy?

What should happen when a winner is discovered to be a cheat?

It is understandable that the headlines will be negative but my first impression when I heard about 23 people retrospectively failing drugs tests from London 2012 was that this is good news. You want everything to be out in the open. You want the sport to be taking effective action and exposing cheats for what they are.

Obviously, that is not to say that when these things do come to light it doesn't make you feel incredibly angry. You have to think about the people who get hurt in the process – people who have spent their entire lives trying to get either on podiums or into finals and they get robbed of those opportunities.

Goldie Sayers [who finished fourth at the 2008 Beijing Olympics behind an alleged Russian drugs cheat] is one of those people and she just typifies why these cheats need to be weeded out. I remember Goldie was in the shape of her life in Beijing and she was let down by the system, the deceit and the cheating. She was robbed of her moment on the podium and that is just awful.

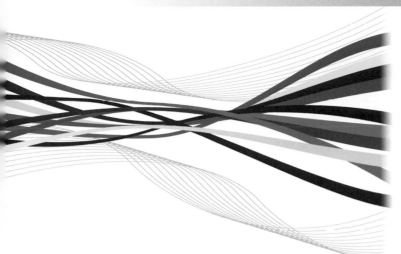

People spend their entire lives trying to get either on podiums or into finals and they get robbed of those opportunities.

Some people are now saying that London was the dirtiest Olympics, but I can't believe that is correct. If you look at the 1980s there was a sense that doping was rife. Athletes were prepared to take chances back then because they felt the rest of the world was engaged in cheating as well. It was widespread. It is just a case that more people are now being caught and, as a lover of our sport, that can only be a good thing.

I do think that when you come so close to achieving your goals and you know the hard work you have put in compared to someone who may have cheated to beat you it's only natural to have suspicions about them. You never like to call people out for it but I'd be lying if I said I never had those feelings at times during my competitive years. But I'm lucky that I sat at the top of the tree when I won gold in Sydney. I got there on my own merit so there's an inclination to say yes, there were cheats out there, but I managed to beat them anyway.

If we look ahead to Rio I just think the only option now is to have greater sanctions. I know there will be a decision made on Russia next month but I think federations,

committees, agents and everyone who is complicit in cheating should miss out. That is the lesson that must be learnt – if you are in any way engaged in drug taking, you will miss Olympic Games. *[In June 2016, Russia's track and field team was barred from competing in the Olympic Games].*

One thing that is so important in all of this is that this news must not tarnish the memory of the London Games. The British public lived off the exuberance and the energy of London 2012 for years after so it would be a crying shame for everybody involved and the athletes who competed cleanly if the memory of the Games is a dirty one. I certainly felt immensely proud of my country and the British athletes that rose to the occasion. For that to now be under a cloud of suspicion and doubt is a real shame.

The danger with this drip-fed news of cheating and drug-taking is that people start to doubt whether it really is possible to win legally. I can assure them that it is. We want to remember London 2012 for things like Super Saturday *[Saturday, 4th August 2012 when Britain won six gold medals and one silver - its most successful day in 104 years of Olympics]* and look across all the Olympic sports and remember the hundreds of amazing performances during an incredible couple of weeks. That's what I will always remember from the London Games. We must never forget that clean athletes do win.

Daily Telegraph, 28 May 2016
© Telegraph Media Group Limited 2016

The danger with this drip-fed news of cheating and drug-taking is that people start to doubt whether it really is possible to win legally.

A desire, a dream, a vision - the making of a champion!

Background and personality

Muhammad Ali grew up as Cassius Clay in Louisville, Kentucky in the southern part of the United States. It was a place and a time in which Black Americans were treated as inferior, not allowed to use the same facilities as white people, expected to be deferential to their 'betters' and at risk of violence if they stepped out of line.

His prodigious talent saw him winning a place at the Olympics when he was just 18. He came home with a gold medal but was still refused service in a 'whites only' restaurant; his sporting achievements did not outweigh his skin colour to earn him respect in that intolerant atmosphere.

Professional boxing

Only eight weeks after winning gold, he fought and won his first bout as a professional boxer. His style was unique - he was fast, flippant, taunting opponents with his speed of movement, dodging and dancing, but with a powerful punch.

"Float like a butterfly, sting like a bee, his hands can't hit what his eyes can't see."

Quick-witted, as well as quick on his feet and with his punches, Ali would taunt his opponents outside the ring too. When he took on the World Heavyweight Champion, Sonny Liston, he mocked the man, who was made in the more traditional style of the big, brutal, incoherent boxer:

"Sonny Liston is nothing. The man can't talk. The man can't fight. The man needs talking lessons. The man needs boxing lessons. And since he's gonna fight me, he needs falling lessons."

He was a gift to the media who hadn't encountered anything like his bravado, which amused and enraged the public but which was backed up by skill in the ring. He beat Liston to become World Champion and beat him again in a rematch lasting a mere 100 seconds.

Perhaps his most famous fight was 'The Rumble in the Jungle" in Zaire. Ali was a 3-to-1 outsider against the new world champion George Foreman, a powerful, hard-hitting heavyweight. Ali used a new tactic he called 'rope-a-dope'. He leaned back against the ropes, taking punishing blows to his body but dodging punches to his head before launching counter attacks with straight right hand shots. In round eight, he knocked the champion out, winning back the world title at the age of 32.

He also fought long-time rival Joe Frazier for a final time in the so-called "Thrilla in Manila" and the two men battled brutally for 14 rounds before Frazier's corner conceded. Ali's taunting had agitated Frazier and the fight was a mental as well as a physical battle. Ali later said the fight was "the closest thing to death" he'd ever experienced and apologised for the name calling that he had used to promote it.

Ali defended his heavyweight title in six fights before losing it to Leon Spinks and then regaining it - the only person to become World Heavyweight Champion three times. He had a brief retirement followed by a brief, regrettable, come back. He retired permanently at age 40, having lost 5 fights and won 56.

Becoming Muhammad Ali

At the beginning of his boxing career Cassius Clay was already a controversial public figure because he was seen by some as loudmouthed and a clown who destroyed the dignity of a noble sport. By racists he was seen as 'uppity', not the quiet, subservient figure that they preferred in black role models.

Muhammad Ali

1942 – 2016

SOME ISSUES:

Why do you think Ali became world famous?

What makes a great champion stand out above other people who have been very successful in sport?

Ali used his celebrity to highlight injustice and inequality. Do all famous people have a duty to do this?

Who is your favourite sports person and why?

"Champions aren't made in gyms, champions are made from something they have deep inside them"

Image © PA Wire/Press Association Images

He was coming to prominence at a time when the Black Power movement was growing and developing. There were many different strands to this - in civil rights, arts, politics and sport. Clay began to meet up with the leaders of the Nation of Islam, a group which proposed that the way to achieve better conditions for black people in America was separate development, rejecting white society and its culture.

After his fight with Sonny Liston, Cassius Clay announced that he was a member of the Nation of Islam and was rejecting his previous identity:

"Cassius Clay is a slave name. I didn't choose it and I don't want it. I am Muhammad Ali."

Although his views on the exact style of Islam to follow and on separate development changed as time went on, Muhammad Ali saw himself throughout his life as standing up for poor and oppressed black people.

Opposing the war in Vietnam

The USA had long been involved in a war against Communist rule in Vietnam. Young men who were called up to serve (via a form of lottery to determine who should go first) were obliged to go, although there were ways to avoid the draft. Views on the war were associated with attitudes to the general liberalisation of society - those who opposed the war were often associated with 'hippy' culture, sexual liberation and racial integration. Those who supported it were often also supporters of the existing, more rigid and segregated structure of society. The USA, and much of the world, polarised around those who 'served their country' and the 'draft dodgers'.

When Muhammad Ali was called up he refused to serve, saying,

"Why should they ask me to put on a uniform and go 10,000 miles from home and drop bombs and bullets on brown people in Vietnam while so-called Negro people in Louisville are treated like dogs and denied simple human rights?"

and

"Man, I ain't got no quarrel with them Viet Cong. No Viet Cong ever called me nigger."

As a result of his stance he was stripped of his World Heavyweight title, banned from boxing and sentenced to five years in prison. While he appealed against the sentence (eventually with success) he gave talks in colleges and universities, where there was a strong protest movement against the war.

Fame, philanthropy and Parkinson's

At the height of his career, Ali was one of the most famous faces on the planet and even now his name would be recognised by people who would be hard pushed to name any other boxer. He was always keen to use his fame to help others - even helping in the release of hostages taken by Saddam Hussein in Iraq.

In his early forties, Ali was diagnosed with Parkinson's disease which his doctors linked to his boxing career but Ali did not. He took on the fight against the disease and its symptoms, raising millions of dollars for the medical centre which was named after him. In the summer of 1996 he appeared before a worldwide audience, lighting the Olympic flame in Atlanta. Millions were moved by the sight of this fragile, trembling, yet absolutely determined figure and in 2012 he appeared again at the London Olympics - to a rapturous reception.

Ali died in 2016. His funeral cortege took a route around his home town of Louisville and the 'people's champion' was given a last round of applause by thousands of ordinary people, while his memorial service was attended by celebrities, heads of state and ex-presidents.

As always, Muhammad Ali must have the last word

"Champions aren't made in gyms, champions are made from something they have deep inside them - a desire, a dream, a vision. They have to have last-minute stamina, they have to be a little faster, they have to have the skill and the will. But the will must be stronger than the skill."

Sources: Various

War &
conflict

I was held hostage by Isis. They fear our unity more than our airstrikes

In Syria I learned that Islamic State longs to provoke retaliation. We should not fall into the trap

Nicolas Hénin

SOME ISSUES:

Is more bombing the right response to terrorist attacks?

How can people be protected against terrorism?

Why are Isis successful in recruiting people?

Social media is used to promote terrorism, can it be used against it?

How does the refugee crisis fit into this situation?

As a proud Frenchman I am as distressed as anyone about the events in Paris*. But I am not shocked or incredulous. I know Islamic State. I spent 10 months as an Isis hostage, and I know for sure that our pain, our grief, our hopes, our lives do not touch them. Theirs is a world apart.

Most people only know them from their propaganda material, but I have seen behind that. In my time as their captive, I met perhaps a dozen of them, including Mohammed Emwazi: Jihadi John was one of my jailers. He nicknamed me "Baldy".

Even now I sometimes chat with them on social media, and can tell you that much of what you think of them results from their brand of marketing and public relations. They present themselves to the public as superheroes, but away from the camera are a bit pathetic in many ways: street kids drunk on ideology and power. In France we have a saying – stupid and evil. I found them more stupid than evil. That is not to understate the murderous potential of stupidity.

All of those beheaded last year were my cellmates, and my jailers would play childish games with us – mental torture – saying one day that we would be released and then two weeks later observing blithely, "Tomorrow we will kill one of you." The first couple of times we believed them but after that we came to realise that for the most part they were bullshitters having fun with us.

They would play mock executions. Once they used chloroform with me. Another time it was a beheading scene. A bunch of French-speaking jihadis were shouting, "We're going to cut your head off and put it on to your arse and upload it to YouTube." They had a sword from an antique shop.

They were laughing and I played the game by screaming, but they just wanted fun. As soon as they left I turned to another of the French hostages and just laughed. It was so ridiculous.

It struck me forcefully how technologically connected they are; they follow the news obsessively, but everything they see goes through their own filter. They are totally indoctrinated, clinging to all manner of conspiracy theories, never acknowledging the contradictions.

Most people only know them from their propaganda material, but I have seen behind that

Much of what you think of them results from their marketing

Everything convinces them that they are on the right path and, specifically, that there is a kind of apocalyptic process under way that will lead to a confrontation between an army of Muslims from all over the world and others, the crusaders, the Romans. They see everything as moving us down that road. Consequently, everything is a blessing from Allah.

With their news and social media interest, they will be noting everything that follows their murderous assault on Paris, and my guess is that right now the chant among them will be "We are winning". They will be heartened by every sign of overreaction, of division, of fear, of racism, of xenophobia; they will be drawn to any examples of ugliness on social media.

Central to their world view is the belief that communities cannot live together with Muslims, and every day their antennae will be tuned towards

finding supporting evidence. The pictures from Germany of people welcoming migrants will have been particularly troubling to them. Cohesion, tolerance – it is not what they want to see.

Why France? For many reasons perhaps, but I think they identified my country as a weak link in Europe – as a place where divisions could be sown easily. That's why, when I am asked how we should respond, I say that we must act responsibly.

And yet more bombs will be our response. I am no apologist for Isis. How could I be? But everything I know tells me this is a mistake. The bombardment will be huge, a symbol of righteous anger. Within 48 hours of the atrocity, fighter planes conducted their most

What they fear is unity

spectacular munitions raid yet in Syria, dropping more than 20 bombs on Raqqa, an Isis stronghold. Revenge was perhaps inevitable, but what's needed is deliberation. My fear is that this reaction will make a bad situation worse.

While we are trying to destroy Isis, what of the 500,000 civilians still living and trapped in Raqqa? What of their safety? What of the very real prospect that by failing to think this through, we turn many of them into extremists? The priority must be to protect these people, not to take more bombs to Syria. We need no-fly zones – zones closed to Russians, the regime, the coalition. The Syrian people need security or they themselves will turn to groups such as Isis.

Canada withdrew from the air war after the election of Justin Trudeau. I desperately want France to do the same, and rationality tells me it could happen. But pragmatism tells me it won't. The fact is we are trapped: Isis has trapped us. They came to Paris with Kalashnikovs, claiming that they wanted to stop the bombing, but knowing all too well that the attack would force us to keep bombing or even to intensify these counterproductive attacks. That is what is happening.

Emwazi is gone now, killed in a coalition air strike, his death celebrated in parliament. I do not mourn him. But during his murder spree, he too followed this double bluff strategy.

After murdering the American journalist James Foley, he pointed his knife at the camera and, turning to the next intended victim, said: "Obama, you must stop intervening in the Middle East or I will kill him." He knew very well what the hostage's fate would be. He knew very well what the American reaction would be – more bombing. It's what Isis wants, but should we be giving it to them?

The group is wicked, of that there is no doubt. But after all that happened to me, I still don't feel Isis is the priority. To my mind, Bashar al-Assad is the priority. The Syrian president is responsible for the rise of Isis in Syria, and so long as his regime is in place, Isis cannot be eradicated. Nor can we stop the attacks on our streets. When people say "Isis first, and then Assad", I say don't believe them. They just want to keep Assad in place.

At the moment there is no political road map and no plan to engage the Arab Sunni community. Isis will collapse, but politics will make that happen. In the meantime there is much we can achieve in the aftermath of this atrocity, and the key is strong hearts and resilience, for that is what they fear. I know them: bombing they expect. What they fear is unity.

Nicolas Henin is author of Jihad Academy, The Rise of Islamic State

* In November 2015 a series of coordinated terrorist attacks in Paris killed 130 people and injured 368. Isis claimed that this was in revenge for French airstrikes.

The Guardian, 16 November 2015
© Guardian News & Media 2015

The real threat of foreign fighters in Syria

The foreign fighter phenomenon is a double-edged sword; it kills and maims on the way into Syria and the way out.

Martin Reardon
@mdreardon79

In its initial report: Foreign Fighters in Syria, released by the Soufan Group in June 2014, it was estimated that approximately 12,000 foreign fighters from 81 countries had travelled there since 2011. Most joined the ranks of the Islamic State of Iraq and the Levant (ISIL), Jabhat al-Nusra, or Ahrar al-Sham.

In a follow up report released by the Soufan Group in December 2015, it was estimated that those numbers more than doubled in the last 18 months to between 27,000 and 31,000 from 86 countries - a stark dose of reality that the foreign-fighter phenomenon has not only exploded in numbers but is global in nature.

Consider: The number of foreign fighters from Western Europe more than doubled in the last 18 months, from 2,500 in 2014, to over 5,000. Most of them come from just four countries - France with 1,700, the UK and Germany with 760 each, and Belgium with 470.

In Russia, those numbers have gone up three fold - from 800 in 2014, to 2,400 by September 2015 - most coming from Chechnya and Dagestan in the North Caucasus. According to Russian President Vladimir Putin, that number is as high as 5,000 to 7,000 when fighters from the former Soviet republics are included.

Startling numbers

In North Africa and the Middle East the numbers are even more startling, with over 16,000 fighters having travelled to Syria and Iraq. Tunisians make up the largest contingent of foreign fighters overall, with an estimated 6,000. That's double the number from 2014. Saudi Arabians make up the next largest contingent with 2,500, followed by Jordanians with 2,000.

Other countries in the region with significant numbers include Morocco - 1,200; Lebanon - 900; Libya - 600; Egypt - 600; and Algeria - 170.

Turkey, too, has had its share of foreign fighters, with approximately 2,100 having gone to Syria and Iraq, although many of them have already returned home. According to Turkish authorities, 500 of its citizens have been imprisoned for joining ISIL, and another 100 for joining Jabhat al-Nusra.

Southeast Asia is not immune to the foreign fighter phenomena either. According to Indonesian officials, 700 of its citizens have fought in Syria and Iraq as of late 2015. In May 2014, they had reported that figure as being only 30 to 60.

Compared to the dramatic increase in numbers of foreign fighters in Europe and elsewhere, the United States and Canada have remained relatively stable since 2014. According to FBI records, about 150 Americans have travelled to Syria as of September 2015, and another 100 have been arrested attempting to do so. Canadian officials report even less, with 130 of its citizens having gone to Syria as foreign fighters.

Why they go

The process of radicalisation and reasons for the foreign fighter flow to Syria and Iraq vary from region to region. In North Africa, which has a long history of foreign fighters dating back to the Soviet occupation of Afghanistan in the 1980s, the deteriorating security situation, high levels of unemployment, and peer-to-peer recruitment by family, friends and influential members of the community are major factors.

For many foreign fighters their motivation is a search for belonging, purpose, adventure, and friendship

In Europe, radicalisation and the foreign fighter flow are driven largely by a sense of marginalisation and alienation among immigrant communities, particularly those from North Africa. French authorities categorise foreign fighters as disaffected, aimless and lacking a sense of belonging - traits that appear common from region to region.

Add to that equation community-based recruiting in European countries with the highest number of foreign fighters, where groups of acquaintances are drawn to a common identity.

Case in point: the Molenbeek neighbourhood of Brussels, where several of the terrorists from the November Paris attacks lived, and knew each other before joining ISIL in Syria, and then eventually making their way back home to carry out the attacks.

For many foreign fighters, regardless of where they come from, their motivation is no more complex than a search for belonging, purpose, adventure, and friendship.

What this means

The most troubling significance with these numbers is that despite a sustained international effort to contain ISIL and stem the flow of foreign fighters to Syria, they have more than doubled in just 18 months, indicating that ISIL's appeal has

not ebbed - and in fact, may be stronger now than it was 18 months ago.

Another disturbing fact in all this is that the issue of foreign fighters is both a near-term threat and a long-term challenge. The Syrian civil war will not end soon, and although ISIL continues to be degraded through concentrated air strikes and military pressure on the ground, it will likely survive in one form or another for a considerable time.

In the meantime, new foreign fighters will continue to join its ranks, and many of those already there will return to their home countries where they pose a very real threat of either carrying out terrorists attacks on their own or at the direction of ISIL or other extremist groups.

For Western countries in particular, where 20-30 percent of foreign fighters return to their home countries, this presents a significant challenge to law enforcement agencies that must first identify them and then assess whatever threat they may pose.

The foreign fighter phenomenon in Syria goes well beyond the civil war there. No doubt, they have been a major factor - one of many - that have changed that country forever. But their impact goes beyond the borders of Syria.

Many will eventually or have already returned to their home countries, whether elsewhere in the Middle East, North Africa, Europe, Asia, North America or any of the 86 countries where they came from. Some will no doubt have had their fill of violence, and want nothing more to do with it.

But other returnees will no doubt be just as - or even more - radicalised and intent on carrying out terrorist attacks against their home countries, as we've already seen throughout the Middle East, North Africa and Europe.

And that's what makes the foreign fighter phenomenon such a dangerous and unpredictable double-edged sword - it kills and maims on both the down stroke in Syria and the upstroke abroad.

www.aljazeera.com

Martin Reardon is a senior vice president with the Soufan Group, a New York-based strategic security and intelligence consultancy, and senior director of Qatar International Academy for Security Studies. He is a 21-year veteran of the FBI and specialised in counter-terrorism operations.

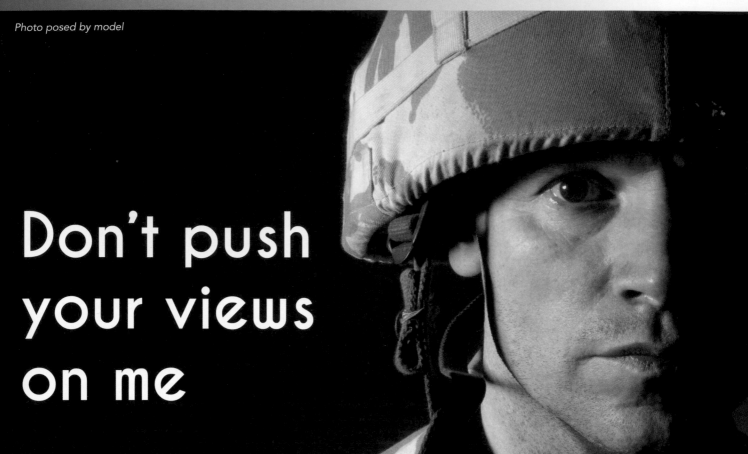

Photo posed by model

Don't push your views on me

A powerful message to those who think he should hate Muslims from a British soldier who lost a leg in Iraq

Chris Herbert, a British soldier who lost his leg in Iraq, became so enraged by the casual racism of people who expected him to hate all Muslims that he wrote a stirring rebuttal on his Facebook page. His powerful message was to those who expected him to share their racism because he "got blown up".

The roadside bomb which blew his vehicle up in Basra, Iraq, killed one friend, injured another and left him without his right leg - a terrible experience and a daunting prospect for someone aged just 19.

Chris Herbert found himself encountering people who expected him to share their Islamophobia as a result of his experience, particularly following the Paris terrorist attacks in November 2015.

His Facebook message, intended to put the bigots right, lists the Muslims who served with him and helped him as well as those white Brits who had abused him.

It ends with the robust advice to "get a grip".

A Muslim Nurse was part of the team that helped me when I returned to the UK

Getting frustrated by some people expecting racism from me, because I got blown up.

HERE IT IS:

Yes. A Muslim man blew me up, and I lost my leg.

A Muslim man also lost his arm that day wearing a British Uniform.

A Muslim medic was in the helicopter that took me from the field.

A Muslim surgeon performed the surgery that saved my life.

A Muslim Nurse was part of the team that helped me when I returned to the UK.

A Muslim Healthcare Assistant was part of the team that sorted out my day to day needs in rehabilitation when I was learning to walk.

A Muslim taxi driver gave me a free ride the first time I went for a beer with my Dad after I came home.

A Muslim doctor offered my Dad comfort and advice in a pub, when he didn't know how to deal with my medicines and side effects.

CONTRARY TO THAT:

A white Brit spat in my girlfriend's face for 'f****** a cripple when you could have me [him]'

A white Brit pushed my wheelchair away from a lift so he could use it first.

A white Brit screamed at my Dad for parking in a disabled bay when I was in the services coming home.

(Although, alot of people helped in my recovery! I don't hate white Brits either! hahaha)

Point is, f*** off. I know who I dislike, and I know who I don't. I know who I appreciate, and I know who I don't.

If you want to hate an entire race of men and women for the actions of a few d***heads feel free, but don't push your views on me, thinking I am an easy target because one d******** decided it was my day to die.

Blaming all Muslims for the actions of groups like Daeshe and the Taliban, is like blaming all Christians for the actions of the KKK or Westboro Baptist Church. Get a grip of your lives, hug your family and get back to work.

– CHRIS HERBERT, 9 December 2015

If you want to hate an entire race of men and women for the actions of a few feel free...
...Blaming all Muslims for the actions of groups like Daeshe and the Taliban, is like blaming all Christians for the actions of the KKK

Sources: Facebook and various

REMEMBRANCE ISN'T ONLY ABOUT THOSE WHO FOUGHT, BUT ALSO THOSE WHO REFUSED

HARRY LESLIE SMITH

WE MUSTN'T LET NOSTALGIA GET IN THE WAY OF A REAL UNDERSTANDING OF THE COSTS OF WAR

SOME ISSUES:

How much do you know about how ordinary people felt at the beginning of World War Two?

Do you think people felt differently about the second world war than they did about the first?

Do you agree with the writer that it is important for people to be able to disagree with decisions, even in times of emergency?

Do you think the past tends to get sugar coated? Is it important to remember harsh realities or should they be put behind us?

How can we make sure that we record and share people's real experiences?

As an RAF veteran of the second world war I know that November is a cruel month for both remembering and forgetting the cost of armed conflict.

During these past few days when the light grows dim, I have stumbled around London and remembered a time when, as a young man, I witnessed our capital face death from swarms of Nazi bomber planes.

In this day and age we like to impose uniformity on our past conflicts. We see them through a nostalgic lens of wartime propaganda films in which the hero gladly sacrifices his life for a green and pleasant land. But the past is not as simple or as clear-cut as our TV presenters like to suggest during Remembrance Sunday services. For every act of unique heroism we remember, we often forget or ignore all those who, because of post-traumatic stress disorder or moral or religious objections, were unwilling to put their lives on the line for king and country.

Today, we forget too easily that our resolve during the first two years of battle with Hitler wasn't as great as popular history likes to imagine. In fact, Lord Halifax*, who was a member of Neville Chamberlain's cabinet, wanted to broker a peace deal

60,000 MEN REGISTERED AS CONSCIENTIOUS OBJECTORS AND MORE THAN 100,000 MEN IN UNIFORM DESERTED THEIR POSTS

between Britain and the Nazis, as did many other aristocrats and business leaders. Moreover, many working-class citizens who had been hit by austerity during the Great Depression didn't feel particularly patriotic about Britain in either peace or war.

I remember that before I volunteered for the RAF my employer begged me to become a conscientious objector. His issues against the war were more about lost commerce than moral outrage at the shedding of blood. Yet despite his promises of promotion and material reward, I didn't take his advice because, although I had grave concerns over the inequalities of 1930s Britain, I still believed my place during a time of national emergency was in uniform.

Many, however, didn't feel as strongly as I and my friends who volunteered, because during the second world war 60,000 men registered as conscientious objectors. Moreover, there were more than 100,000 men in uniform who during the course of the conflict against Nazism deserted their posts or failed to return from leave.

It is unfortunate that too many in this present age look upon these men as cowards whose objections to battle are best forgotten. But I believe it is important that we remember those who dissent in a time of war even if we believe our struggle to be true and just. How a nation treats those who oppose their war aims is the true measure of its enlightenment.

Present-day Britain has a lot to learn from our second world war history because, despite popular myth, conscientious objectors weren't always shunned by society but compelled to contribute to the war effort through ambulance and paramedic work or rebuilding neighbourhoods that had suffered extensive bomb damage. Even the treatment of deserters was more humane in the second world war than the

first, when many were shot out of hand. Still, there is no question that deserters and their families were treated harshly by both the police and government authorities during the second world war. Fortunately, many were able to get on with their lives in postwar Britain with no lasting stigma.

This is but one of the reasons I will no longer wear the poppy today: it represents only what is seen as the "courage" of war – those who stood and fought, but not those who stood and disagreed. It is the reason why, when I recently went to see the ceramic poppies that surround the Tower of London like a turgid lake of blood, I recalled not only lives lost in battles from ancient and modern wars but also those that were changed irrevocably by the consequences of having an individual conscience during a time of collective insecurity. I feel we must find a way to remember them too.

The Guardian, 9 November 2014
© Guardian News & Media 2014

* Lord Halifax was Foreign Secretary in the Conservative government between 1938 and 1940. Neville Chamberlain was Prime Minister from May 1937 to May 1940. This government first tried to appease Hitler and did not oppose his invasion of part of Czechoslovakia but after the invasion of Poland in 1939, war was declared.

MANY WORKING-CLASS CITIZENS DIDN'T FEEL PARTICULARLY PATRIOTIC ABOUT BRITAIN

Wider world

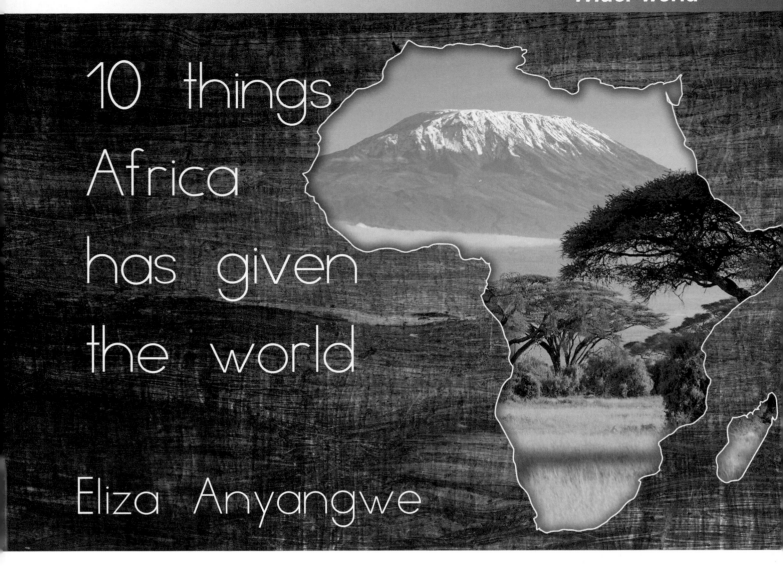

10 things Africa has given the world

Eliza Anyangwe

From coffee beans to polyrhythms, transplants and the world's oldest mathematical objects, here are some of our favourite things from the vast continent

SOME ISSUES:

Were you aware that all of these things came from Africa?

Is it important to know where things come from?

Where do our impressions of far off places come from?

Is it important to challenge clichés?

Twitter nearly gave itself an aneurysm over Taylor Swift's latest music video Wildest Dreams, which had all the usual clichés that make its location immediately identifiable as idyllic, romanticised "Africa": sunsets, wildlife, safari boots and definitely no natives. You start to wonder, is that all there is to this vast continent? Are Africans good for nothing else?

So I've ventured into the dark recesses of the web to discover how Africa shaped our world and gave us some of our favourite things. Hold on to your pith helmets.

Coffee

Italians gave it to us short and strong, Americans served it filtered then ratcheted up the calories by adding syrups, whipped cream and even pumpkin. But everyone's favourite stimulant originates from Ethiopia, where it grows wild. It possibly dates back to the 10th century, when nomadic people would have eaten the red cherries rather than making a beverage with them.

Modern art

Africa's contemporary artists are having a bit of moment, but the world still largely ignores the continent's role in inspiring celebrated artists such as Picasso, Matisse or Kirchner. In the early 1900s the aesthetics of traditional African sculpture became what the Met Museum in New York describes as "a powerful influence among European artists who formed an avant-garde in the development of modern art".

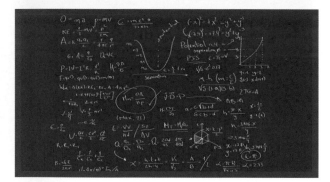

Mathematics

The history of mathematics is so Eurocentric that most accounts of ancient mathematical systems seem to begin and end in Egypt. But the Lebombo bone, found in Swaziland, and the Ishango bone, discovered on the border between Uganda and Zaire, both baboon fibulas, are the world's two oldest mathematical objects – the former at least 35,000 years old. The Ishango bone may be the oldest table of prime numbers.

Mobile phones

Not all of it, obvs, but in the inner workings of your most precious possession lie bits of the Democratic Republic of Congo in the form of the mineral cobalt, which is used to make rechargeable batteries. According to the Extractive Industries Transparency Initiative, the DRC "holds almost half of the world's cobalt reserves". And that's not all: the DRC is among the world's largest producers of cobalt, copper, diamonds, tantalum and tin.

Ubuntu

In the face of refugee crisis, the word "ubuntu" has never been more important. Popularised by Archbishop Desmond Tutu and Nelson Mandela as a way to heal post-apartheid South Africa, the ancient Bantu word encapsulates the idea of shared humanity: "I am, because we all are." Here's how the New World Encyclopedia defines the word that is also used in Uganda, Tanzania, Burundi and Zimbabwe: "It implies an appreciation of traditional beliefs, and a constant awareness that an individual's actions today are a reflection on the past, and will have far-reaching consequences for the future. A person with ubuntu knows his or her place in the universe and is consequently able to interact gracefully with other individuals."

Nando's

Yes, Nando's, "the home of the legendary Portuguese flame-grilled peri-peri chicken" and the coveted black card. Since its humble beginnings in Johannesburg, South Africa, in 1987, Nando's blend of chicken, hot sauce and African music has spread across the globe. At last count there was a Nando's on every continent except Latin America, some 1,000 restaurants in 30 countries. No chicken-loving nation is safe.

Jazz

It's all about the polyrhythms – two or more different rhythms happening at the same time – which European folk music also has but African music spread. The Pulitizer prize-winning composer and author Gunther Schuller wrote that "every musical element – rhythm, harmony, melody, timbre, and the basic forms of jazz – is essentially African in background and derivation".

But Africa didn't only give us blue notes, it may also have given us Beethoven. This year, a group of musicians revived the question about Beethoven's ethnicity, arguing that his piano music should be played polyrhythmically and that, as played by most classical pianists, the left hand appears to have almost no rhythm, no soul. Ouch.

Shae butter

Chances are you've bought soap, lip balm, skin lotion or even shaving cream that contains shea butter, which grows in 19 countries across the continent from Senegal in the west to Sudan in the east. Skincare brand L'Occitane calls it "nature's miracle beauty balm; the perfect quick fix for almost anything". Cleopatra, who knew a good thing when she saw it (hello, Marc Antony!) is said to have used the butter, making it a very valuable commodity during her reign.

Transplants

After performing the first heart transplant in 1967, South African surgeons scored another first by this year carrying out the world's first transplant of the male organ. The nine-hour operation in March 2015 allowed its 21-year-old recipient to become sexually active, and he wasted no time in proving its efficacy. In June head surgeon André van der Merwe announced that the young man's partner was pregnant.

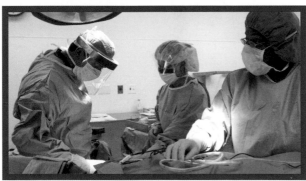

Jollof rice

Now that Jamie Oliver has written a recipe for Jollof, the rice dish may soon reach such dizzying heights of popularity that its west African origins will be forgotten. Just don't ask which particular country introduced it to the world. Cameroon, Ghana, Nigeria, Senegal – its origins continue to be hotly contested.

The Guardian, 8 September 2015 © Guardian News & Media 2015

Egypt's women-only taxi service promises protection from male drivers

Pink Taxi is a response to widespread sexual harassment but critics say it segregates women without addressing the problem

Nour Youssef in Cairo

Egypt's Pink Taxi – a new service marketed as a safe way for women to travel in Cairo, where sexual harassment and assaults have become increasingly commonplace – is surprisingly neither pink, nor a taxi.

"This is not a taxi. It's a limousine service," says Reem Fawzi, the founder of the service. The name is simply marketing, she adds.

Appearing on influential TV talk shows, Fawzi promises Egyptian women "privacy and safety" from male taxi drivers. "Just enter 'taxi driver' into Google [in Egypt] and it will suggest 'taxi driver kills'; 'taxi driver rapes'; 'taxi driver steals'," she says.

Fawzi hopes to eliminate some of the risks for women and families travelling in public: Pink Taxi is operated exclusively by female drivers, and must be ordered in advance. Customers are required to send in a scan of their national ID "for the safety of the driver," Fawzi adds.

The company's vehicles also come with an internal camera and a microphone to record every ride – and a so-called "kill" button to remotely stop the car if needed.

According to the UN, 99.3% of women in Egypt fall victim to sexual harassment.

Last month, there were 447 incidents of sexual harassment in downtown Cairo during the four days of the Muslim holiday Eid al-Adha, according to a pressure group gathering evidence of assault.

Customers are required to send in a scan of their national ID - for the safety of the driver

SOME ISSUES:

The service hopes "to eliminate the risks for women and families travelling in public". What are these risks?

In what ways would this service help?

Are women-only services, of all kinds, a complete solution to this problem?

Could such services be useful in other countries?

Image from https://www.facebook.com/PinkTaxiEg/

Maram Hany, a college student, speaks fondly of the three months she's spent learning how to drive and change tyres at Pink Taxi, but admits there are still some problems with the service.

"We get harassed more [by other male drivers] driving the taxi than we do in normal cars," she says. "But we are trained on how to deal with it." The training, she explains, comprises of one instruction: keep driving.

Mervat al-Badry, a former flight attendant who has also joined up, said driving on Cairo's streets is a challenge: "Men make fun of us [saying] 'you can barely drive' and 'God save us'."

"But we took it as a challenge... women fly planes, why not drive a taxi?"

The service has drawn criticism from women's rights activists, who accuse Fawzi of infantilising her customers with the choice of vehicle colour and design, dismissing the service as the latest in a continuing trend toward segregation.

"Pink Taxi and segregation in general says [to women]: 'Harassment is inevitable. Here is how you can adapt [to it]'," says Dalia Abdel-Hameed, head of the gender program at the Egyptian Initiative for Personal Rights.

Egypt's public schools have long been segregated along gender lines but in recent years women-only metro cars, cafes, gyms, pools and beaches have also emerged. Some argue this reinforces the notion that women can't be in public without needing special protection.

"[Fawzi] is fear-mongering for profit. I am in cabs all day, it is fine," says Basma Mohamed, one of the many women's rights activists to note that harassment mostly occurs on the street, which Pink Taxi customers have to brave anyway.

"If she really wanted to help the women of Egypt, [Pink] Taxi would go everywhere and these would not be their prices," says Mohamed.

The cheapest ride on offer by Fawzi's service is for 35 Egyptian pounds (£2.90) with the prices going up to 210 pounds (£17), a significant cost when minimum wage across the country – not always applied – is 1,200 pounds a month.

But for some, money is not the main concern.

"Clothing is the determinant factor," says college student Maha Mohamed. "If I am going to a party wearing revealing clothes then I would definitely pay double [for the Pink Taxi] price."

The Guardian, 7 October 2015
© Guardian News & Media 2015

Some argue this reinforces the notion that women can't be in public without needing special protection

What Muslim pilgrims travelling to Mecca can teach us about the refugee crisis

Living a frugal life on the Hajj helps us understand the plight of those who have nothing to rely on but each other

Sajda Khan

SOME ISSUES:

What can non-Muslims learn from the annual pilgrimage?

Would it be a good thing if people followed some religious behaviours, even if they were not religious themselves?

How can Europe and the international community organise a better response to the refugee crisis?

While Europe grapples with a surge of desperate refugees fleeing conflict, persecution and poverty, the annual Muslim pilgrimage to Mecca dawns upon us again.

Hajj is no conventional journey, it is a voyage to the land of the prophets of God where the pilgrims symbolically re-enact the rites and rituals of these great prophets. Hajj is also an expedition that is deeply spiritual, with lessons that are universal and very relevant to the present. The pilgrimage is a manifestation of the solidarity and humanitarian principles that are desperately needed today as we are faced with the worst refugee crisis of the 21st century.

The simple clothing worn by every pilgrim - whether prince or pauper, black or white - demonstrates the principle of equality, because all wear the same attire. The Prophet of Islam, Muhammad said: "You do not believe until you love for others what you love for yourself" - with the "others" referring to all of humanity despite religious and cultural backgrounds.

More than a million other people, from all corners of the earth, converge for the pilgrimage - together representing a multitude of races, languages,

Hajj has lessons that are universal and very relevant to the present.

ethnicities, and cultures. This is truly overwhelming as a human tide, so disparate in appearance and background, is totally unified in expressing solidarity in their purpose and aspiration.

It is this diversity and plurality that strengthens the bond of humanity. As the Prophet Muhammad once said: "Man is either your brother in faith or your brother in humanity."

Pilgrims undertaking the Hajj live a very simple life, travelling with few possessions, spending nights in tents, sharing what they have, just like those who have left Syria with nothing to begin their own journeys. This spirit of selflessness,

and putting others first, leads to empathy and compassion - the very qualities that all Europeans need to call upon now in the search for a solution to the plight of refugees.

The harrowing Syrian catastrophe should not be the responsibility of Europe alone, but the world as a whole; it needs a united response from the international community.

The body of three-year-old Syrian boy Aylan Kurdi washed ashore on a Turkish beach was heart-rending and sparked outrage. The Syrian refugee crisis is a moral imperative for us all - and we must not flunk it.

The outcome of the Hajj is spiritually enlightening. The journey cultivates three human virtues: humility, equality and compassion. A society based on these values will always respond to others who find themselves on their own tragic journey, and are in desperate need of solidarity.

The Independent, 17 September 2015
www.independent.co.uk

This spirit of selflessness, and putting others first, leads to empathy and compassion - the very qualities that all Europeans need

Refugee voices

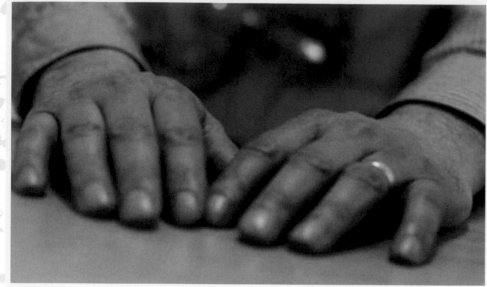

Image © Refugee Action

In Syria, Omar was a successful businessman who lived happily with his family...

War took his home, his livelihood and separated him from his loved ones. Now he's struggling to bring them to safety.

Omar's home in Syria "was like a paradise," he says. But everything changed when war broke out. Violence reached his neighbourhood; anti-government graffiti was sprayed on his house. Omar and his nephew were arrested, beaten and imprisoned for thirteen days. Later, his nephew was shot and killed.

Enough was enough. Omar and his family fled to a town on Turkish side of the Turkey/Syrian border. They hoped they'd soon be able to go home. "We lost everything that we owned," Omar recalls.

For three years, Omar and his family lived in Turkey. Life was tough. "We had no income, no rights to live there. They didn't respect us at all," he says. With his savings running out and his family facing a hopeless future, he took drastic action – selling his car to pay for a passage to Europe.

The cost of the journey was so high, the sale of Omar's car only paid for one person's travel. His hope was that if he made it to a country that respected refugees' rights, his family would be able to join him legally later. He said goodbye to his loved ones and set out on the perilous journey.

In the Mediterranean, the boat Omar took - "plastic, like a balloon" – was sabotaged by its driver, who was afraid of being arrested. Omar found himself in open water, swimming for thirty terrifying minutes until another boat rescued him. The only possessions he was carrying were lost in the sea.

Omar wanted to reach a country that respected refugees and would help him reunite his family. He decided on Britain. "I knew that [the UK] gave rights to people," said Omar. "I wanted to come here and work and start from zero". With the last of his savings, he paid to be smuggled here in a lorry.

In Dover, he was picked up by the police – who immediately took him to hospital. "I was overwhelmed," he says. "I swear now, I cried because they treated me so kindly, they treated me with respect. They gave me a glass of water, they let me sit down. The doctor gave me a check. They looked after me really, really well. It made me forget about everything I had been through."

As a Syrian, Omar was quickly granted asylum. But his dream of reuniting his family has proved harder than he expected. Under UK rules, only his wife

SOME ISSUES:

When you hear about refugees what do you think?

How do you think the media contribute towards the negative image of refugees?

Why is it important to understand the situations refugees are coming from?

What can we do to find out more about their plight?

How can we help those fleeing from danger and seeking safety?

"Britain gave me another life," he says. "All the people I've met have been nice to me."

and youngest son are potentially eligible to join him in Britain. The rest of his family – his older children, his mother and his grandchildren – are unlikely to be able to come to the UK.

Omar doesn't want his family to risk their lives. One of his sons and his daughter-in-law are already missing, kidnapped by people smugglers trying to make the crossing to Greece. If his family cannot be reunited, "I'll be destroyed," he says. "I want them to come here and live with me. Life is short and we have always lived together. I would give my life for them to come here."

Despite his problems, Omar is hugely grateful to the UK – and still hopes his family will one day find safety here too. "Britain gave me another life," he says. "All the people I've met have been nice to me. In my religion [Islam] the values are to respect people. We have to respect; we have to help each other. I have not seen that [in many countries]. But I see it in the UK."

Image © Refugee Action

My name is Alima. I am a refugee from Iraq...

Before the war in my country, I was a doctor in Baghdad. I worked in the x-ray department. Life was good before the war. We had a house and cars and everything was alright.

When the war came it became unsafe to go outside. Even if you stayed at home, you never knew if you were safe. People were being attacked for being Shia, or working with the government or with the Americans or British. It became hell - it was not the Baghdad I knew.

I was forced to flee in July 2007. I came to the UK and was granted refugee status at the beginning of September. When I got status, the feeling of safety and security was wonderful. But the practicalities of life as a refugee were worrying.

When I received refugee status, I only had 28 days to leave my temporary accommodation and find somewhere new to live. I had no idea how to do this. I wanted to retrain as a doctor and look for work too. But I didn't know where to start.

Luckily, I found Refugee Action. First, they helped me find a place to live. Then they directed me to the Job Centre and helped me plan my future.

The person I spoke to was really friendly. He helped me write a CV and put me in contact with an organisation that helps retrain refugee doctors. The concept of looking for work was completely new to me. In Iraq, the authorities would tell you where to work – you never looked for work by yourself.

Getting refugee status is like getting a new birth certificate. You have to start your life again and it's not easy. For me, the most frustrating thing is being on financial benefits and not being able to find a job.

But that's made me even more determined to re-qualify in my profession. I've now passed all my exams. I'm hopeful that I will be able to work here as a doctor soon.

Source: Refugee Action, www.refugee-action.org.uk

Having refugee status is like getting a new birth certificate... For me, the most frustrating thing is being on financial benefits and not being able to find a job.

Pussy Riot perform in a metal cage at Banksy's Dismaland attraction in Weston-super-Mare. Photograph: Ben Birchall / PA Archive/Press Association Images

'Dismantle Europe's borders': Pussy Riot speaks up for refugees -
Nadya Tolokonnikova

Pussy Riot is a Russian feminist punk rock protest group which specialises in provocative performances which are also protests.

One of the protest band's members explains why the migration crisis is 'the defining issue of our generation'

SOME ISSUES:

Do you think ordinary citizens do more to make positive changes than the government?

If businesses and financial services are international, is the idea of national borders really out of date?

Why do people rely on governments rather than acting themselves?

What can we all do to make positive changes in our society?

In the early 1900s the suffragettes fought for the right to vote. In the 1960s tens of thousands of people united to fight for civil rights. More recently, the issue of LGBT equality has raged in Russia and beyond.

In each of these instances it was not governments or the media who led the way. It was ordinary people; people dedicated to fighting injustice even when doing so meant breaking the law, risking possible imprisonment.

REFUGEES ARE FORCED TO JUMP ONTO MOVING TRAINS and hide under LORRIES as THERE IS NO OTHER WAY

Now we face a new challenge, a new injustice to fight: the refugee crisis, which has become the defining issue of our generation.

Hundreds of thousands of men, women and children are seeking sanctuary in Europe. These innocent people are fleeing war, famine and persecution by brutal dictatorships. They have undertaken epic and life-threatening journeys from their home countries in the hope of finding safety.

Paris attacks

This is a troubling time for Europe. Citizens are mourning for Paris, scared of where and when the next attack will come.

But if Europe – egged on by extreme right politicians such as Marine Le Pen – closes its borders, Islamic state will have won. This period of grief should not be the time when we betray our humanity.

The Russian attitude towards refugees is hostile and irrational. Registering for asylum is a slow process and cases are seldom granted.

Take the case of Khasan Aman Ando and his family who fled their home in Iraq after it was besieged by Isis.

They are stuck in limbo at Sheremetyevo airport, where they have been for more than 60 days. They are seeking asylum in Russia but will immediately be refused if they leave the airport, for crossing the border illegally.

This irrationality is mirrored in the UK, where refugees cannot seek asylum from outside the country, but are prevented from entering by the UK government. They are forced to jump onto moving trains and hide under lorries as there is no other way.

The border obsession

Our governments still believe in the power of borders – that's why Europe closes itself to refugees, and Putin annexed Crimea.

The global economy is built on the ideals of nomadism, and global financial flows of capital know no borders. But governments and their laws are lagging behind.

We have to step away from this logic. This is the century of ideas, not razor wires and refugee camps. If we really are living in a global society, where is the free movement of people?

Throughout the 18th and 19th century huge numbers from Sweden, Ireland and Italy emigrated across the Atlantic to find work, and the US became a shining example of how dynamic a country of immigrants can be.

If David Cameron calls migrants "a swarm of people" then to counter his rhetoric we have to show migrants our warmth and solidarity.

We can fundraise, create apps for migrants to use and build houses and shelters in the "jungle" refugee camp in Calais. Or, like the people of Iceland offering safety to 10,000 refugees, we can open up our homes.

We as citizens must not wait for our governments, who are too slow, too inert and steered by populist votes and tendencies. Let's take control of the situation ourselves, create networks and use technology to do what our own governments can't do.

Let's show that democratic nations are not only capable of sending bombs in international

WE as CITIZENS MUST NOT WAIT FOR OUR GOVERNMENTS!

response, but capable too of welcoming millions of new citizens and working together with them.

This crisis is not something to be afraid of, it is an opportunity to remind ourselves what humanity is capable of.

The Guardian, 18 November 2015
© Guardian News & Media 2015

LET'S CREATE NETWORKS and use TECHNOLOGY TO do what OUR OWN GOVERNMENTS can't do.

Why are white people expats when the rest of us are immigrants?

Surely any person going to work outside their country is an expatriate? But no, the word exclusively applies to white people
Mawuna Remarque Koutonin

SOME ISSUES:

What do you think of when you hear 'expat' and what do you think of when you hear 'immigrant'?

Why do you think Europeans like to think of themselves as 'expats'?

The terms 'immigrant' and 'immigration' should be neutral. How has the media contributed towards them becoming negative?

In the lexicon of human migration there are still hierarchical words, created with the purpose of putting white people above everyone else. One of those remnants is the word "expat".

What is an expat? And who is an expat? According to Wikipedia, "an expatriate (often shortened to expat) is a person temporarily or permanently residing in a country other than that of the person's upbringing. The word comes from the Latin terms ex ('out of') and patria ('country, fatherland')".

Defined that way, you should expect that any

person going to work outside of his or her country for a period of time would be an expat, regardless of his skin colour or country. But that is not the case in reality; expat is a term reserved exclusively for western white people going to work abroad.

Africans are immigrants. Arabs are immigrants. Asians are immigrants. However, Europeans are expats because they can't be at the same level as other ethnicities. They are superior. Immigrants is a term set aside for 'inferior races'.

Don't take my word for it. The *Wall Street Journal*, the leading financial information newspaper in the world, has a blog dedicated to the life of expats and recently they featured a story 'Who is an expat, anyway?'. Here are the main conclusions: "Some arrivals are described as expats; others as immigrants; and some simply as migrants. It depends on social class, country of origin and economic status. It's strange to hear some people in Hong Kong described as expats, but not others. Anyone with roots in a western country is considered an expat … Filipino domestic helpers are just guests, even if they've been here for decades. Mandarin-speaking mainland Chinese are rarely regarded as expats … It's a double standard woven into official policy."

Africans are immigrants. Arabs are immigrants. Asians are immigrants...

The reality is the same in Africa and Europe. Top African professionals going to work in Europe are not considered expats. They are immigrants. Period. "I work for multinational organisations both in the private and public sectors. And being black or coloured doesn't gain me the term "expat". I'm a highly qualified immigrant, as they call me, to be politically correct," says an African migrant worker.

Most white people deny that they enjoy the privileges of a racist system. And why not? But our responsibility is to point out and to deny them these privileges, directly related to an outdated supremacist ideology. If you see those

"expats" in Africa, call them immigrants like everyone else. If that hurts their white superiority, they can jump in the air and stay there. The political deconstruction of this outdated worldview must continue.

Mawuna Remarque Koutonin is the editor of SiliconAfrica.com, where this blog was first published. Follow @siliconafrica on Twitter.

The Guardian, 13 March 2015
© Guardian News & Media 2015

...however, Europeans are expats!

Australian dream?

Journalist, Stan Grant, whose heritage includes both indigenous people and a deported Irish rebel, spoke out against bigotry and racism. In a powerful speech he urged Australians to live up to their national anthem.

The Australian national anthem, Advance Australia Fair, like many anthems, speaks of the beauty and richness of the land and the ambition of its people. But for one group of people, the original indigenous inhabitants, the words ring hollow. When others sing:

Australians all let us rejoice,
For we are young and free;
We've golden soil and wealth for toil;
Our home is girt by sea;
Our land abounds in nature's gifts
Of beauty rich and rare;
In history's page, let every stage
Advance Australia Fair.

Words like 'Australians all', 'our land' and 'history's page' must stick in the throats of Aboriginal people who have inhabited the continent for 45,000 years but who feel that their land, culture and opportunities have all been taken away. But individuals who have a voice have begun to speak out for their culture and people.

We usually say that the British 'discovered' Australia in 1787 but what actually happened was an invasion of a land which had been occupied for thousands of years. The result, as so often, was a catastrophe for the indigenous people. Their land was stolen, they were massacred or died from new diseases, their whole way of life was almost totally obliterated. Even in the supposedly more enlightened times of the 20th century there was a policy of forcibly removing aboriginal children from their parents so that they could be absorbed into white society. Until 1973, Australia had a 'whites only' immigration policy, and while that degree of institutional racism has been abolished, racist attitudes have been shown to be deep and pervasive by the case of Adam Goodes.

Goodes, a highly skilled player of Australian Rules Football, who has twice been voted player of the year, had been loudly booed at matches all over the country. This reaction apparently stemmed from incidents in which he either defended or celebrated his aboriginal origins.

In the first of these, in May 2013, a 13 year old girl in the crowd at a match called Goodes an ape. He identified her to police and she was removed from the ground. The girl later apologised and Goodes urged people not to condemn her but to condemn the ethos that made her think her behaviour was acceptable. He also spoke out after watching a documentary, by acclaimed journalist John Pilger, about 'the first people' and what happened to them when Britain established a colony in Australia. In 2014, when he was awarded

SOME ISSUES:

What do you think a national anthem says about a country?

Should alternative interpretations of history be taught in schools?

What do you think about the UK's role in Australian history?

Why do you think there are still such inequalities in Australia?

And then I realised. McDonald's is supposed to be a job for people who can't do anything else. I noticed that the majority of entry level jobs didn't hire people who looked like the people I worked with.

At McDonald's there were people with disabilities, overweight people, people who weren't conventionally attractive, people that couldn't speak much English, young teenagers, and a lot of racial diversity. These people made up the backbone of the store. They were respected as some of our best workers.

Then I would look at a store like Starbucks and the majority of the time I would see people that looked like me. White, early twenties, reasonably attractive, slim, English speakers.

This was the bias that both me and the people around me were applying to my job. I meet the criteria for a 'good' job at a clothing store. People who come from good backgrounds aren't supposed to end up in McDonald's alongside those who couldn't do better if they tried.

If you're a white girl in your early 20s you will be ridiculed for working at McDonald's. But I don't think the same applies for disabled people, or middle-aged immigrant women. Their friends aren't quietly snickering, 'When are you going to get a real job?' Because this is the job we expect them to have.

McDonald's is gross and greasy. But my humiliation, and that of my friends and my family wasn't because I made burgers. It was because I was supposed to be better than that. Supposed to be more intelligent, more hard working and more talented than the people I worked with. I deserved a 'good' job. I had an inflated sense of self that comes with being a person of privilege.

I realised this attitude was way more gross than shovelling fries. Because I am not better than a McDonald's worker.

Sure, maybe I have different skills. I have no muscles and I fluster under that kind of pressure. I'm always going to be better at desk jobs than labour jobs. But this is not because I'm more intelligent or more skilled or worth more than a great McDonald's employee.

There are different types of labour, and just because we treat the work done by marginalised people as worthless doesn't mean it's true.

I am not as hard working as my co-workers, who sometimes pull twenty hour shifts to make sure no customer has to miss out on their midnight hamburger.

I am not as smart as our manager-turned-engineer. He learned how to fix all the machines so we didn't have to call a mechanic.

I am not as organised as those who predict and order the ingredients for thousands of customers a week, knowing that if they screw up, it's not just an angry boss to deal with. Customers always wait in the wings, ready to scream, throw drinks and use racial slurs over a lack of ketchup. I'm not patient enough to deal with that.

These things are skills.

And if you think you are better than those people, because you work in retail or organise files in a reception, you are wrong.

For me my time at McDonald's was invaluable. Yeah, I never want to scoop fries or make burgers again, but I learnt something more important. I started to chip away at my arrogance. I challenged the ways I dehumanised people for their job. I stopped equating dislike for big shitty companies with dislike for their foot soldiers. I developed more empathy.

And if that is supposed to be an embarrassing blip in my resumé, I really don't get it.

Huffington Post, 4 December 2015

A version of this post originally appeared on medium.com.

I realised this attitude was way more gross than shovelling fries. Because I am not better than a McDonald's worker.

The 18-year-old care worker:

'I've never felt so worthwhile'

Jodie Gornall

> The job needs unrelenting energy and is physically and emotionally demanding, but every day I know I've made a difference to someone's life

SOME ISSUES:

Why is this type of work important?

Is three days enough training for this job?

How much do you think people caring for others should be paid?

Is it important to have a job that makes you feel worthwhile?

An 18-year-old care worker. Not exactly my expectation, but for now, the reality. The routine of a six-hour school day gone after 14 years.

My schedule now? I assist an older lady with her morning shower. I make a widow her breakfast. I dress a gentleman. I hoist an immobile woman from her bed. I give medication, I escort people to hospital appointments, I provide companionship, I care.

After unsuccessfully applying to study medicine last year, I wanted a job involving people that would immerse me in the health and social care world without requiring a degree. I searched for roles as healthcare assistant, volunteer, anything that didn't involve only a desk and a computer. I uploaded my fresh CV to some sites. Then homecare company Bluebird Care contacted me.

Training was completed in three days. A week later I had my tunic, fleece, gloves and aprons ready in a plastic bag (I like to think of them collectively as my super suit). My alarm set for 6am, I slept, nervously anticipating my first day.

I need to be patient, tolerant, completely calm and understanding at all times. I stand there with 18 years of a life lived, but in front of me is a whole life lived, an abundance of stories and memories, still being lived – and my responsibility. Service users surely have prejudged my abilities given my age. Many clients ask how old I am when I walk in: a pale, rosy-cheeked girl with impractically long, red hair. I reply boldly, "18". Their eyes widen, showing worry and surprise – understandably so. I like to prove their assumptions wrong from this exact point. This is the time to eradicate any negative judgement and disapproval by kicking arse at the job I am proud to be doing. So far, no complaints have been filed.

I need to be patient, tolerant, completely calm and understanding at all times.

Photo posed by model

Despite the demands and fatigue, I love the job. The people I meet make it all worthwhile, the stories I collect.

The uniform has quite an impact on how I am perceived in public. As a teenager, I am used to averted eyes, judgmental sighs and prejudice. When in uniform, people make way, glance a smile, look comforted, thinking if they dropped down right then on the pavement I'd be able to save their lives.

I've never truly appreciated the benefits of a good night's sleep before now. The job requires unrelenting energy, complete attention, and is physically and mentally demanding too. I'm caring for lives, so I need to be at my best. The added pressures of teenagedom don't make the naps any less frequent: friends, family, hormones, boyfriends, broken hearts, nights out, hangovers,

university applications. I'm exhausted, rushing through this year of my life, an age many of my service users refer to as "the good times".

The truth is though, I wouldn't have it any other way. Despite the demands and fatigue, I love the job. The people I meet make it all worthwhile, the stories I collect. I come home every day, knowing I've made a positive difference to at least one person's life. There are moments that make me laugh until my sides split, and others when I can't help but cry. My eyes

have been opened to the stark reality of what many people's lives come to. I have matured, by demand, and taken on responsibilities many people I know would not, and could not, cope with. I never imagined how this job would affect my life. My perspective has changed on everything, my behaviour too. My priorities, values and morals have all been rearranged. I'm trying to appreciate this time of my life, after being advised multiple times by my clients "don't grow old".

So yes, at 18, I am a full-time care worker. The school holidays are long gone, emotions are erratic, partying in town is rare, but I've never felt so worthwhile in all my years.

The Guardian, 25 November 2015
© Guardian News & Media 2015

I come home every day, knowing I've made a positive difference to at least one person's life.

Ten things you should know about the gender pay gap

Sick of hearing "women shouldn't have babies if they're going to complain"? Here are some myth-busting truths about unequal pay

Laura Bates

According to the Fawcett Society, 9 November marked Equal Pay Day - the date from which women in Britain effectively work for free until the end of the year, due to the 14.2% gender pay gap. Myths and misconceptions still persist around unequal pay. (This week alone I've heard "the gender pay gap doesn't exist", "women shouldn't have babies if they're going to complain" and "women aren't paid less, they just earn less".) So in the interests of clearing up some confusion, here are 10 facts you might not know about the pay gap ...

1. It starts young ... really young

A website set up to allow parents to pay pocket money to their children via online accounts revealed that boys were paid 15% more than girls for doing the same chores. The gap widened for homework, where boys received more than double the amount of pocket money girls did for completing an assignment.

2. It's an intersectional problem

Research by Race for Opportunity found that black, Asian and minority ethnic (Bame) workers make up a disproportionate number of people in low-paid jobs, with almost a quarter (23%) of Pakistani employees and a fifth of Bangladeshi, Chinese and Black Caribbean workers earning less than £25,000 per year. It also found that a white British employee has an average of almost 4 promotions during their career, compared to just 2.5 for British African, Indian and Pakistani employees. Figures from the Low Pay Commission found that 15.3% of Pakistani/Bangladeshi workers earned the minimum wage - more than twice the number of white workers in minimum wage jobs. And the pay gap is wider for older women than for their younger colleagues, with women in their fifties earning nearly a fifth less than men of the same age.

Research also suggests that trans women are more economically vulnerable and can earn almost a third less after transitioning.

3. It's complicated

The pay gap exists for many and complex reasons. As well as both direct and indirect discrimination, there are issues such as occupational segregation, and the devaluation of jobs primarily associated with female labour. The fact that women make up the majority of part-time and low-paid workers, and the relative lack of promotion opportunities for part-time workers, are also factors. Among part-time workers, women are still more likely to be lower paid than men.

SOME ISSUES:

What can be done to stop gender inequality in the workplace?

This article is about the inequality women face in the workplace, but how do you think these attitudes affect men and their lives?

What should be done to make more people aware of these issues?

What impact does inequality have on business, industry and the economy?

5. It's not performance-based

Talking of football, the US national teams recently provided a stunning, high-profile example of pay failing to correlate to performance. In the World Cup, the women's team were victorious, winning the whole championship, while the men's team went out in the first round. But the women's team won prize money of $2 million, while the men won $8 million just for being eliminated at the first hurdle.

6. While working mothers lose out, working fathers actually benefit

We all know that the motherhood penalty can have a huge negative impact on women's careers. Mothers are less likely to get jobs in the first place, and less likely to be paid as well as their similarly qualified male colleagues. But to add insult to injury, working fathers actually see a boost to their salaries, with their earnings increasing an average of over 6% when they have children, compared to mothers, whose salaries decrease 4% for each child on average.

4. It happens across a huge variety of professions

Attention has recently been drawn to the wage gap between male and female stars in Hollywood. But the gender pay gap affects everybody from architects to athletes. Recent research from the Office for National Statistics revealed that female architects are paid a whopping 25% less than their male counterparts. And while members of the England women's football team earn around £20,000 per year, male Premier League players earn an average of £1.6 million per year.

A white British employee has an average of almost 4 promotions during their career, compared to just 2.5 for British African, Indian and Pakistani employees.

All photos posed by models

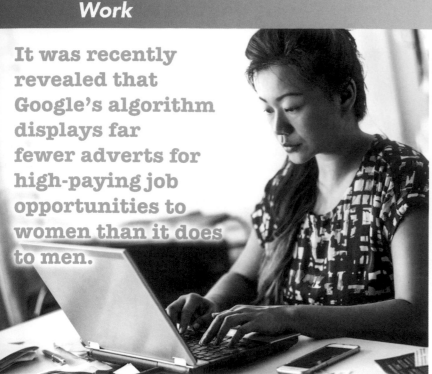

It was recently revealed that Google's algorithm displays far fewer adverts for high-paying job opportunities to women than it does to men.

7. It affects graduates too

Much has been made recently of the diminishing pay gap among younger workers. But studies still show a graduate pay gap, where women can earn up to £8,000 less in their starting salaries than their male peers who took the same degree. According to the Higher Education Careers Service Unit, one in five men are paid more than £30,000 after their degree, compared with just 8% of women who earn the same. And research from the Higher Education Statistics Agency found that the average graduate salary is £2,000 higher for male graduates than for female graduates.

8. Not all work "counts"

As Katrine Marçal points out in her recent book Who Cooked Adam Smith's Dinner? the very methods by which we measure and value labour have long disregarded the enormous contribution and impact of the unpaid domestic and caring work predominantly carried out by women.

9. It can arise from subtle bias

When we think of the pay gap, it's easy to imagine a villainous boss deliberately choosing to pay a female employee less than her male counterparts. But while that can happen, discrimination can also be more complex. A study published in the journal PNAS submitted identical applications for laboratory manager jobs, but assigned female-sounding names to half the applications and male-sounding names to the other half. In a randomised double-blind study, participants not only considered the "male" applicants more competent and hireable, but were also likely to offer them a higher starting salary.

10. Even technology isn't immune from discriminatory practices

It was recently revealed that Google's algorithm displays far fewer adverts for high-paying job opportunities to women than it does to men. So the next time someone tries to tell you feminism is unnecessary and the gender pay gap doesn't exist, fix them with a beady stare, talk them through its complexities, and if all else fails, hit them with Twitter user @LauraLuchador's viral joke:

 Lau Ree
@LauraLuchador

🐦 Follow

If I had a pound for everytime I was told I didn't need feminism I'd have 85p each time. @EverydaySexism

4:09 PM - 28 Nov 2014 · Edinburgh, Scotland, United Kingdom

🔁 1,871   ❤ 1,738

The Guardian, 10 November 2015

The class ceiling is worse than the glass ceiling ever was

Louise Cooper

I was 17 when I first suffered British class discrimination. I had just sat my A-level Maths early and achieved an A. I had also achieved straight As in my mock A level exams, in biology, chemistry and physics. I don't write this to be boastful; I know I got lucky genetically – I have brains, and I come from a family of grafters. But I don't come from money, class or privilege. My school was called Yateley Comprehensive, not St Paul's or Roedean.

I applied for university through a sponsorship programme and was interviewed by a white male middle manager. He asked me what grades I expected. I replied As or Bs as I felt I should downplay my expectations. (I did get four As.)

At the end of the interview he told me I was arrogant, boastful and talked too much. He was about 50 and in a position of power. I was a teenage girl, and not. I cried all the way home. In this man's view, someone from my background should not expect to do well. A girl from a comp should not have aspirations.

Much has been written about the glass ceiling for women, but the class ceiling is just as difficult to break through. For me, in fact, it was the greater barrier.

These class ties that still hold us back are rarely discussed. Yet new research has uncovered the existence of a "class-origin pay gap" of around £7,350 a year in highly prized jobs such as law, medicine and finance. The LSE academics behind the study summed it up perfectly when they said their findings suggest class still casts a "long shadow" over our life chances.

I learnt this the hard way, through shame, embarrassment and humiliation. The following 28 years have confirmed my initial, teenage experience.

I've worked every year of my life since I was 13. I was a national/international-level swimmer and an academic high achiever - everything employers say they want. But after graduating from City University (now CASS) with a First Class degree in Business Studies and Finance, not one British investment bank offered me a job. They were places for privately educated men, and occasionally, a few women. The only job offers I got were from American banks, which are far more meritocratic.

More than a decade later I attended another interview, this time at a posh private bank. Before me was a panel of plummy-voiced men discussing

SOME ISSUES:

Do you think your background will affect how well you can do in life?

What can be done to make sure that children from less privileged backgrounds have the same opportunities in life?

What can educational establishments and companies do to encourage people from less privileged backgrounds to achieve more?

What should the government do to promote equality?

I was everything employers say they want... But after graduating with a First Class degree not one British investment bank offered me a job

a society wedding they had all been to the preceding weekend. Trevor Phillips, former Chairman of the Commission for Racial Equality, calls this "signalling" - a message that I didn't fit in. One of the interviewees (titled) questioned why I even bothered to apply: "You do know the culture here, don't you?"

In June, research from The Social Mobility Foundation found that "elite firms are systematically excluding working class applicants from their workforce". That bright "working class applicants struggle to get access to top jobs in the UK" in the highly paid professions of law, accounting and finance. It also found that state school applicants needed higher grades than their privately educated contemporaries to get the same job. And even if a disadvantaged graduate breaks into such a career, they won't be promoted as readily as their advantaged and wealthier colleagues.

According to a government report called Elitist Britain, 71% of senior judges, 62% of senior armed forces officers, 43% of newspaper columnists, 33% of MPs and 26% of BBC executives all went to private schools, compared to 7% of the public as a whole. Diplomats, Lords, those in television, influential voices on radio, CEOs of public bodies, Permanent Secretaries - those who run this country, make its laws and dominate its national debates - predominantly come from a small, so-called "elite" group. In short, we are wasting 93% of this country's talent in order to give the top jobs to the already

privileged but not automatically more capable.

So why don't we, the majority, scream and shout at such social injustice? Do something to ensure our children get the same opportunities as the wealthy and lucky few? Karl Marx said religion is the opiate of the masses. The Romans kept the plebs quiet by distributing free bread and staging huge spectacles – "bread and circuses". So which soporific in the 21st century keeps Britons similarly diverted? Could cake and talent shows be the new palliatives to stop us demanding a more just and fair society?

In some ways I have been lucky. After my initial setbacks, I spent seven years at Goldman Sachs and then a decade at BBC World Service. I now work for myself as a writer and broadcaster. It could have been so different if I'd given in, and given up hope.

I wish not to rage blindly against the upper class machine now. I wish to inspire others like me to kick the doors down, rip up the rule book and keep fighting. Those without benefits of title, privilege, usefully connected parents and an expensive education can still try and make a difference. They won't be elevated straight to the 10th floor like those from Eton and Roedean; they will have to start at the bottom rung of the

Success

...They were places for privately educated men, and occasionally, a few women.

ladder and climb. It will be harder and tougher, but they will always know they got there despite their background, not because of it.

Self-help books and amateur psychologists recommend that in the event of a childhood trauma, you should visualise yourself going back and comforting your younger self. If I could, I would go back and look my younger self in the eye and say: "Feel the humiliation, the insult, the shame. Be hurt and sad and cry. Because it will make you the woman you become. It will make you a fighter and a tryer."

Daily Telegraph,
9 November 2015
© Telegraph Media Group Ltd 2015